新时代商务英语专业系列教材
New Era Business English Series

总主编/翁凤翔　郭桂杭

Electronic Commerce

电子商务

主　编/邹　莉

副主编/沈红兵　李　慧

编　者/何嗣锋　贺方成

马　东　黄亚丽

于　苗　杨　烁

重庆大学出版社

Indicative Abstract

This book expounds the characteristics and advantages of e-commerce, analyzes the current situation, trends and principles of e-commerce development, and studies the close relationship between the current information technology development and e-commerce.

Based on the domestic information technology development environment, this book conducts a comprehensive and in-depth study of e-commerce, mainly includes the electronic market structure and mechanism, products and services, online customer management, system and technology innovation, as well as electronic commerce law and electricity supplier safety. This book puts forward several commercial developments in the birth of business forms, such as B2B and OTA, to give readers a more detailed understanding of the development of e-commerce.

图书在版编目(CIP)数据

电子商务：英文/邹莉主编. -- 重庆：重庆大学出版社，2017.8

商务英语专业系列教材

ISBN 978-7-5689-0699-9

Ⅰ.①电… Ⅱ.①邹… Ⅲ.①电子商务—英语—高等学校—教材 Ⅳ.①F713.36

中国版本图书馆 CIP 数据核字(2017)第 182114 号

电子商务

DIANZI SHANGWU

主 编 邹 莉

责任编辑:张春花 版式设计:高小平

责任校对:姜 凤 责任印制:张 策

*

重庆大学出版社出版发行

出版人:易树平

社址:重庆市沙坪坝区大学城西路 21 号

邮编:401331

电话:(023)88617190 88617185(中小学)

传真:(023)88617186 88617166

网址:http://www.cqup.com.cn

邮箱:fxk@cqup.com.cn (营销中心)

全国新华书店经销

重庆升光电力印务有限公司印刷

*

开本:787mm×1092mm 1/16 印张:15 字数:368 千

2017 年 8 月第 1 版 2017 年 8 月第 1 次印刷

ISBN 978-7-5689-0699-9 定价:39.00 元

总序

商务英语作为本科专业获得教育部批准进入我国大学本科教育基本目录已经好些年了。商务英语本科专业的身份与地位获得了我国官方和外语界的认可。迄今为止,据不完全统计,有300所左右的大学开设了商务英语本科专业。各种商务英语学术活动也开始活跃。商务英语专业与英语语言文学专业、翻译专业成为我国英语教学的“三驾马车”。商务英语教学在全国已经形成较大规模,正呈良性发展态势,越来越多的大学正在积极准备申报商务英语本科专业。可以预计,将来在我国,除了研究性大学外的大部分普通本科院校的外语学院都可能开设商务英语本科专业。这是大势所趋,因为随着我国改革开放和经济全球化、世界经济一体化进程的加快,各个融入经济一体化的国家和地区急需有扎实英语功底的,熟悉国际商务基本知识的,具备国际商务领域操作技能的跨文化商务交际复合型、应用型商务英语人才。

高校商务英语专业教育首先必须有充足的合格师资;其次,需要有合适的教材。目前,虽然市面上有很多商务英语教材,但是,完整的四年商务英语本科专业教材并不多。重庆大学出版社出版的商务英语本科专业系列教材一定程度上能满足当前商务英语本科专业的教学需要。

本套系列教材能基本满足商务英语本科专业1—4年级通常开设课程的需要。商务英语专业不是商务专业而是语言专业。所以,基础年级的教材仍然是英语语言学习教材。但是,与传统的英语语言文学专业教材不同的是:商务英语专业学生所学习的英语具有显著的国际商务特色。所以,本套教材特别注重商务英语本科专业教育的特点,在基础阶段的英语技能教材中融入了商务英语元素,让学生在学习普通英语的同时,接触一些基础的商务英语语汇,通过听、说、读、写、译等技能训练,熟悉掌握商务英语专业四级和八级考试词汇,熟悉基础的商务英语篇章,了解国际商务常识。

根据我国《高等学校商务英语本科专业教学质量国家标准》(以下简称《标准》),本套教材不仅包含一、二年级的基础教材,还包含高年级的继续夯实商务英语语言知识的教材,如《高级商务英语教程》1—3册等。此外,还包括英语语言文学专业学生所没有的突出商务英语本科专业特色的国际商务知识类教材,如《国际商务概论》《国际贸易实务》《国际贸易法》《市场营销》等。本套教材的总主编都是教育部商务英语专业教学协作组成员,参与了该《标准》的起草与制定,熟悉《标准》的要求,这为本套教材的质量提供了基本保障。此外,参与编写本套教材的主编及编者都是多年从事商务英语教学与研究的有经验的教师,因而,在教材的内容、体例、知识、练习以及辅助教材等方面,都充分考虑到了教材使用者的需求。教材的编写宗旨是:力求传授实用的商务英语知识和国际商务有关领域的知识,提高学生的商务英语综合素质和跨文化商务交际能力以及思辨创新能力。

教材编写考虑到了以后推出的全国商务英语本科专业四级和专业八级的考试要求。在教材的选材、练习、词汇等方面都尽可能与商务英语本科专业四级、八级考试对接。

本套教材特别适合培养复合型、应用型的商务英语人才的商务英语本科专业的学生使用,也可作为商务英语爱好者学习商务英语的教材。教材中若存在不当和疏漏之处,敬请专家、学者及教材使用者批评指正,以便我们不断修订完善。

翁凤翔

2016 年 3 月

Preface

Over the past decade, e-commerce practices are developing rapidly in China and around the world, and many new business models, methods, technologies and laws and regulations are emerging. Academic theorists are also constantly summing up and exploring the knowledge and rules of e-commerce. The education sector is actively promoting the development of e-commerce education.

With the acceleration of global economic integration, more and more traditional enterprises are speeding up the implementation of e-commerce. It is predicted that, in the next few years, with the rapid promotion of e-commerce, China will have nearly 3,000 small and medium-sized enterprises to implement e-commerce business transformation. The competition of industry is the competition of talents. The rapid development of e-commerce will give birth to a great demand for talents of this new busniess. However, in recent years, one side is the continued demand for e-commerce talents, and the other side is higher vocational e-commerce graduates "employment without doors". The 20% employment rate of e-commerce graduates is far below the national average employment rate of 70%. The fundamental cause of this phenomenon lies not in the profession itself, but in the vocational education itself. As a vocational education, the current discipline-based professional training mode is still prevalent. Especially as an interdisciplinary e-commerce major, there is a "big and all", "universal" talent training tone. The gap between the training target and the market demand leads to the "unsalable" pattern of talents.

Members involved in this book are: Zou Li, Shen Hongbing (Chongqing Technology and Business University); Li Hui, He Sifeng, Yang Shuo, He Fangcheng (Chongqing University of Education); Huang YaLi (Chongqing University of Arts and Science); Ma Dong (Panzhihua University); Yu Miao (Chengdu Neusoft University).

During the preparation of this book, we received friendly help and support from many scholars, experts, teachers and students, to whom we express our sincere thanks. Suggestions from you, our dear readers, are warmly welcomed too.

August, 2017

Preface

Contents

Chapter 1 Introduction to Electronic Commerce 1

Chapter 2 E-marketplace: Structures and Mechanisms 15

Chapter 3 Retailing in Electronic Commerce 34

Chapter 4 Online Consumer Behavior, Customer Relationship Management 50

Chapter 5 B2B Electronic Commerce 68

Chapter 6 Innovative EC Systems 87

Chapter 7 E-supply Chains 104

Chapter 8 E-commerce Security 122

Chapter 9 E-commerce Payment System, Order Fulfillment and Other Support Service 140

Chapter 10 E-commerce Development and Trends in China 160

Chapter 11 Electronic Commerce Laws 180

Chapter 12 Online Marketing Research and Advertisement ... 197

Chapter 13 Online Travel Agent 215

Chapter 1 Introduction to Electronic Commerce

本章导读

2016 年中国电子商务交易市场规模稳居全球第一，电子商务交易额超过 20 万亿元，占社会消费品零售总额比重超过 10%。其中一线城市仍占据主力消费区域的头把交椅，二三线城市互联网消费市场与一线城市的差距正在逐步缩小，而三线以下城市及乡镇市场在家电、通信产品等大宗物件的消费能力直逼一线城市，特色电商一枝独秀的潜力也开始显现。另外，B2B市场交易规模达7.9万亿元，网络零售市场交易规模2.3万亿元。网络零售市场中移动端成为主战场，逐渐成为网购主要形态。在电子商务从业人员上，截止到 2016 年 6 月，中国电子商务服务企业直接从业人员超过 285 万人，由电子商务间接带动的就业人数，已超过 2 100 万人。本章将介绍电子商务的内涵定义、架构分类、发展历史以及电子商务在中国的发展历史及发展趋势。

Business Terms

①**Value-added Network (VAN)**: a hosted service offering that acts as an intermediary between business partners sharing standards based or proprietary data via shared business processes

②**Wide Area Network (WAN)**: a telecommunications network or computer network that extends over a large geographical distance. Wide area networks are often established with leased telecommunication circuits.

③**Local Area Network (LAN)**: a computer network that interconnects computers within a limited area such as a residence, school, laboratory, university campus or office building and has its network equipment and interconnects locally managed

④**Worldwide Interoperability for Microwave Access (WiMAX)**: a family of wireless communication standards based on the IEEE 802.16 set of standards, which provide multiple physical layer (PHY) and Media Access Control (MAC) options

⑤**Request for Proposal (RFP)**: a document that solicits proposal, often made through a bidding process, by an agency or company interested in procurement of a commodity, service or valuable asset, to potential suppliers to submit business proposals

⑥**Request for Information (RFI)**: a standard business process whose purpose is to collect written information about the capabilities of various suppliers. Normally it follows a format that can be used for comparative purposes.

⑦**Request for Quotation (RFQ)**: a standard business process whose purpose is to invite suppliers into a bidding process to bid on specific products or services

⑧**Digital Subscriber Line (DSL)**: a family of technologies that are used to transmit digital data over telephone lines

Introductory Case

Advertising of E-commerce Websites Took the Lead in China's Online Advertising Market

In 2016, share of search engine advertising in online advertising market declined 5% to 27.2%, ranking the second in online advertising market. Meanwhile, e-commerce websites surpassed search engines and became the most popular online advertising media with a share of 30.0%, and it's expected to maintain the share in the near future. Portal websites and information advertising (excluding non-portal function content) took up 7.4%; Advertising of online video websites took up 11.0%; and social networking advertisements took a share of 8.3% with a rapid YoY growth. As the relationship between social networking service and scenarios gets increasingly intimate, advertising resources and forms of news feeds were continuously optimized, the share of social networking advertising will keep rising.

In 2016 the calculating scope of advertising of portal websites and information websites changed. Their online advertising revenue no longer included non-portal content revenue. Under such scope, the revenue reached 21.41 billion Yuan with a high YoY growth of 36.4%. Mobile apps were still the trend of traditional portal websites in 2016, and portal websites stared to explore the upstream and downstream industries. In the upstream, they improved the amount of their high-quality content and we-media resources; while in the downstream, they offered more targeted information to users with the help of advanced algorithm, and the continuous trials in the whole industry chain provided commercialization of the industry with more chances.

Questions for Discussion

①What is the status and trend of advertising of Chinese e-commerce websites in 2016?

②What are the main factors that contribute to a considerable growth in advertising development of Chinese e-commerce websites?

③Could you cite a specific example of online advertising to support the theme of the passage?

1.1 OVERVIEW OF ELECTRONIC COMMERCE

Electronic commerce, commonly written as eCommerce or e-commerce, is the trading or facilitation of trading in products or services using computer networks, such as the Internet. Electronic commerce draws on technologies such as mobile commerce, electronic funds transfer, supply chain management, Internet marketing, online transaction processing, electronic data interchange (EDI), inventory management systems, and automated data collection systems. Modern electronic commerce typically uses the World Wide Web for at least one part of the transaction's life cycle, although it may also use other technologies such as e-mail.

E-commerce businesses may employ some or all of the following:

- Online shopping websites for retail sales direct to consumers;
- Providing or participating in online marketplaces, which process third-party business-to-consumer or consumer-to-consumer sales;
- Business-to-business buying and selling;
- Gathering and using demographic data through Web contacts and social media;
- Business-to-business electronic data interchange;
- Marketing to prospective and established customers by e-mail or fax (for example, with newsletters);
- Engaging in pretail for launching new products and services;
- Online financial exchanges for currency exchanges or trading purposes.

1.2 FRAMEWORK OF ELECTRONIC COMMERCE

Electronic commerce (EC) framework involves many activities, organization units and technologies under the environment of e-commerce. Generally, EC's framework comprises "3 levels" and "2 columns". "3 levels" refers to network level, information publishing level and information transmission level, business service level and e-commerce application level. "2 columns" refers to public and legal regulation column and technical standard column.

Network level

Network level is the network hardware infrastructure, namely an information transmission system. It includes telecom, cable TV, wireless access, Internet, VAN, WAN, LAN, intranet, extranet, Wi-Fi and WiMAX.

Information publishing level and information transmission level

Network level decides the route of e-commerce information transmission. However, information publishing level and information transmission level deal with the questions concerning how to transmit information and what information to be transmitted. The most popular information publish mode is publishing information on WWW in the form of HTML or XML. Java or XML can facilitate publishing information on various network systems, various equipments and various operating system platforms. From the technical perspective, the whole process of e-commerce system revolves around information publishing and transmission.

Business service level and e-commerce application level

Business service level actualizes normal online business activities and services, such as online advertisement, online retail, online directories, electronic payment, online client service, electronic certification (certificate authority, CA) and e-commerce information security. Among them, CA is the most important element. Since e-commerce is the business activities conducted online and all parties involved in online business would not see each other in person, identity confirmation and security become extraordinarily important.

On network level, information publishing level, information transmission level and business service level, people can realize all kinds of e-commerce applications, such as the information systems of supply chain management, enterprise resource planning, client relation management, and enterprise knowledge management as well as competing intelligence activities that are conducted on the basis of the said information systems. The main parties engaging in e-commerce activities like supplier, distributor, cooperating partners, and governments are interacting in all aspects with enterprises on this level.

1.3 CLASSIFICATION OF ELECTRONIC COMMERCE

Business-to-Business (B2B) refers to a situation where one business uses e-commerce to make a commercial transaction with another. This typically occurs when a business uses the computer and Internet:

- to source materials for their production process;
- to acquire the services of another for operational reasons;
- to re-sell goods and services produced by others;
- to fulfill the payment and conclude the transactions with others.

An example that illustrates B2B concept is automobile manufacturing. Many of a vehicle's components are manufactured independently and the auto manufacturer must purchase these parts separately. For instance, the tires, batteries, electronics, hoses and door locks may be manufactured elsewhere and sold directly to the automobile manufacturer.

B2B is often contrasted against business-to-consumer (B2C). In B2B commerce it is often the case that the parties to the relationship have comparable negotiating power, and even when they don't, each party typically involves professional staff and legal counsel in the negotiation of terms, whereas B2C is shaped to a far greater degree by economic implications of information asymmetry.

B2C refers to a transaction that occurs between a company and a consumer. The term may also describe a company that provides goods or services for consumers. B2C can reduce intermediaries and labor costs, shorten transaction times, improve customer service and expand market.

While most companies that sell directly to consumers can be referred to as B2C companies, the term became immensely popular during the dotcom boom of the late 1990s, when it was used mainly to refer to online retailers, as well as other companies that sold products and services to consumers through the Internet. Although numerous B2C companies became victims to the subsequent dotcom bust as investors interest in the sector dwindled and venture capital funding dried up, their leaders such as Amazon and Taobao survived the shakeout and went on to rank among the most successful companies in the world.

Business-to-Business-to-Consumer (B2B2C) is an emerging e-commerce model that combines B2B and B2C for a complete product or service transaction. B2B2C is a business model where online, or e-commerce, businesses and portals reach new markets and customers by partnering with consumer-oriented product and service businesses. The consumer-oriented businesses have their own clients, to whom the product or service is provided without adding any value to it. B2B2C is a collaboration process that, in theory, creates mutually beneficial service and product delivery channels.

As an example of a B2B2C model, Business A pays Business B for users, leads or sales generated by Business B's business or website. Business A then uses Business B's channels to locate prospective customers. Business B provides its customers with new and relevant services, facilitating an increased customer base and earned revenue for sold products and services.

Business-to-Government (B2G) is a derivative of B2B marketing and often referred to as a market definition of "public sector marketing" which encompasses marketing products and services to various government levels through integrated marketing communications techniques such as strategic public relations, branding, marcom, advertising, and Web-based communications.

B2G networks provide a platform for businesses to bid on government opportunities which are presented as solicitations in the form of RFPs in a reverse auction fashion. Public sector organizations (PSOs) post tenders in the form of RFPs, RFIs, RFQ, Sources Sought, etc. and suppliers respond to them. In addition, PSOs also play a micro-readjustment, guidance and supervision role in the form of e-commerce: Via network and other information technology, PSOs can obtain comprehensive information promptly and make correct decisions and quick feedbacks; Sending control information as well as laws and regulations to enterprises, PSOs can strength the management and service function.

Consumer-to-Business (C2B) is a business model in which consumers (individuals) create value and businesses consume that value. C2B model, also called a reverse auction or demand collection model, enables buyers to name or demand their own price, which is often binding, for a specific good or service. The website collects the demand bids and then offers the bids to participating sellers. Another form of C2B is the electronic commerce business model in which consumers can offer products and services to companies and the companies pay the consumers. This business model is a complete reversal of the traditional business model in which companies offer goods and services to consumers. We can see the C2B model at work in blogs or Internet forums in which the author offers a link back to an online business thereby facilitating the purchase of a product.

Consumer-to-Consumer (C2C) is a business model which provides an environment where customers can sell these goods or services to each other. C2C electronic commerce involves the electronically facilitated transactions between consumers through some third party. A common example is the online auction, in which a consumer posts an item for sale and other consumers bid to purchase it; the third party generally charges a flat fee or commission. The sites are only intermediaries, just there to match consumers. They do not have to check quality of the products being offered.

Government-to-Consumer (G2C) is to offer a variety of information and communication technology services to citizens in an efficient and economical manner, and to strengthen the relationship between government and citizens using technology.

Two-way communication of G2C allows citizens to send instant messages directly to public administrators, and cast remote electronic votes (electronic voting) and instant opinion voting. Transactions such as payment of services, city utilities can be completed online or over the phone. Mundane services such as name or address changes, applying for services or grants, or transferring existing services are more convenient and no longer have to be completed face to face.

1.4 A BRIEF HISTORY OF ELECTRONIC COMMERCE

History of e-commerce dates back to the invention of the very old notion of "sell and buy", electricity, cables, computers, modems, and the Internet. E-commerce became possible in 1991 when the Internet was opened to commercial use. Since that date thousands of businesses have taken up residence at web sites.

At first, the term e-commerce meant the process of execution of commercial transactions electronically with the help of the leading technologies such as Electronic Data Interchange (EDI) and Electronic Funds Transfer (EFT) which gave an opportunity for users to exchange business information and do electronic transactions. The ability to use these technologies appeared in the late 1970s and allowed business companies and organizations to send commercial documentation electronically.

Although the Internet began to advance in popularity among the general public in 1994, it took approximately four years to develop the security protocols (for example, HTTP) and DSL which allowed rapid access and a persistent connection to the Internet. In 2000 a great number of business companies in the United States and Western Europe represented their services in the World Wide Web. At this time the meaning of the word e-commerce was changed. People began to define the term e-commerce as the process of purchasing of available goods and services over the Internet using secure connections and electronic payment services. Although the dot-com collapse in 2000 led to unfortunate results and many of e-commerce companies disappeared, the "brick and mortar" retailers recognized the advantages of electronic commerce and began to add such capabilities to their web sites (e. g., after the online grocery store Webvan came to ruin, two supermarket chains, Albertsons and Safeway, began to use e-commerce to enable their customers to buy groceries online). By the end of 2001, the largest form of e-commerce, B2B model, had around $700 billion in transactions. By the end of 2007, e-commerce sales accounted for 3.4 percent of total sales.

History of e-commerce is unthinkable without Amazon and eBey which were among the first Internet companies to allow electronic transactions. Thanks to their founders we now have a handsome e-commerce sector and enjoy the buying and selling advantages of the Internet.

1.5 DEVELOPMENT OF CHINESE ELECTRONIC COMMERCE

Since 1995, China's e-commerce has experienced from the "tool", "channel" to "infrastructure" these three expanding and deepening development process. In 2013, e-commerce of the "infrastructure" further spawned a new business ecology and new business landscape, further influenced and accelerated the traditional industry e-commercialization, further expanded its economic and social impact. "E-commerce Economy" began to rise.

China and the United States become the world's most dazzling Internet economy "Gemini". According to S&P Capital data, among the global Internet top 10 companies, the United States accounts for 6 and China accounts for 4. In the world's 25 largest Internet companies, the ratio of the United States to China is 14:6 seats (data from KPCB). The US Internet companies such as Apple, Google, Amazon and Facebook are still leaders, but the Chinese Internet companies such as Tencent, Baidu, Alibaba, Jingdong Mall, Vip. com are catching up.

Tool stage (1995-2003)

This stage is the exploration period or the enlightenment period of Internet entering China. In the early days, e-commerce enterprises and individuals mainly used e-commerce as a tool to optimize business activities or business processes, such as information dissemination, information collection and mail communication. Its application was limited to a business "point".

On May 9, 1995, Ma Yun founded the Chinese Yellow Pages and it became the first Internet company to provide services for the creation of web pages. The China Chemical Network was established in 1997 and 8848. com, Ctrip, eBay, Alibaba, Dangdang and a number of e-commerce sites have been founded in 1999. The end of 1999 reached the climax of Internet development, witnessing the birth of more than 370 domestic B2C companies, and until 2000, the number became 700. However, with the Internet bubble burst in 2000 and NASDAQ sharp decline, 8848. com and a number of e-commerce business failed. Then e-commerce experienced a relatively long "ice age".

Channel stage (2003-2008)

At this stage, e-commerce application was extended from the enterprises to the individuals. In 2003, SARS ravaged many industries, but brought a good fortune to the e-commerce. The e-commerce community has undergone a series of major events: On May 2003, Alibaba Group set up Taobao and began to march toward the C2C market. In December 2003, HC Hong Kong GEM listed became the first domestic B2B e-commerce listed companies. On January 2004, Jingdong set to be involved in the field of e-commerce. In November 2007, Alibaba Network Co., Ltd. was successfully listed on the Main Board in Hong Kong. The state has also issued a series of major documents on the development of e-commerce: in March 2004, the State Council executive meeting voted for the adoption of "People's Republic of China Electronic Signature Law (Draft)"; in January 2005, the State Council issued "A Number of Opinions on the Development of E-commerce" (more known as "Document No. 2"); In June 2007, the National Development and Reform Commission and the State Council Information Office jointly issued China's first e-commerce development plan "E-commerce Development Eleventh Five-Year Plan". It is the first time that China proposed the development plan for e-commerce services; In 2007, the Ministry of Commerce issued the "Opinion on Online Trading (Interim)" and "Opinions of the Ministry of Commerce on Promoting the Development of Electronic Commerce". Then the policy ecology of e-commerce development was constructed.

At the same time, with the rapid growth of Internet users and e-commerce transactions, e-commerce became a new trading channel for many enterprises and individuals, such as the traditional store's online store, the traditional enterprise's e-commerce department and the traditional bank's Internet banking. Many companies opened up the online channels besides the offline channels. In 2007, China's online retail trade scale was about 56.1 billion Yuan. With the rising e-business, e-commerce gradually extended to the supply chain links. It promoted the growth of the logistics, online payment and other e-commerce support services.

Infrastructure phase (2008-2013)

The economic changes triggered by e-commerce made the core element "information" increasingly and widely used in economic activities. It speeded up the information penetration in business, industry and agriculture, greatly changed the consumer behaviors, corporate forms and social value creation modes, effectively reduced the social transaction costs, promoted the social labor division, detonated social innovation, improved the efficiency of the allocation of social resources, profoundly impacted on the retail industry, manufacturing, logistics industry and other traditional industries, became an important information economy infrastructure or new business infrastructure. On and through e-commerce platform of the new commercial infrastructure, more and more enterprises and individuals could reduce transaction costs, share business resources and innovate business services, which greatly promoted the development of e-commerce in turn.

In July 2008, China had the world's largest "Internet population". According to China Internet Network Information Center (CNNIC) statistics, at the end of June 2008, the number of Chinese Internet users reached 253 million, for the first time outnumbering the United States and ranking first in the world. During the two sessions in 2010, Premier Wen Jiabao's "Government Work Report" was clearly put forward to strengthen the business system and other infrastructure construction, and actively develop e-commerce, which is the first time in the national government work report clearly putting forward vigorously supporting electronic commerce. In October 2010, McCaw forest landed NASDAQ and became the first Chinese B2C e-commerce concept stock. In December of the same year, Dangdang was listed on the New York Stock Exchange in the United States. In 2011, the rapid development of the group purchase sites witnessed the situation of thousands of wars and the number of Chinese group purchase users were more than 42.2 million. In 2012, Taobao Mall was renamed "Tmall" with independent operation and the brand discount site Vip.com was listed in the NYSE transactions. Also in 2012, Taobao and Tmall's transaction volume exceeded 1 trillion Yuan. On the day "Double Eleven", the transaction size valued about 36.2 billion Yuan. In 2013, Alibaba and Intime Group, Fosun Group, Fuchun Group, SF Express logistics enterprises built the "rookie", planning to build a network of intelligent logistics to support 30 billion daily retail scales on average within 8-10 years, so that packages can be delivered to customers within 24 hours in any region of China.

Economy stage (after 2013)

China overtook the United States in 2013 and became the world's largest online retail market. In 2013, China's e-commerce transactions exceeded 10 trillion Yuan, the scale of network retail transactions valued about 1.85 trillion Yuan, equivalent to 7.8% of total retail sales of social consumer goods. In February 2014, China Employment Promotion Association released "Network

Entrepreneurship Employment Statistics and Social Security Research Project Report", which showed the online shops in China facilitated direct employment of a total of 9 million 620 thousand people and indirect employment over 120 million, reaching a new growth point of employment. In June 2014, China's online shopping users reached 332 million and the proportion of Internet users in China to use online shopping was 52.5%. In April 2014, Jumei. com was listed on the NYSE. In May, Jingdong Group was listed on the US NASDAQ officially. In September, Alibaba was officially listed on the NYSE and the issue price was 68 US dollars per share, being the largest IPO in the US history in terms of financing. In 2014, China's express delivery business volume was nearly 14 billion, ranking first in the world. China's express delivery business has a cumulative increase on the average of more than 50% for 44 consecutive months. According to iResearch, China's e-commerce GMV totaled 20.2 trillion Yuan in 2016, increasing by 23.1% compared with 2015. Online shopping with growth rate of 23.9% and local life O2O with growth of 28.2% were important roles which fueled the development of e-commerce in 2016.

The rapid development of online retail has promoted the development of production service industry, such as broadband, cloud computing, IT outsourcing, network third party payment, network marketing, online shop operation, logistics express delivery and consulting service, and formed a huge e-commerce ecosystem. E-commerce infrastructure is increasingly improved and e-commerce's economic and social impact is stronger than before. E-commerce, on the basis of the "infrastructure", has spawned new business ecology and a new business landscape, influenced and accelerated the traditional industry e-commercialization, and promoted the overall transformation and upgrading of the economy.

SUMMARY

This chapter mainly discusses issues related to electronic commerce (EC), which is the trading or facilitation of trading in products or services using computer networks, such as the Internet. EC framework involves many activities, organization units and technologies under the environment of e-commerce. Generally, EC's framework comprises "3 levels" and "2 columns". "3 levels" refers to network level, information publishing level and information transmission level, business service level and e-commerce application level. "2 columns" refers to public and legal regulation column and technical standard column. EC is classified into B2B, B2C, B2B2C, B2G, C2B, C2C, G2C etc. This chapter also discusses EC's history, and Chinese EC's history and development.

Words and Expressions

①**access**: the act of approaching or entering 接近,进入

②**bid**: a formal proposal to buy at a specified price 投标

③**brick and mortar**: existing in reality; substantial 实际存在的;实体的

④**demographic**: relating to or concerning demography 人口统计学的
⑤**dissemination**: the act of dispersing or diffusing something 传播
⑥**infrastructure**: the stock of basic facilities and capital equipment needed for the functioning of a country or area 基础设施
⑦**intermediary**: a negotiator who acts as a link between parties 中间人
⑧**logistics**: the management of the flow of things between the point of origin and the point of consumption in order to meet requirements of customers or corporations 物流
⑨**manufacturing**: the act of making something (a product) from raw materials 制造业
⑩**Marcom**: public relation department 公关部
⑪**mundane**: very ordinary and not at all interesting or unusual 平凡的
⑫**NASDAQ**: National Association of Securities Deal Automated Quotations 纳斯达克
⑬**newsletter**: report or open letter giving informal or confidential news of interest to a special group 通信
⑭**outsourcing**: If a company outsources work or things, it pays workers from outside the company to do the work or supply the things. 外包
⑮**protocol**: a set of rules for exchanging information between computers 协议
⑯**retail**: the selling of goods to consumers 零售
⑰**revenue**: money that a company, organization, or government receives from people (公司、组织的)收入,收益
⑱**telecom**: systems used in transmitting messages over a distance electronically 电信
⑲**transaction**: the act of transacting within or between groups (as carrying on commercial activities) 交易

Exercises

Ⅰ. **Key Terms** (Explain the following terms.)

①electronic commerce

②business-to-business

③business-to-consumer

④business-to-government

⑤government-to-consumer

Ⅱ. **Multiple Choice Exercises** (Choose the correct answer to the following questions from A, B, C and D. There is only one correct answer.)

①Electronic commerce draws on technology such as ________.

A. social media　　B. third-party sales　　C. mobile commerce　　D. retail sales

②Modern electronic commerce typically uses the ________ for at least one part of the transaction's life cycle.

A. World Wide Web　　B. Baidu　　C. telex　　D. HTML

③Which is not included in Network level of EC?

A. Wire Access.　　B. Cable TV.　　C. Extranet.　　D. WiMAX.

④B2B would not occur when a business uses the computer and Internet to ________.

A. fulfill the payment and conclude the transactions with others

B. source materials for their production process

C. re-purchase goods and services produced by others

D. acquire the services of another for operational reasons

⑤Which statement is incorrect about the description of B2B2C?

A. B2B2C is an emerging e-commerce model that combines B2B and B2C for a complete product or service transaction.

B. B2B2C provides clients with the value-adding products and services.

C. B2B2C is a collaboration process.

D. B2B2C creates mutually beneficial service.

⑥Which statement is correct about the advantage of EC?

A. Organizations can expand their markets to national and international markets with minimum capital investment.

B. E-commerce cannot help organization to reduce the cost to create process, distribute, retrieve and manage the paper based information.

C. E-commerce improves the brand image of the company.

D. E-commerce helps organization to provide better customer services.

⑦When did e-commerce become possible?

A. 2007.　　B. 2001.　　C. 1994.　　D. 1991.

⑧Which of the following statements is incorrect concerning EC's history?

A. The dot-com collapse in 2000 led to unfortunate results and many of e-commerce companies disappeared.

B. Although the Internet began to advance in popularity among the general public in 1994, it took approximately four years to develop the security protocols and DSL.

C. In 1997, the "brick and mortar" retailers recognized the advantages of electronic commerce and began to add such capabilities to their web sites.

D. By the end of 2001, the largest form of e-commerce, B2B model, had around $700 billion in transactions.

Ⅲ. Review Questions

①What is the framework of e-commerce?

②Could you explain "B2B2C model" with one example?

③Could you briefly introduce the tool stage of Chinese EC?

Ⅳ. Online Practice

①Visit dangdang. com and finish the following tasks:

- Find the five top-selling books on EC.
- Find a review of one of these books.
- Review the customer services you can get from Dangdang website and describe the benefits you can get by shopping there.
- Review the products directory.

②Go to qyer. com and design your own travel plan. Share with your classmates the advantage of the activity.

③Go to jc56. com website and find information about recent EC projects that are related to logistics and supply chain.

④Find some typical websites as models for B2B, B2C, B2B2C, B2G, C2B, C2C and G2C.

Ⅴ. Case Study

Logistics Revolution in China: Will Delivery Companies Deliver?

Express delivery in China is cheap and fast. Buy something online and most likely you'll have a *kuaidi* (Chinese word for delivery) at your door step in just a day or two for a small delivery fee of as little as RMB 10 ($1.5). The country has more than 35,000 courier delivery companies that make this speedy delivery possible. They whiz through cities on their three-wheeled electric trucks, and go door-to-door delivering parcels for slim profits.

But having so many companies competing for such low margins has created a fiercely competitive logistics industry. Many companies center their business model on delivering parcels, and very few venture on other value-added services. Aiming at only being quick-and-cheap doesn't leave much room or time for any other customer-friendly initiatives. T. L. Yip, the associate director of Hong Kong-based C. Y. Tung International Centre for Maritime Studies, says, "The market is so big that delivery companies have to sacrifice efficiency to meet the demand."

This comes at a price. In 2012 the Chinese postal authority cancelled the permits of 116 express delivery companies amid growing reports of customers complaining about losses, theft, poor handling of parcels and massive delays, especially during peak times. In 2011 the State Post Bureau received a whopping 366.1% more complains than the previous year! Half of them were caused by delayed deliveries. This seriously affects e-commerce companies whose inability to control delivery may end up tarnishing their prospects of growth and affecting the loyalty of their customers.

Alibaba, the world's biggest B2B online platform, is probably the one facing the biggest challenge. It has a popular C2C online marketplace (Taobao receives more than 20 million orders a day, accounting for 70% of China's deliveries). The parcels are delivered by third-party providers that have to deal with China' underdeveloped delivery infrastructure. This is a common problem the whole industry is facing, prompting other e-commerce player like Jingdong Mall (JD. com which was formerly known as 360buy. com), Suning and Vancl to invest in self-owned and managed logistics systems to ensure they are in control of the whole process.

In contrast, Alibaba is not interested in owing its delivery network and since 2011 it has been lobbying for what it sees as a "logistics revolution". In May 2013, it announced the formation of a new company, Cainiao Network Technology. With Alibaba's former CEO, Jack Ma, as the Chairman, Cainiao is an alliance of logistic companies, courier and e-commerce companies such as Yintai Group, Alibaba Group and SF-Express, which are willing to collectively work for the development of a nationwide IT logistics platform. An Alibaba group spokesperson told *CKGSB Knowledge* that the company is "spearheading the project in cooperation with industry partners with a common goal of enhancing the existing logistic network, whether it is on the IT or physical delivery and warehousing levels". With a planned initial investment of $16.3 billion, the consortium marks a critical step in Alibaba's vision of developing what it calls a China Smart Logistics Network within this decade. The ultimate aim is to solve a common problem that the company describes as a "key industry bottleneck for e-commerce growth in China", the spokesperson says.

Questions for Discussion

①What was the background of the formation of Cainiao Network Technology?

②What challenges are the logistics companies in China facing?

Chapter 2 E-marketplace: Structures and Mechanisms

本章导读

市场在经济中处于中心地位，它方便货物、信息、服务的交换与支付，在这一过程中，市场为买方、卖方、中介乃至社会提供了经济价值。电子市场是基于 Internet 通信技术和其他电子化通信技术，通过一组动态的 Web 应用程序和其他应用程序把交易的双方集成在一起的虚拟交易环境。电子市场的主要构成和参与者包括顾客、卖方、产品和服务、基础设施、前端、后端、中介等。本章主要探讨什么是电子市场、电子市场的主要参与者、电子市场的主要类型、电子市场的机制以及电子商城、电子商店、信息门户网站等电子市场的重要组成部分。由于电子商务不同于传统商业模式，其对商业的中间环节进行了改革和再造，于是有了"非居间化"或"脱媒"。传统商业在电商的冲击下遭遇了巨大的挑战，一些企业却把这个当成了商机，作为第三方向企业和消费者提供网络服务，是为"再居间化"或"重媒"。电子目录、搜索引擎和购物车等也是电子商务必要的构成部分。随着电子商务进一步纵深发展，中国涌现出了一批规模庞大的 B2B 电商企业，其中阿里巴巴、环球资源、中国制造和敦煌门户等在营收方面位居前列。

Business Terms

①**e-marketplace**: an online market place where buyers and sellers can do business electronically

②**storefront**: the facade or entryway of a retail store located on the ground floor or street level of a commercial building, typically including one or more display windows

③**e-mall**: an online shopping location where many stores are located

④**intermediary**: an individual or firm that brings together buyers and sellers for a fee without taking part in actual sale transactions

⑤**portal**: a mechanism that is used in e-marketplaces, e-stores, and other types of EC

⑥**infomediaries**: web sites that gather and organize large amounts of data and act as intermediaries between those who want the information and those who supply the information

⑦**broker**: a person whose job is to buy and sell shares, foreign money, or goods for other people

Introductory Case

The revenue of China's B2B platforms for small and medium enterprises (SME) increased steadily. According to the latest data from iResearch, the revenue of China's B2B platforms for SME totaled 23.59 billion Yuan in 2016, up 17.1% from 2015.

iResearch holds the opinion that the revenue was influenced by three factors. The first is the capital market. 169 B2B companies had raised 15 billion Yuan financing in total until December 2016, indicating that B2B platform companies were popular in capital market.

The next is the export and import market. In 2016, China's exports and imports totaled 24.3 trillion Yuan, falling 1.1% from 2015. This downtrend in foreign trade market exerted a certain influence on the import and export businesses of SME.

The last is the strategy of B2B platforms. Many platforms adjusted their strategies and businesses in 2016 to pursue a diversified development. Alibaba started to pay attention to the revenue of their platform and raised the fee for membership; DHgate enhanced the registration regulation on the platform; HC360 invested in more market segments; Cogobuy established IngDan platform to explore intelligent hardware field. What's more, the B2B platforms integrated resources in the supply chain and increased their investment in B2B 2.0 businesses, such as online trade, O2O businesses and Internet finance, which will accelerate their revenue growth.

In 2016, top 9 core companies took up 72.9% of SME' B2B e-commerce market. Alibaba maintained its leading position with a share of 47.5%; Global Resource and JQW ranked the second and the third with a share of 5.6% and 5.1% respectively. The fourth and fifth were DHgate and HC360 with a market share of 4.8% and 4.6%. They both adjusted their businesses in 2016, but it will take some time to take effect. Other B2B e-commerce platforms had steady growth and their market share remained unchanged.

Questions for Discussion

①Which factors influenced the revenue of China's B2B platforms for SME in 2016?

②What were the strategies the B2B platforms applied to successfully boost their revenues?

③How do you think the next stage of Alibaba?

2.1 OVERVIEW OF E-MARKETPLACE

According to Bakos (1998), electronic markets played a central role in the economy, facilitating the exchange of information, goods, services, and payments. In the process, they created economic value for buyers, sellers, market intermediaries, and for society at large.

The major place for conducting EC transaction is the electronic market (e-market). An e-marketplace, also called e-marketspace, is a virtual marketplace in which sellers and buyers meet and conduct different types of transactions. Customers exchange their goods and services for money (or other goods and services if bartering is used). The functions of an e-market are the same as that of a physical marketplace; however, computerized systems tend to make e-markets much more efficient by providing more updated information to buyers and sellers.

In recent years, markets have seen a dramatic increase in the use of IT and EC. EC has increased market efficiency by expediting or improving the functions listed in the following table. Furthermore, EC has been able to significantly decrease the cost of executing these functions.

Functions of a Market

Matching of Buyers and Sellers	Facilitation of Transactions	Institutional Infrastructure
• Determination of product offerings Product features offered by sellers Aggregation of different products • Search (of buyers for sellers and of sellers for buyers) Price and product information Organizing bids and bartering Matching seller offerings with buyer preferences • Price discovery Process and outcome in determination of prices Enabling price comparisons	• Logistics Delivery of information, goods, or services to buyers • Settlement Transfer of payments to sellers • Trust Credit system, reputations, rating agencies like Consumers Reports and BBB. Special escrow and trust online agencies	• Legal Commercial code, contract law, dispute resolution, intellectual property protection Export and import law • Regulatory Rules and regulations, monitoring, enforcement

Source: "The Emerging Role of Electronic Marketplaces on the Internet" by Y. Bakos, in *Communications of the ACM*. 1998 by ACM Inc.

The emergence of electronic marketplaces, especially Internet-based ones, changed several processes used in trading and supply chains. These changes, driven by technology, result in even greater economic efficiency.

2.2 E-MARKETPLACE COMPONENTS AND PARTICIPANTS

The major components and players in a marketplace are sellers, customers, goods and services, infrastructure, a front end, a back end, intermediaries, other business partners and support services.

Sellers There are millions of storefronts on the Internet, advertising and offering a huge variety of items. These stores are owned by companies, government agencies or individuals. But in a B2B e-marketplace, these storefronts are owned by companies.

Customers There are 668 million people in China, 3. 174 billion worldwide (CNNIC, July 2015) who surf the Internet. They are potential consumers of the goods and services offered or advertised on the Internet. These consumers are looking for bargains, customized items, collectors' items, entertainment, socialization, and so on. They are in the driver's seat. They search for detailed product and service information, then compare, bid, or negotiate.

Goods and services One of the major differences between marketplace and e-marketplace is the possible digitization of products and services. Although both types of markets can sell physical products, the e-marketplace also can sell digital products, which can be transformed to digital format and instantly delivered over the Internet.

Infrastructure The e-marketplace infrastructure includes the Internet, intranet, hardware, software, and the like.

Front end The front end composes of the seller's portal, electronic catalogs, a shopping cart, a search engine, an auction engine, and a payment gateway.

Back end The back end refers to the activities that support online order fulfillment, inventory management, purchasing from suppliers, payment processing, packaging and delivery.

Intermediaries An intermediary is a third party that acts as a conduit for goods or services offered by a supplier to a consumer. Typically the intermediary offers some added value to the transaction that may not be possible by direct trading. Intermediaries of all kinds offer their services on the Internet. The role of the online intermediaries is quite different from that of regular intermediaries, such as wholesalers. For example, online intermediaries create and manage the online markets. They help match buyers and sellers, provide some infrastructure services, and help consumers and/or sellers to institute and complete transactions. They also support the vast number of transactions that exist in providing services. Most of these online intermediaries operate as computerized systems.

Other business partners Apart from intermediaries, there are also other types of partners, such as shippers, using the Internet to collaborate, mostly along with the supply chain.

Support services There are many different support services, ranging from certification and escrow services to content providers.

2.3 TYPES OF E-MARKETPLACE AND MECHANISMS

According to different classification criteria, there are several types of e-marketplace. The major B2C e-marketplaces are storefronts and Internet malls (e-malls). B2B e-marketplaces include private sell-side e-marketplaces, buy-side e-marketplaces, and exchanges. The gateways to these e-marketplaces are the portals.

2.3.1 Electronic Storefronts

An electronic storefront refers to a company's web site where products and services are sold. It is an electronic store. The storefront may belong to a manufacturer, to a retailer, to individual selling from home, or to another type of business. Companies that sell services (such as tourism) might refer to their storefronts as portals. In general, all storefronts have their own portals.

A storefront includes several mechanisms that are necessary for conducting the sale. The most common mechanisms are an electronic catalog; a search engine that helps the consumer find products in the catalog; and electronic cart for holding items until checkout; e-auction facilities; a payment gateway where payment arrangements can be made; a shipment court where shipping arrangements are made; and customer services, including product and warranty information.

Please go to the website of Tmall and find out the mechanisms of its storefront: the e-catalog, the search engine, the e-cart, the e-auction facilities, the payment gateway, the shipment court, and the customer services. If possible, try to identify all of them during a personal buy experience.

2.3.2 Electronic Malls

Besides buying at individual storefronts, consumers can shop in electronic malls, usually, called e-malls. Similar to the physical malls, an e-mall is an online shopping location where many stores are located. For example, Tmall. com is an e-mall that aggregates various stores and millions of products and services are sold and offered. It contains a directory of product categories and the stores in each category. When a consumer indicates the category he or she is interested in, the consumer is transferred to the appropriate independent storefront. Some malls only provide directory services for consumers, and some provide shared ones; some are actually large click-and-mortar retailer, and some are virtual retailers only.

2.3.3 Types of E-stores and E-malls

The e-stores and e-malls are also of several different types.

General stores/malls. These are large marketspaces that sell all types of products and offer kinds of services, such as Alibaba, Tmall, Jingdong, Amazon; and the major public portals, such as Alipay. All department and discount stores also fall into this category.

Specialized stores/malls. These refer to the stores/malls only sell one or a few types of products, such as books, flowers, wine, cars, or pet toys. Dangdang started as a specialized online bookstore, but today it is a generalized store.

Regional versus global stores. Some e-stores, such as e-grocers or sellers of heavy furniture, only serve the customers who live nearby. However, some local stores will sell to customers overseas if the customer is willing to pay the shipping, insurance, and other costs.

Pure-play online organizations versus click-and-mortar stores. Stores can be pure online organizations, such as Amazon and Dangdang. They do not have physical stores. Others are physical (brick-and-mortar) stores that also sell online, such as Gome with Gome. com, Sunning with Sunning. com. The second category is called click-and-mortar.

2.3.4 Type of E-marketplace

There are many different types of e-marketplace based on a range of business models. They can be broadly divided into categories based on the way in which they are operated.

Independent e-marketplace. An independent e-marketplace is usually a B2B online platform operated by a third party which is open to buyers or sellers in a particular industry. By registering on an independent e-marketplace, you can access classified ads or requests for quotations or bids in your industry sector. There will typically be some form of payment required to participate.

Buyer-oriented e-marketplace. A buyer-oriented e-marketplace is normally run by a consortium of buyers in order to establish an efficient purchasing environment. If you are looking to purchase, participating in this sort of e-marketplace can help you lower your administrative costs and achieve the best price from suppliers. As a supplier you can use a buyer-oriented e-marketplace to advertise your catalog to a pool of relevant customers who are looking to buy.

Supplier-oriented e-marketplace. Also known as a supplier directory, this marketplace is set up and operated by a number of suppliers who are seeking to establish an efficient sales channel via the Internet to a large number of buyers. They are usually searchable by the product or service being offered. Supplier directories benefit buyers by providing information about suppliers for markets and regions they may not be familiar with. Sellers can use these types of marketplace to increase their visibility to potential buyers and to get leads.

Vertical and horizontal e-marketplaces. Vertical e-marketplaces provide online access to businesses vertically up and down every segment of a particular industry sector such as automotive, chemical, construction or textiles. Buying or selling using a vertical e-marketplace for your industry sector can increase your operating efficiency and help to decrease supply chain costs, inventories and procurement-cycle time. A horizontal e-marketplace connects buyers and sellers across different industries or regions. You can use a horizontal e-marketplace to purchase indirect products such as office equipment or stationery.

2.3.5 Information Portals

A portal is a mechanism that is used in e-marketplaces, e-stores and other types of EC (e. g., intrabusiness, e-learning etc.). With the growing use of intranets and the Internet, many organizations encounter information overload at a number of different levels. Information is scattered across numerous documents, e-mail messages, and databases at different locations and in disparate systems. It is becoming more and more time-consuming to find relevant and accurate information.

As a consequence, organizations lose a lot of productive employee time. One solution to this problem is the use of portals. A portal is an information gateway. It attempts to address information overload by enabling people to search and access relevant information from disparate IT systems and the Internet, using advanced search and indexing techniques, such as Google's desktop search and Baidu's desktop search, in an intranet based environment. An information portal is a single point of access through a Web browser to critical business information located inside and outside of an organization. Many information portals can be personalized for the users.

2.3.6 Types of Portals

There are many descriptions and shapes of portals. One way to distinguish them is to look at their content, which can vary from narrow to broad, and their community or audience, which also can vary.

Commercial/public portals. These portals are the most popular ones on the Internet, and they offer content for diverse communities. Although they can be customized by the user, they are still intended for broad audiences and offer fairly-priced contents, some in real time. Examples of such sites are Yahoo, Tencent and the like.

Corporate portals. Corporate portals coordinate rich content within relatively narrow corporate and partners' communities. They are also known as enterprise portals or enterprise information portals.

Publishing portals. These portals are intended for communities with specific interests. Theses portals involve relatively little customization of content, but they provide extensive online search features and some interactive capabilities. Examples of such sites are TechWeb, and ZDNet.

Personal portals. These target specific filtered information for individuals. They offer relatively narrow content and are typically very personalized.

Mobile portals. These are portals that are accessible from mobile devices, such as cell phones, pads and so on. Although most of the other portals mentioned here are PC based, increasing numbers of portals are accessible via mobile devices. One example of such a mobile portal is ifeng. com.

Voice portals. Voice portals are web sites, usually portals, with audio interfaces. This means that they can be accessed by a standard telephone or cell phone. AOL by phone is an example of a service that allows users to retrieve e-mail, news, and other content from AOL via telephone. It uses both speech recognition and text-to-speech technologies. Companies such as Tellme. com and Be Vocal. com offer access to the Internet from telephones and tools to build voice portals. Voice portals are especially popular for 1—800 numbers that provide self-service to customers with information available in Internet databases.

According to another classification, the types of portal and their major characteristics are as follows:

Access portal: associated with ISP

Horizontal or functional portal: offers a range of services; for example search engines, directories, news, recruitment, personal information management, shopping

Vertical portal: covers a particular market, such as construction, with news and other services

Media portal: mainly focuses on consumer or business news

Geographical portal: horizontal or vertical

Marketplace portal: horizontal, vertical or geographical

Search portal: focuses on search (Google, Ask, etc.)

Media type portal: voice or video and delivered by streaming media or download of files (Youtube, Viemo, etc.)

2.4 INTERMEDIATION AND SYNDICATION IN E-COMMERCE

Intermediaries, also called brokers, play an important role in commerce by providing value-added activities and services to buyers and sellers. There are many types of intermediaries. The most well-known intermediaries in the physical world are wholesalers and retailers. On the Internet, there are, in addition, intermediaries that provide and/or control information flow. Theses e-intermediaries (online intermediaries) are known as infomediaries. The information flows to and from buyers and sellers via infomediaries, as shown in the following chart. Frequently, intermediaries aggregate information and sell it to others.

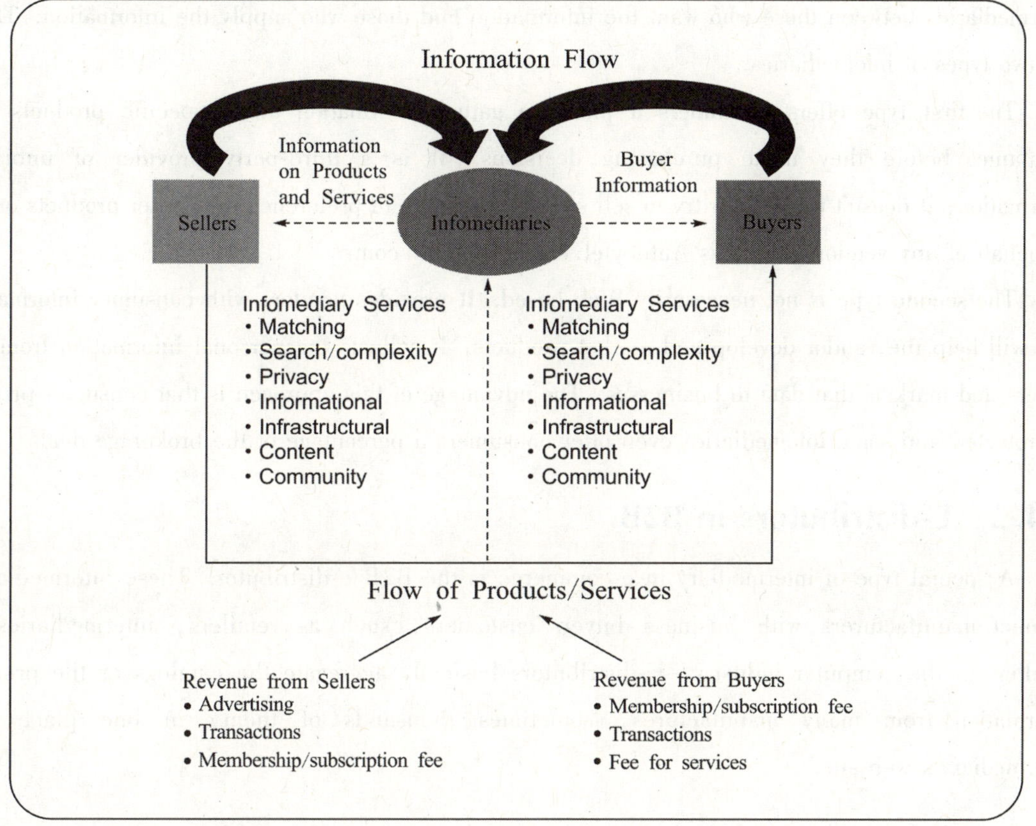

Source: Grover. v., and J. Teng. "E-Commerce and the Information Market." *Communications of the ACM*. 2001 by ACM Inc.

2.4.1 Brokers and Infomediaries

A broker is a company that facilitates transactions between buyers and sellers. Different types of brokers are as follows:

Buy/sell fulfillment. A corporate that helps consumers buy and sell orders, such as eTrade.

Virtual mall. A company that helps consumers buy from a variety of stores, such as Yahoo! Stores.

Metamediary. A firm that offers customers accesses to a variety of stores and provides them with transaction services, such as financial services. For example, Amazon zShops.

Search agent. A company that helps consumers compare different stores, such as Shopping. com.

Shopping facilitator. A company that helps consumers use online shops by providing currency conversion, language translation, payment features and delivery solutions, and potentially is a user-customized interface, such as MyOrbital. com.

Infomediaries are web sites that gather and organize large amounts of data and act as intermediaries between those who want the information and those who supply the information. There are two types of infomediaries.

The first type offers consumers a place to gather information about specific products and companies before they make purchasing decisions. It is a third-party provider of unbiased information; it doesn't promote or try to sell specific products in preference over other products or act on behalf of any vendors, such as Autobytel. com, BizRate. com.

The second type is not necessarily Web-based. It provides vendors with consumer information that will help the vendor develop and market products. It collects the personal information from the buyers and markets that data to businesses. The advantage of this approach is that consumer privacy is protected and some infomediaries even offer consumers a percentage of the brokerage deals.

2.4.2 E-distributors in B2B

A special type of intermediary in e-commerce is the B2B e-distributor. These intermediaries connect manufacturers with business buyers/customers, such as retailers, intermediaries or resellers in the computer industry. E-distributors basically aggregate the catalogs or the product information from many manufactures, sometimes thousands of them, in one place—the intermediary's web site.

2.4.3 Disintermediation and Reintermediation

Disintermediation is the removal of intermediaries in economics from a supply chain, or cutting out the middlemen in connection with a transaction or a series of transactions. Instead of going through traditional distribution channels, which have some type of intermediary (such as a distributor, wholesaler, broker, or agent), companies may now deal with customers directly, for example via the Internet. Disintermediation may decrease the total cost of servicing customers and may allow the manufacturer to increase profit margins and/or reduce prices. Disintermediation initiated by consumers is often the result of high market transparency, in that buyers are aware of supply prices direct from the manufacturer. Buyers may choose to bypass the middlemen (wholesalers and retailers) to buy directly from the manufacturer, and pay less. They can alternatively elect to purchase from wholesalers. Often, a business-to-consumer electronic commerce

(B2C) company functions as the bridge between buyer and manufacturer.

Reintermediation can be defined as the reintroduction of an intermediary between end users (consumers) and a producer. This term applies especially to instances in which disintermediation has occurred first. At the start of the Internet revolution, electronic commerce was seen as a tool of disintermediation for cutting operating costs. The concept was that by allowing consumers to purchase products directly from producers via the Internet, the product delivery chain would be drastically shortened, thereby "disintermediating" the standard supply model middlemen. However, what largely happened was that new intermediaries appeared in the digital landscape (e. g., Amazon and eBay). Reintermediation occurred due to many new problems associated with the e-commerce disintermediation concept, largely centered on the issues associated with the direct-to-consumers model. The high cost of shipping many small orders, massive customer service issues, and confronting the wrath of disintermediated retailers and supply channel partners all presented real obstacles. Huge resources are required to accommodate pre-sales and post-sales issues of individual consumers. Before disintermediation, supply chain middlemen acted as salespeople for the producers. Without them, the producer itself would have to handle procuring those customers. Selling online has its own associated costs: developing quality websites, maintaining product information, and marketing expenses all add up. Finally, limiting a product's availability to Internet channels forces the producer to compete with the rest of the Internet for customers' attention, a space that is becoming increasingly crowded.

2.5 ELECTRONIC CATALOGS, SEARCH ENGINES AND SHOPPING CARTS

2.5.1 Electronic Catalog

Electronic catalog is a unique Web tool, consisting of a product database, directory and search capabilities, and can be interactive. It is the backbone of most e-commerce sales site. For vendors, e-catalog is to advertise and promote products and services. For customers, it is to locate information on products and services.

E-catalog offers following features to all the users:

- facilitate product selection
- avoid selection mistakes
- create complete documentation

E-catalogs can be classified on three dimensions:

- The dynamics of the information presentation

- The degree of customization
- Integration with business processes

2.5.2 Search Engines

Search engine is a software system that is designed to search for information on the World Wide Web. The search results are generally presented in a line of results often referred to as search engine results pages (SERPs). The information may be a mix of web pages, images, and other types of files.

Google, Alta Vista, and Baidu are popular search engines. Portals as AOL, Yahoo, and MSN also have their own search engines.

2.5.3 Electronic Shopping Carts

A e-shopping cart is an order-processing softuare that allows customers to select items they wish to buy while they continue to shop. The software program of an electronic shopping cart allows customers to select items, review what has been selected, make changes, and then finalize the list.

2.6 ONLINE AUCTIONS

An online auction is an auction which is held over the Internet. What makes online auctions so powerful is that, with Internet technology, vast numbers of business or individuals can bid, allowing sellers to get the best price. Two main types of auction are:

- Forward auction: where lots are sold to the highest bidder.
- Reverse auction: where suppliers compete on price and the lowest bid for a tender wins the business.

2.6.1 Forward Auction

Selling using a forward auction can be a cost-effective way for your business to acquire new customers, test new products or establish pricing points. Excess inventory can be disposed of quickly and sales costs are reduced because of the minimal amount spent on marketing. You can price your goods according to demand and stock level.

Some business trade solely online using forward auction on web sites such as eBay.

Forward auction can also bring benefits when buying for your business. You may be able to source non-critical supplies, e. g. acquire stationery and office furniture, or acquire specialist, second-hand equipment at a more competitive rate. By setting up automated searches and bid alerts you can reduce the time spent on procurement.

2.6.2 Reverse Auction

If you are a supplier to large companies, you may be asked to compete for their business in a reverse auction. Businesses that supply their goods through reverse auctions benefit by being able to compete for businesses globally. They can also make savings by gaining access to customers who are ready to buy, without having to launch a sales campaign. Reverse auctions are a good way to offload stock or build market share; however, they are normally by invitation only.

2.7 B2B E-MARKETPLACE IN CHINA

2.7.1 The Main B2B E-Commerce Marketplace in China

The top 5 China e-commerce marketplaces are Alibaba, Global Sources, HC360, Made-in-China, and DHgate. (China Internet Watch, May 15, 2015).

◇ Alibaba (Alibaba Group Holding Limited) is a Chinese e-commerce company that provides C2C, B2C and B2B sales services via Web portals. It also provides electronic payment services, a shopping search engine and data-centric cloud computing services. The group began in 1999 when Jack Ma founded the website Alibaba. com, a B2B portal to connect Chinese manufacturers with overseas buyers. In 2012, two of Alibaba's portals handled 1. 1 trillion Yuan ($170 billion) in sales. Suppliers from other countries are supported (with more stringent checks than for Chinese companies), but the company primarily operates in China. At closing time on the date of its initial public offering (IPO), 19 September 2014, Alibaba's market value was $231 billion. It is the world's largest retailer, whose online sales and profits surpassed all US retailers (including Walmart, Amazon and eBay) combined in 2015. It also has been expanding into media and entertainment industry, with revenues rising 3-digit percent year on year.

◇ Global Sources is a Hong Kong based B2B media company. It facilitates trade between China and the world. The company provides sourcing information to volume buyers and integrated marketing services to suppliers. In addition, Global Sources verifies the quality of the manufacturer. The company was founded in November 1970 by Merle A. Hinrichs and C. Joseph Bendy as Trade Media Ltd., its first publication, *Asian Sources* magazine, was launched three months later. At September 1974, the company's first spin-off publication—*Asian Sources Electronics* appeared. More industry-specific titles were subsequently added. In 1996, Global Sources launched the industry's first B2B website, *Asian Sources Online* and its monthly CD-ROW. Both were designed to supplement and complement the company's trade publications. The company launched its

China Sourcing Fairs in 2003. Today, more than 1 million international buyers, including 95 of the world's top 100 retailers, use Global Sources services to obtain products and company information to help them source profitably from overseas supply markets.

2.7.2 The B2B E-commerce Market Share in China

China's B2B e-commerce market reached 5.48 billion Yuan ($883 million) in Q1 2015, a decrease of 1.6% QoQ according to Analysis International.

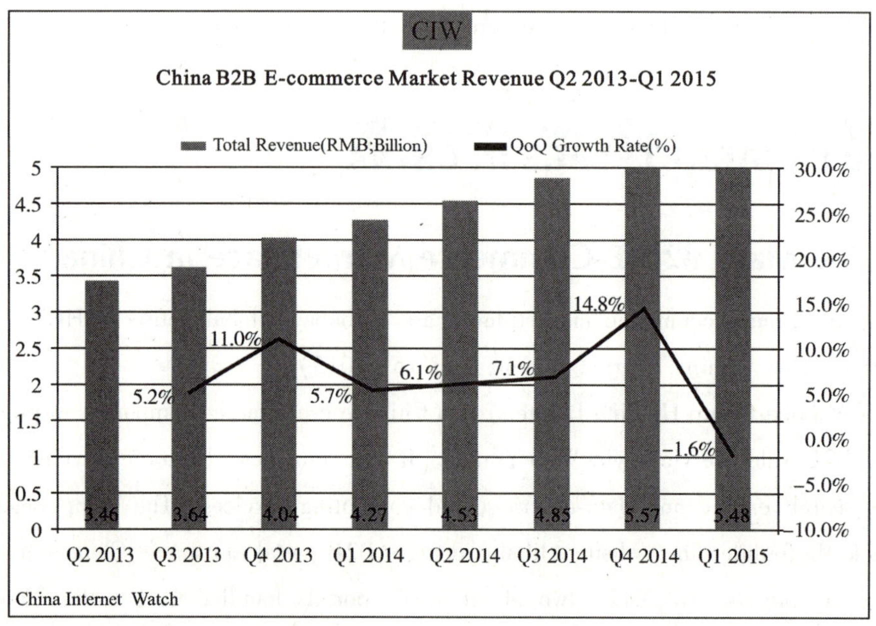

Source: Analysis International, May 2015

The first quarter of year normally sees slow growth in China B2B market considering the fiscal year cycle, enterprise purchase cycles, holidays and etc. In addition, China's international trade market had some negative impact. The total value of China's import and export trading was down by 6% QoQ in Q1 2015.

China's international trading trade B2B platform completely enters a transaction era; and, the value of credit guarantee service entered the stage. Cross-channel collaborations have become new means for B2B e-commerce platforms to enhance the competitiveness.

Alibaba still dominates China's B2B market with revenues of 44.13% market share, followed by HC360 (4.86%) and Global Sources (4.69%).

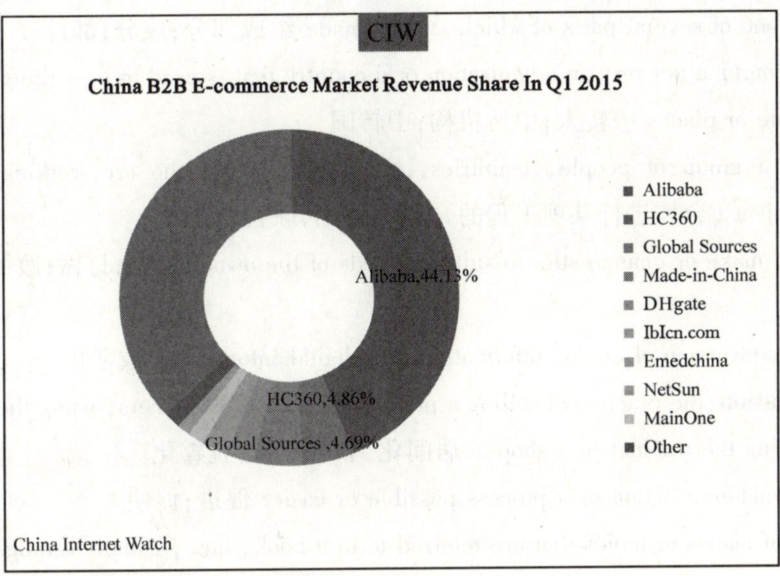

Source: Analysis International, May 2015

SUMMARY

This chapter mainly discusses e-marketplaces and components, the role of intermediaries, the major types of e-marketplaces, electronic catalogs, search engines, shopping carts, types of auctions and their characteristics, as well as the major B2B marketplaces in China. E-marketplace is a virtual market that does not suffer from limitations of space. Its major components include customers, sellers, products, infrastructures, frontend processed and backend activities, electronic intermediaries, other business partners and support services. The intermediaries will change as e-markets develop: Some will be eliminated and others will change their roles. According to different classification, there are different types of e-marketplace. E-catalogs, search engines, and shopping carts are other important mechanisms in e-marketplace. There are some very influential B2B markets in China, such as Alibaba, Global Sources.

Words and Expressions

①**bargain**: thing bought for less than the usual price 减价品;便宜货

②**barter**: to exchange goods, property, services, etc. for other goods, etc. without using money (同某人)以物易物;以(财产或劳务等)作交换

③**catalog**: a complete list of items, for example of things that people can look at or buy 目录;目录簿

④**click-and-mortar**: 既开展线上销售又有传统门店销售的企业

⑤**component**: one of several parts of which sth. is made 组成部分;成分;部件

⑥**conduit**: (*formal*) a person, an organization or a country that is used to pass things or information to other people or places 中转人;中转机构;中转国

⑦**consortium**: a group of people, countries, companies, etc. who are working together on a particular project (合作进行某项工程的)财团,银团,联营企业

⑧**customize**: to make or change sth. to suit the needs of the owner 订制,订做,改制(以满足顾主的需要)

⑨**digitization**: conversion of analog information into digital information 数字化

⑩**disintermediation**: the practice of selling a product directly to customers, using the Internet rather than first selling the product to a shop 非居间化,非中介化,脱媒化

⑪**facilitate**: to make an action or a process possible or easier 促进;促使

⑫**index**: a list of names or topics that are referred to in a book, etc., usually arranged at the end of a book in alphabetical order or listed in a separate file or book 索引

⑬**interface**: the way a computer program presents information to a user or receives information from a user, in particular the layout of the screen and the menus 界面(尤指计算机屏幕布局和菜单)

⑭**intranet**: a computer network that is private to a company, university, etc. but is connected to and uses the same software as the Internet 内联网,企事业单位内部互联网(公司、大学等的内部网络,但与互联网相接并共享软件)

⑮**obstacle**: a situation, an event, etc. that makes it difficult for you to do or achieve sth. 障碍;阻碍

⑯**procurement**: the process of obtaining supplies of sth., especially for a government or an organization(尤指为政府或机构)采购,购买

⑰**profit margin**: the difference between the cost of buying or producing sth. and the price that it is sold for 利润;利润幅度;毛利

⑱**reintermediation**: the reintroduction of an intermediary between end users (consumers) and a producer 再中介化,中介重建

⑲**warranty**: a written agreement in which a company selling sth. promises to repair or replace it if there is a problem within a particular period of time (商品)质保单

⑳**wrath**: (*formal*) extreme anger 盛怒;震怒;怒火

Exercises

Ⅰ. **Key Terms**(Explain the following terms.)

①e-marketplace

②e-catalog

③e-mall

④search engine

⑤e-auction

Ⅱ. Multiple Choice Exercises (Choose the correct answer to the following questions from A, B, C and D. There is only one correct answer.)

①One of the major differences between the marketplace and the e-marketspace is the possible ________ of products and services in a e-marketspace.

A. globalization B. virtualization C. digitalization D. realization

②________ are in the driver's seat in e-commerce.

A. Producers B. Suppliers C. Clients D. Customers

③An independent e-marketplace is usually a ________ online platform operated by a third party.

A. B2B B. C2C C. B2C D. G2B

④As a supplier you can use a ________ e-marketplace to advertise your catalog to a pool of relevant customers who are looking to buy.

A. seller-oriented B. supplier-oriented C. buyer-oriented D. a third party

⑤________ are the most popular ones on the Internet, and they offer content for diverse communities.

A. Commercial portals B. Private Portals

C. Corporate portals D. Personal portals

⑥Some portals are web sites, usually portals with audio interfaces, and they can be accessed by a standard telephone or cell phone. These portals are ________.

A. public portals B. private portals C. voice portals D. video portals

⑦A ________ is a company that facilitates transactions between buyers and sellers.

A. buyer B. seller C. broker D. intermediary

⑧The biggest B2B market in terms of revenue is ________.

A. Alibaba B. Global Sources C. Made-in-China D. DHgate

Ⅲ. Review Questions

①What are the functions of e-commerce?

②What roles do intermediaries play in EC?

③How do you understand the relationship between disintermediation and reintermediation? Do they conflict with one another?

Ⅳ. Online Practice

①Visit the websites of Amazon and Alibaba and figure out the differences between them in the perspective of customers, sellers, and goods.

②A dealer of general mechanical equipment and accessories is looking for some oversea suppliers on the Internet. Would you like to recommend some e-marktplaces?

③Go to the websites of Alibaba and Tmall and find the similarities and differences between them in terms of customers, sellers, and goods.

④Study some different B2B marketplaces, and try to figure out the trend of e-marketplaces.

Ⅴ. Case Study

Bringing the Construction Industry into E-commerce

Though last among a list of 20 industries in readiness for e-commerce, concrete and other contractors are getting more online with HD Supply.

Construction contractors—those working with concrete and other building materials—were dead last in a study last year by *Harvard Business Review* of how 20 industries were digitally transforming their operations.

Nonetheless, HD Supply Construction & Industrial White Cap, a provider of building supplies, is finding ways to bring contractors into e-commerce. Ian Heller, vice president, marketing and e-business, said in a presentation during the B2B workshop at the Internet Retailer Conference & Exhibition 2015 in Chicago last week.

Total sales for HD Supply Construction & Industrial White Cap, were $1.5 billion last year, up 15% from $1.3 billion in 2013. The company sells through a business-to-business e-commerce site and through 156 physical branches across 31 states. It also channels sales through 455 outside account managers. It provides specialty hardware, tools, safety equipment and safety products for mid-sized to large contractors.

Heller said the company, a unit of industrial products distributor HD Supply Inc., is using new mobile and desktop e-commerce offerings to bring more customer orders online, as construction personnel and managers are using new online buying tools to get what they need, when and where they need it on job sites. The company does not break out online sales.

But HD Supply Construction & Industrial's traditional customer base and its manner of processing many orders through account managers have made it difficult to move customers into ordering online, Heller said.

He cited the most notable challenges:

A highly mobile customer base located on job sites;

Many purchases were made via a bidding process;

Many sales were handled by HD Supply's account managers;

Most contractors are small business;

HD Supply delivers most orders on its own trucks to job sites.

The company sought to address these challenges with a mobile site to complement its transactional web site, Heller said. The mobile site lets buyers browse among more than 20 product categories—including fasteners, building materials, electrical supplies and power tools—and arrange for delivery at specific job site locations and times, and arrange for copies of orders and order confirmations to be routed to supervisors and accounts payable personnel at the customer's company. The site also routes those documents to account managers at HD Supply, who can check if the customer ordered all that it needed.

The mobile site is also designed to be easy to navigate by the small businesses who buy from HD Supply. It offers such features as a help section where customers learn how to click to pay online invoices or to apply online for a credit application. Other features include a mobile calculator for determining the amount of price of concrete needed on a job site.

To make buying easier for customers, HD Supply's account managers can set up product lists for each customer based on their business and purchasing history. Customers can purchase quickly from lists of frequently purchased items.

Customers can also enter purchase order numbers to maintain records in their financial management systems, and instantly view running totals of the numbers of SKUs ordered and expenses.

Customers also receive order confirmations via e-mail, with copies sent as necessary to such additional customer personnel as accounts payable managers and project managers as well the buyer.

Questions for Discussion

①What is new about the offerings of HD Supply Inc. ?

②What challenges are HD Supply Inc. facing when they offer their products online?

Chapter 3 Retailing in Electronic Commerce

本章导读

中国电子零售业发展迅猛,2015 年中国零售业电子商务销售额达到了 5 896.1 亿美元,相比 2014 年,增长了 33.3%,占全国零售业销售额的 10.1%。据预测到 2018 年,中国零售业电子商务市场总交易额将超过 10 110 亿美元,届时将占零售业销售额的 16.6%,将比全球第二大电子商务市场美国的两倍还多。电子零售并非传统实体零售的分支和延展,而是与实体零售一起同属于商业流通领域的一种新商业经营业态,电子零售可以由实体零售商双线经营(如沃尔玛在线),同时也有提供纯网络零售服务的电子零售商(如卓越、当当等)。电子零售主要是商家对个人顾客开展零售业务,而电子商务涵盖的范围很广,主要包括 B2C 和 C2C 等多种电子商务模式。本章将对电子零售进行介绍,包括电子零售的概念、种类、商业模式等;同时,本章将讨论中国电子零售市场的发展情况,如:中国电子零售中热销产品和服务的种类、在线消费者的特点、电子零售市场的增长趋势等;此外,本章将对 B2C 和 C2C 两种电子零售模式进行深入探讨,讨论这两种电子零售模式的特点、盈利模式等。最后,本章将探讨电子零售业发展中所面临的问题和挑战,这些挑战给电子零售商提出了新的要求,他们应当不断更新经营思想和管理方法来面对电子零售业中日新月异的变化。

Business Terms

①**B2C commerce**: B2C e-commerce includes transactions of products or services from businesses to individual buyers.

②**business model**: It is a description of how an organization achieves profitability and sustainability through its business operations.

③**C2C commerce**: Consumer-to-consumer electronic commerce (C2C EC) refers to a kind of electronic commerce in which both the buyers and the sellers are individuals, not businesses.

④**direct marketing by manufactures**: It means manufactures market their products and services directly online from company websites to individual customers.

⑤**e-tailing**: Retailing conducted online over the Internet

⑥**Internet online mall**: It refers to online shopping location where many stores are located.

⑦**revenue model**: It is a framework for generating revenues. It identifies which revenue source to pursue, what value to offer, how to price the value, and who pays for the value. It is a key component of a company's business model.

⑧**third-party B2C transaction platforms**: They are run by professional third party electronic marketing operators, on which businesses and customers make transactions together.

Introductory Case

Taobao—China's Dominating C2C E-Commerce Platform

For young Chinese consumers it must be hard to imagine a life without Taobao—China's biggest C2C e-commerce portal. Taobao completely changed the way Chinese shop and it has become so dominant that it now accounts for an estimated 80% of online transactions in China. Launched by Alibaba Group in 2003 to combat eBay's entry into China, Taobao has come to define e-commerce in China. According to Alibaba, as of June 2012, Taobao boasts more than 800 million product listings and more than 500 million registered users. The site is listed by Google as the 14th most visited website in the world.

A critical element to understand about Taobao is that it has allowed everyone with a factory or manufacturing facility in China a channel to sell directly to consumers. As things have funny ways of finding their way out of factories in China, this also means that, like it or not, your brand's products will be sold on Taobao.

Taobao managed to conquer eBay who closed its China operations in 2006 by initially offering their service for free, but more importantly by tailoring the platform specifically to the needs and behavior of Chinese (young) consumers. Most fashion companies, including those not even operating in China yet, will be alarmed at the amount of their products being sold in China through Taobao. A healthy portion of these may be genuine products being resold through unauthorized vendors, yet a large percentage will be outright fakes. Although China's growing middle class and large numbers of rich have no trouble with buying genuine products, there is still millions of people who don't mind buying fake goods at all, and Taobao caters to these customers with ease.

Controlling the online trade in fake products is one of Taobao's biggest problems and is a taint to its international reputation. Since December 2011, Taobao has been listed on the US Trade Representative Office's list of companies notorious for selling fake brand goods. Alibaba has taken note of this and is taking steps aimed at improving its image including prison terms for merchants selling fake goods. To rectify consumer mistrust over fake products on Taobao in 2008, Alibaba Group set up Tmall —a B2C market place where brands can operate with proven legitimacy. Brands such as Gap, Uniqlo and Nike have all set up official pages on Tmall.

Earlier this year Taobao begun their international expansion into Hong Kong and Taiwan and also enabled the use of Visa and Mastercard for payments on the site. Taobao is currently only available in Mandarin limiting the service to China. While the company certainly has its sites set on the international market, it's likely to be a few years yet until Taobao is available in English and starts to operate around the world.

Questions for Discussion

①What are the features of Taobao online shopping mall?

②What are the defaults of Taobao online shopping mall?

③Taobao is a successful online retailer in China. What is the future trend of Taobao online shopping mall?

3.1 OVERVIEW OF ELECTRONIC RETAILING

A retailer is a sales intermediary that operates between manufactures and customers. In the physical world, retailing is done in stores that customers must visit in order to make a purchase. For example, Unilever that manufactures a large number of products must use retailers for efficient distribution. However, with the popularization of the Internet, retailing has moved from the physical world to the invisible online world. Retailing conducted online over the Internet is called electronic retailing, or e-tailing. People who conduct retail business online are called e-tailers. E-tailing makes it easier for manufactures to sell directly to customers by cutting out intermediaries.

3.2 E-TAILING BUSINESS MODELS

A business model is a description of how an organization achieves profitability and sustainability through its business operations. E-tailing business models can be classified into various types based on different classification standards.

3.2.1 Classification by the Relationship Among Participants

B2C e-tailing model. The business-to-consumer (B2C) model includes transactions of products or services from businesses to individual buyers. In a broader sense, B2C e-commerce accounts for a larger proportion of e-tailing, compared to C2C model.

C2C e-tailing model. In the consumer-to-consumer (C2C) model, consumers transact directly with other consumers. Examples of C2C include individuals selling residential property, cars, knowledge and expertise online.

3.2.2 Classification by Distribution Channels

Click-and-mortar retailers. There are two types of click-and-mortar retailers, which depend on how the business is originally founded. Originally, many click-and-mortar retailers start life as traditional psychical retail businesses and over time develop websites and adopt online transaction to support their business activities (e. g. Suning and Walmart). Recently, a small number of successful e-tailers that have business online are now creating physical storefronts, leveraging the brand power of the online environment to support more traditional trading activities via stores. This is the new type of click-and-mortar retailers. For example, Dell, a pioneer of e-tailing and one of the largest sellers of computers online, has also opened psychical stores.

Pure-play retailers. Pure-play retailers are businesses that sell directly to consumers online without maintaining physical stores. Amazon is an example of a pure-play e-tailer. Pure-play e-tailers have the advantage of low overhead costs and streamlined processes. However, the disadvantage may be a lack of established infrastructure to support the online activities.

Direct marketing by manufactures. Direct marketing by manufactures means manufactures market their products and services directly online from company websites to individual customers. Most of the manufactures are click-and-mortar e-tailers and some of the manufactures are pure-play e-tailers. In direct marketing, the manufactures can have a better understanding of the markets through the direct connection to consumers. At the same time, customers can get more information about the products because of the direct connection to the manufactures.

Internet online malls. An Internet online mall is an online shopping location where many stores are located, for example Taobao. When a customer goes to Taobao and clicks on "cosmetics", a large range of cosmetics brands will be displayed for shoppers. You can see the brand name, the company name, the price, the simplification and etc.

3.2.3 Classification by the Scope of the Items Handled

General e-tailers. General e-tailers sell a vast range of goods and services online; capitalize on the Internet to offer such variety to a diverse group of customers geographically without the need to maintain a large physical retail store, for example, Jindong, Tmall and etc.

Specialty e-tailers. Specialty e-tailers operate in a very narrow market and sell a certain type of products and services online. For example, Cattoys specializes in selling cat toys.

3.2.4 Classification by the Scope of the Sales Region Covered

Global e-tailers. Global e-tailers market products and services online in many countries around the world. For example, Amazon sells books to customers around the world, which demands good logistics and supply chain management.

Regional e-tailers. Regional e-tailers sell products and services online locally or in a country, also known as local e-tailers. Take Dangdang as an example. It makes transactions online only in China.

3.3 THE E-TAILING INDUSTRY IN CHINA

E-tailing has been developing rapidly to become one of the most popular channels for day-to-day shopping among consumers in China. According to the findings of the *Survey on China's Middle-Class Consumers* conducted by HKTDC, 83% of the respondents have shopped online, and 27% of these consumers would shop online once a month on average, indicating that China's consumers have formed the habit of online shopping. The improved security of electronic payment systems and the enhanced efficiency of delivery services have boosted consumers' desire for shopping online in China. From the perspective of e-tailers, unlike physical stores, online stores are not subject to location and space constraints. A full range of goods can be made available to consumers across the country through online stores.

3.3.1 Growing Share of Online Consumption

The share of online transactions in total retail sales is growing rapidly in China, from 1.4% in 2008 to 7.8% in 2013, indicating that e-tailing makes up an increasing share in China's retail market. The average annual online spending of China's online consumers has also increased from RMB 1, 632 in 2008 to RMB 5, 203 in 2012, representing an average annual growth rate of 33.6%. According to the projection of iResearch Consulting, the average annual spending of online consumers is about RMB 6, 865 in 2013. It is believed that the increasing number of brands and retailers operating online sales, their expanding business scale, as well as the growing diversity in the products and services available online have stimulated the purchase desire and consumption frequency of consumers. This is evidenced by the increase in the average number of online purchase made within a six-month period from 14.5 times in 2011 to 18 times in 2012.

With the gradual perfecting of related laws and regulations, e-tailing is expected to meet the projection of the Ministry of Commerce in that "transaction value of online retail sales will exceed RMB 3,000 billion in 2015, accounting for more than 10% of total retail sales".

Share of Online Transactions in Total Retail Sales

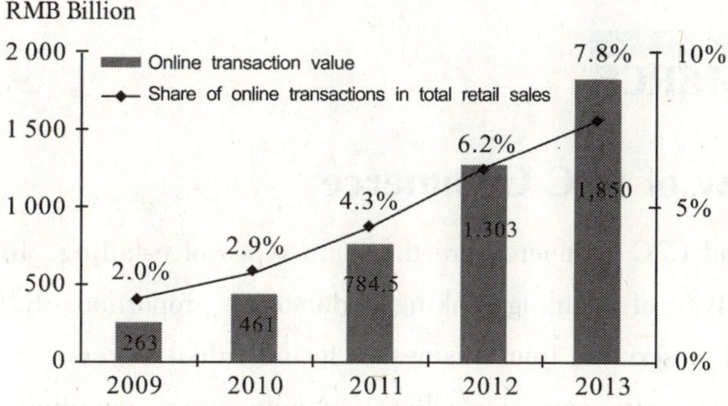

Source: iResearch Consulting

3.3.2 Popular Products and Services Online

In general, standardized products such as computers (29.6%) and electrical appliances (22.9%) are more suitable for e-tailing because consumers can ascertain if their functions, performance and qualities meet their expectations. However, the most popular items purchased online by consumers in China are clothing, footwear and headwear (81.8%). These products are popular among online shoppers probably because the fashion of clothing and accessories is changing all the time and the price-performance ratio of clothing and accessories purchased online is high while their damage rate during delivery is low. Although clothing available for online sale does not allow any fitting, many online stores do provide free return service where consumers can make the purchase first and return any products that do not fit subsequently.

Products Purchased by Online Shoppers

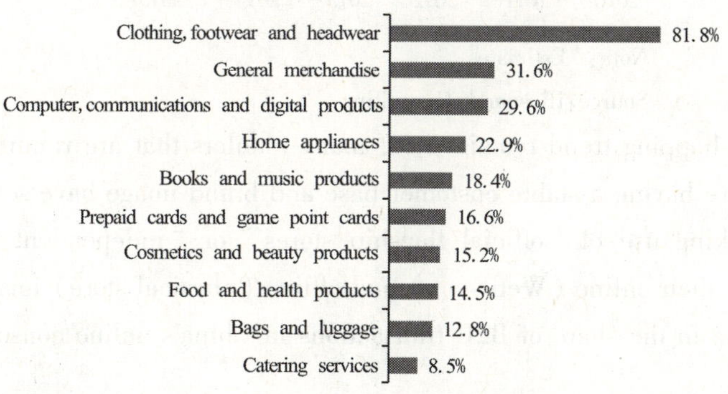

Source: *China Online Shopping Research Report 2012*

It should be noted that in the past, online sales mainly involved products because consumers can determine their suitability through the description and pictures provided. Yet in recent years, many consumer services, such as catering, beauty, movie and travel tour, begin to sell gift certificates, packages and tickets through the Internet, which in turn boosts the share of services in online sales.

3.4 B2C COMMERCE

3.4.1 Overview of B2C Commerce

B2C commerce and C2C commerce are the main types of e-tailing. In a broader sense, B2C commerce is the main type of e-tailing, taking a dominant proportion. B2C e-commerce includes transactions of products or services from businesses to individual buyers.

In B2C shopping sites, the corporate sellers (manufacturers, suppliers, retailers, and etc) are financially more robust and able to offer more comprehensive products, after-sales services and guarantees, so B2C transactions are gaining shares in the online consumption market. According to the following figure, from 2010 to 2015, the B2C retail transactions are increasing sharply, from 13.7% to 45.7%.

Share of China's Online Retail Transactions

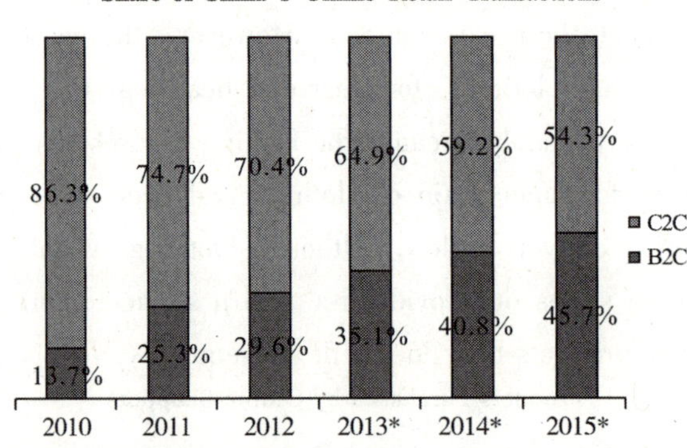

Note: * Estimates

Source: iResearch Consulting

As the online shopping trend remains hot, many retailers that are running their business with physical stores and are having a stable customer base and brand image have set up online shops in a B2C format. By making use of "official flagship stores" or "independent websites", they can consolidate and unify their online (Web store) and offline (physical store) images. Meanwhile, this has led to an increase in the share of B2C transactions in China's online consumption market.

3.4.2 Types of B2C Commerce

B2C commerce can be divided into various types based on different classification criteria. According to different business entities of B2C websites, B2C commerce can be categorized into "independent B2C websites" and "third-party B2C transaction platforms".

Independent B2C websites. Independent B2C websites are created and operated by B2C businesses. The merits of independent B2C websites include meeting the individual requirements of businesses. However, businesses need to spend a large amount of money on promoting and popularizing the independent B2C websites to attract many customers to visit the website. Examples of independent B2C websites are Lenovo. com, Huawei. com and etc. The market share of independent B2C websites is shrinking rapidly, as they are now joining in the third-party B2C transaction platforms under the fierce market competition in e-tailing field.

Third-party B2C transaction platforms. Third-party B2C transaction platforms are run by professional third party electronic marketing operators, on which businesses and customers make transactions together. However, electronic marketing operators do not participate in the actual online transactions. According to a McKinsey Global Institute report, third-party transaction platforms are the main e-tailing format in China, accounting for 90% of the e-tailing market while independent online shops account for 10%. In contrast, such platforms have only a 24% market share in the United States while independent websites account for a 76% share. It can be seen therefore that third-party transaction platforms play a dominant role in China's online consumption market.

Most third-party transaction platforms are run as comprehensive online marketplaces. Like brick-and-mortar shopping malls, all sorts of products and services under different brands are available on one website. They usually classify their merchandise by product category (such as clothing, electronic products and home appliances). Some of them even further divide the categories by brand. Because of the diverse product varieties, the greatest advantages of comprehensive online marketplaces are their huge user communities and high browse rates. Some large websites may even have discount sales corners to attract Internet users to browse and shop. Among the numerous third-party transaction platforms, Tmall's transaction volume accounts for more than half of China's B2C market. According to the following pie chart, Tmall (51.1%), Jingdong (17.5%), Tencent (6.0%), Suning (4.74%), Amazon China (2.6%) are the top 5 companies by share in Chinese B2C online shopping market in 3Q2013. Although the competition pattern of the B2C market is bound to evolve over time, the B2C platform Tmall and the proprietary B2C website Jingdong will still occupy the leading positions firmly in the short term. However, the market share of other B2C websites will change with product strategy direction, marketing promotion and customer relationship management.

Transaction volume of China's B2C e-tailing sites in 3Q2013, by share

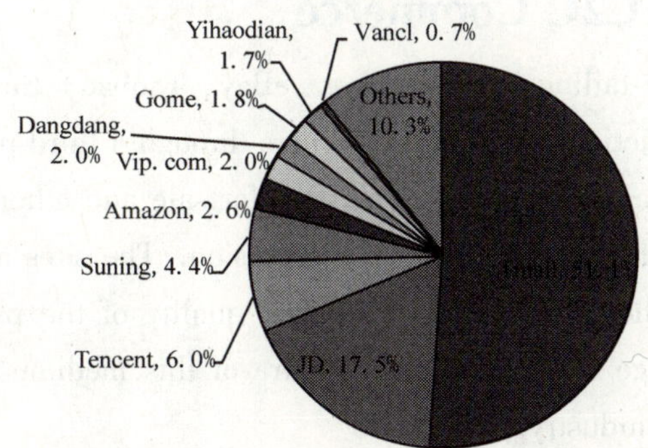

Source: iResearch Consulting

3.4.3 Revenue Models of B2C Commerce

A revenue model is a framework for generating revenues. It identifies which revenue source to pursue, what value to offer, how to price the value, and who pays for the value. It is a key component of a company's business model. It primarily identifies what product or service will be created in order to generate revenues and the ways in which the product or service will be sold.

- Transaction-fee models

Many B2C businesses make profits by earning the price difference between the purchase price and the sales price as well as the service fees based on the level of transaction offered, for example, Dangdang, Haier. com and etc.

- Advertising-supported models

Many individual B2C websites or third-party B2C transaction platforms charge fees to advertisers instead of customers, for putting the advertising information on the B2C platform. The advertising fee is the main source of revenue for B2C businesses. The success of the advertising-supported model depends on whether the online advertising can attract customers' attention to visit their B2C platform.

- Rental virtual shop models

Most third-party B2C transaction platforms make profits by renting virtual shops online, for example Taobao, Jingdong and etc.

- Subscription models

B2C websites also charge online consumers subscription fee for service monthly or annually. YouTube just announced in 2016 that it would charge a subscription fee for some channels. The fees range from 99 cents to $7.99 a month.

3.5 C2C COMMERCE

3.5.1 Overview of C2C Commerce

An emerging sector in e-tailing is C2C (e. g. eBay, Taobao) transaction. C2C involves the electronically facilitated transactions between consumers through a third party. A common example is the online auction, in which a consumer posts an item for sale and other consumers bid to purchase it; the third party generally charges a flat fee or commission. The sites are only intermediaries, just there to match consumers. They do not have to check quality of the products being offered. This sector is able to take advantage of the hypertext nature of this medium to evolve into a potentially major sector within the retail industry.

Craigslist is one of the top C2C websites in the world and the leading service for classified ads. Consumers not only buy, sell and trade items, but also conduct other transactions such as housing and job searches. The site is very user-friendly, allowing consumers to register and list an item for sale within minutes. For consumers looking to make a purchase, they simply go to the "for sale" category and choose the appropriate subcategory (computers, furniture, books, etc.).

3.5.2 Revenue Models of C2C Commerce

Most C2C sites make money from fees or commissions charged to sellers for listing items for sale. C2C sites act simply as intermediaries, matching buyers to sellers, and they have little control over the quality of the products being sold. Although it's free to shop and place bids, sellers place fees to list items for sale, add on promotional features, and successfully complete transactions.

Many C2C sites have expanded and developed existing product categories by introducing category-specific bulletin boards and chat rooms, integrating category-specific content, advertising its service in targeted publications and participating in targeted trade shows. For example, eBay specifically has also broadened the range of products that it offers to facilitate trading on the site, including payment services, shipping services, authentication, appraisal, vehicle inspection and escrow services.

3.5.3 Advantages and Disadvantages of C2C E-commerce

C2C has a number of benefits for users. There are minimal costs involved with the lack of retailers and wholesalers, keeping the margins higher for sellers and prices lower for buyers. There is also the convenience factor—instead of trying to sell items in person at a brick-and-mortar store, consumers can simply list their products online and wait for the buyers to come to them. Buyers don't need to drive around and search through stores for an item they want—they just have to search for it on a C2C site.

But C2C is not without its problems. Credit card payments can be difficult, as the platforms are not necessarily secure and able to process such payments. There is a lack of quality control—since the sellers are consumers themselves, there is little recourse for poorly made or misrepresented products. On the flip side, because the buyers are consumers themselves, the payment guarantees can be hard to enforce.

3.6 E-TAILING ISSUES

3.6.1 Logistics, Distribution and Customer Service Issues

E-tailing can facilitate the transaction. Unless the transaction involves a digital product (software, music etc.), the delivery of the product needs to be considered. Many e-tailers have focused on significant marketing efforts to attract customers in order to execute transactions, but have not focused on the less glamorous, but equally important, aspect of keeping the customers, by facilitating flawless delivery. Not only is it important to follow through and make sure the delivery is facilitated, but companies can use the Web to enhance delivery via customer service by allowing customers to track the status of the transaction. So it is not simply a case of allowing for delivery, but enhancing the delivery experience with the Web.

Once this relationship is formed (via the transaction), the e-tailer can follow up with a solicited marketing program to keep the customers engaged. Customer service should be considered a high priority as it impacts the long-term relationship between the customer and the e-tailer. Customer service should be proactive to ensure prompt delivery leading to satisfaction with the product and subsequently offer a medium of dialog to the customer with the e-tailer. Recently, more attention has been paid to the delivery aspect of the entire transaction.

3.6.2 Payment Issues

Credit card transactions are becoming the preferred mode of payment for the Web at this point. Credit card providers take a percentage of the transaction, and this is higher for the Web than for a traditional retail store. They can rationalize this as the Web is perceived as higher risk, as the e-tailer does not capture the signature of the purchaser.

For markets to grow to their full potential, a medium of exchange needs to standardize, to reduce the friction in markets. This was the case as we moved from a trading environment based on a barter system (which relied on both parties having something interesting to exchange) to a trading environment based on a monetary exchange. With respect to the Web, we need to develop a medium that becomes a standard to increase the participation rates of e-tailers and consumers. Since credit cards have the lead, they may become the standard. They do not facilitate microtransactions, which clearly would open up new markets that will be exclusive to the Web. This is an area where we not only need to develop a medium to facilitate exchange, but also determine the likely goods (Web content, music etc.) that will become viable for the exchange.

3.6.3 Privacy VS. Personalization Issues

There is a conflict between the need for privacy on the part of the consumer, and the need to be able to personalize the offering on the part of the e-tailer (which in turn should provide a better experience for the consumer). It is an interesting question to pose, who owns your identity? While the reasonable answer is yourself, that would imply you have complete knowledge of the use of your identity, who has access to the information, who is selling it (and are you getting paid for that transaction). Companies such as Etrust are positioning themselves as intermediaries that focus on certifying e-tailers and their use of the data that is gathered from transactions.

Most current personalization solutions focus on personalization based on the user experience with the individual website. E-tailers need to develop schemes that allow them to develop a personalization scheme that takes advantage of a wider scope of user behavior. Systems need to be developed that allows for personalization across multiple websites (the entire Web) and the connection between the e-tailer and its physical presence.

3.6.4 Global and Legal Issues

E-tailing exists as a global bazaar. Rules for commerce, and its legal framework, have evolved within geographically limited borders (nation, state and local laws and tax systems). For e-tailing to grow, a legal framework needs to evolve that makes sense for a global marketplace. This is perhaps the most challenging aspect to overcome in order to help growth develop. Currently there is a moratorium on taxes for e-tail transactions with businesses that have no physical presence. Clearly this biases against traditional retailers and those that are adopting the Web, and is potentially a major source of revenue loss for states and countries that would have received those revenues.

With so many hurdles around for e-tailing, it would take time before it really catches up. But, the trend has surely begun. In the future, we will see a peaceful and complementary co-existence of conventional retailing and e-tailing.

3.7 E-TAILING—CHALLENGES AND RESPONSES

Challenges	Response
• Inventory and order management systems are not integrated across all channels;	• Internally prioritizing integrated, multi-channel data management strategies;
• Customer data is not integrated or shared across all channels;	• Bringing in outside expertise to drive internal business process change;
• The dominant channel fears sales cannibalization;	• Creating an ROI-based case to gain more resources to integrate business processes;
• There are budgetary constraints to create integrated processes;	• Changing the organizational structure to be brand-specific rather than channel-specific;
• Channel specific, instead of brand-specific, merchandising organization;	• Changing compensation incentives to be brand-specific rather than channel-specific;
• Cannot change fast enough to keep up with customer expectations.	• Outsourcing programming to improve system integration.

SUMMARY

This chapter mainly discusses issues related to online retailing. Retailing conducted online over the Internet is called electronic retailing, or e-tailing. People who conduct retail business online are called e-tailers. E-tailing makes it easier for manufactures to sell directly to customers by cutting out intermediaries. E-tailing business models can be classified into various types based on different classification standards. The most common classification is based on the classification by the relationship among participants. Then e-tailing can be divided into B2C commerce and C2C commerce. In addition, e-tailing can be classified by distribution channels, the scope of the items handled and by the scope of the sales region covered. B2C commerce has particular features and can be divided into independent B2C websites and third-party B2C transaction platforms. C2C e-commerce differs from a business-to-business model or a business-to-consumer model because consumers interact directly with each other. Most C2C sites make money from fees or commissions charged to sellers for listing items for sale. C2C sites act simply as intermediaries, matching buyers to sellers, and they have little control over the quality of the products being sold. However, there are also a lot of problems involved in the growth of e-tailing, for example, logistics, distribution and customer service issues, payment issues, privacy vs. personalization issues, global and legal issues and etc. With the quick development of electronic commerce, e-tailing is facing a lot of challenges from inventory and order management systems, updating and etc. E-tailers need to update their management ideas and operating methods everyday to adapt to the quick development of electronic commerce industry.

Words and Expressions

①**auction**: a public sale where goods are sold to the person who offers the highest price 拍卖

②**consolidate**: to strengthen it so that it becomes more effective or secure 加强;巩固

③**commission**: a sum of money paid to a salesperson for every sale that he or she makes 佣金

④**distribution channel**: way of selling a company's product either directly or via distributors 分销渠道

⑤**inventory**: the goods and materials that a business holds for the ultimate goals to have a purpose of resale 库存

⑥**manufacturer**: a business or company which makes goods in large quantities to sell 生产商

⑦**personalization**: sometimes known as customization, consists of tailoring a service or a product to accommodate specific individuals, sometimes tied to groups or segments of individuals 个性化

⑧**profitability**: the quality of affording gain or benefit or profit 收益性; 利益率

⑨**pure play retailers**: businesses that sell directly to consumers online without maintaining physical stores 完全电子零售商

⑩**retailer**: a person or business that sells consumer goods or services to customers through multiple channels of distribution to earn a profit 零售商

⑪**shrink**: to become smaller in size, usually as a result of being washed 收缩;缩小

⑫**streamline**: to make something work more effectively by stripping off nonessentials 精简

⑬**supply chain**: a system of organizations, people, activities, information, and resources involved in moving a product or service from supplier to customer 供应链

⑭**subscription**: an amount of money that you pay regularly in order to belong to an organization, to help a charity or campaign, or to receive copies of a magazine or newspaper 会员费；用户费；捐助款；订阅费

⑮**supplier**: a person, company, or organization that sells or supplies something such as goods or equipment to customers 供应商

Exercises

Ⅰ. **Key Terms** (Explain the following terms.)

①e-tailing

②business models

③pure-play retailers

④brick-and-mortar retailers

⑤third-party B2C transaction platforms

Ⅱ. **Multiple Choice Exercises** (Choose the correct answer to the following questions from A, B, C and D. There is only one correct answer.)

①Retailing conducted online over the Internet is called ________.

A. retailing B. click-and-mortar store C. e-tailing D. e-commerce

②According to the relationship among participants, e-tailing can be classified into ________.

A. B2B e-tailing and B2C e-tailing B. B2B e-tailing and C2C e-tailing

C. C2C e-tailing and B2C e-tailing D. C2C e-tailing and B2G e-tailing

③________ are businesses that sell directly to consumers online without maintaining physical stores.

A. Internet online malls B. Pure-play retailers

C. Click-and-mortar retailers D. Direct marketing by manufactures

④According to different business entities of B2C websites, B2C commerce can be categorized into ________.

A. independent B2C websites and general e-tailers

B. global e-tailers and third-party B2C transaction platforms

C. general e-tailers and general e-tailers

D. independent B2C websites and third-party B2C transaction platforms

⑤Which of the following is not the feature of B2C commerce?

A. Heavy advertising required to attract large numbers of customers.

B. High investment in terms of hardware/software.

C. Support or good customer service.

D. Consumers interact directly with each other.

⑥Which of the following is not a third-party B2C transaction platform?

A. Walmart. com.
B. Tmall. com.
C. Amazon. com.
D. Jingdong. com.

⑦What of the following is not the problem of C2C commerce?

A. There is a lack of quality control of products.
B. There is a lack of retailers and wholesalers.
C. The payment guarantees can be hard to enforce.
D. A legal framework needs to evolve that makes sense for a global marketplace.

⑧Which of the following is not the issue of e-tailing?

A. Logistics, distribution and customer service issues.
B. Payment issues.
C. Security issues.
D. Global and legal issues.

Ⅲ. Review Questions

①Why do so many traditional entrepreneurs start business in the online retailer sector initially?

②What are the business models of e-tailing?

③What are the barriers in the development of e-tailing?

Ⅳ. Online Practice

①Online travel industry is one of the earliest online retailing industries in China and now it is a thriving sector in e-tailing. Please visit several online travel businesses and then analyze their services and their operating features.

②Please visit one e-tailing platform, such as Amazon, Dangdang, and then analyze their revenue models.

③Try to build an online WeChat shop. What products or services are you planning to sell? What are the features of your online WeChat shop?

Ⅴ. Case Study

Chinese E-tailers Going Global

China is set to become the world's largest online retail market in the year 2013, according to the Ministry of Commerce, but this isn't stopping China's e-tailers from expanding to all corners of the globe.

Chinese e-commerce companies tend to provide an English website targeting U. S. and

European customers when they start to go global. Vancl is, and will be, focused on its domestic market, but the intention to go global is quite natural, whether it's the brand or the manufacturing that goes outside China. Vancl launched its English website in 2010. It branched out to the Vietnamese market by partnering with the Vietnamese online payment company ECPay, creating a Vietnamese website and local operations. Vietnam is quite representative of Asian markets: Fast-growing with a considerable market size and similar in culture. According to Nnan Dan newspaper, 31 million people, or 34 percent of the country's population, were accessing the Internet in Vietnam by the end of September. The China Internet Network Information Center reported that by June, 538 million people (almost 40 percent of the population) were accessing the Internet.

Another Chinese e-commerce site with serious growth potential is Jingdong Mall, which many insiders call China's Amazon. While Jingdong Mall's English-only website just launched this past October, the company ships to 35 countries and has begun attracting markets in North America, Australia, and Western Europe. They also have a Russian-language website and a local distribution partner there.

Unlike Vancl, Jingdong Mall buys made-in-China goods that it sells overseas, rather than expanding into local operations around the globe. Jingdong also plans to build warehouses overseas to eventually shorten the delivery period. The brand strives to be like Amazon, doing business in different country locally and having diverse sources of products.

Amazon is the world's largest retailer by user number, according to research firm comScore Inc, and 60 percent of its customers come from countries outside of North America. As of June, almost all of the 60 million registered Jingdong users were from the Chinese mainland.

PayPal reported astonishing sales figures for Latin American and Eastern European markets targeted by Chinese e-commerce businesses: from July 2011 to June 2012, exports by Chinese e-commerce companies to Argentina increased by 96 percent, to Israel by 72 percent and to Ukraine by 71 percent.

Going global will be part of the future, something you need to do other than your main business in China even though it's not urgent now. Compared with the domestic market, e-commerce players are likely to have higher profit margins in the international market.

Questions for Discussion

①Why are a lot of e-tailers going global, such as Vancl, Jingdong, Amazon?

②What are the challenges facing the e-tailers now? What are the trends of e-tailing?

Chapter 4 Online Consumer Behavior, Customer Relationship Management

本章导读

我国互联网在近二十年中快速发展,网民数量从1997年的62万发展到2016年的7.01亿,手机网民的数量也达到6.56亿。互联网是一个革命性的媒介,其起源是为消费者收集信息、比较产品、价格及在网上购买的可能性创造全新的体验,使消费者能够扩大他们购买范围内的替代品。互联网和移动互联网改变了人们的传统消费方式。企业越来越多地研究网络消费者的行为,以调整企业的销售和营销策略,增加消费者在互联网的购买量。客户的信任是电子商务成功的关键因素之一,如何建立良好的客户关系,取得他们的信任是从事电子商务业务的企业必须考虑的。在互联网上的营销人员要能预测消费者的行为,了解消费者如何买、在哪里买和为什么在线消费,研究消费者购买决策过程的特定阶段。明确了这些答案,营销人员才能更好地提供消费者想买、会买的产品。本章将从网络消费的行为特点、购买动机、消费者购买决策过程、网络购买环境影响消费者购买行为的关键因素、在线消费者的品牌忠诚度等方面对网络购物消费者的行为加以研究,探讨网上购物与消费者购买行为的各种特性之间的关系。电子商务企业只有在互联网上提供更好的消费者服务,并建立网站和消费者之间的协同效应,维护消费者关系,减少消费者的风险,才能建立品牌忠诚度,实现企业的持续发展。

Business Terms

①**consumer psychology**: a specialty area that studies how the thoughts, beliefs, feelings, and perceptions influence people's buying behavior

②**customer experience**: In commerce, it is the product of an interaction between an organization and a customer over the duration of their relationship. This interaction is made up of several parts: the customer journey, the brand touchpoints, the customer interacts with, and the environments the customer experiences (including digital environment) during their experience. A good customer experience means that the individual's experience during all points of contact matches the individual's expectations.

③**customer relationship management (CRM)**: an approach to managing a company's interaction with current and potential future customers

④**customer service**: It is the provision of service to customers before, during and after a purchase. The perception of success of such interactions is dependent on employees "who can adjust themselves to the personality of the guest". Customer service concerns the priority an organization assigns to customer service relative to components such as product innovation and pricing.

⑤**instant messaging office (IMO)**: Instant messaging (IM) is a type of online chat that offers real-time text transmission over the Internet. Short messages are typically transmitted between two parties, when each user chooses to complete a thought and select "send". Some IM applications can use push technology to provide real-time text, which transmits messages character by character, as they are composed. More advanced IM can add file transfer, clickable hyperlinks, voice over IP, or video chat.

⑥**online consumer behavior**: It describes the process of online shopping from a consumer's perspective. It is often described as the study of trends, including the influence of online advertising, consumer willingness to click on links, the prevalence of comparison shopping.

⑦**search engine**: A Web search engine is a software system that is designed to search for information on the World Wide Web. The search results are generally presented in a line of results often referred to as search engine results pages (SERPs). The information may be a mix of Web pages, images, and other types of files.

⑧**social media**: computer-mediated technologies that allow the creating and sharing of information, ideas, career interests and other forms of expression via virtual communities and networks

Introductory Case

E-book Buyers Are Loyal to Specific Retailers

The walls are indeed high and hard to climb for readers living in the e-book retail walled gardens of Kindle, Nook and IBooks, according to new data from Codex Group, a New York-based book industry research firm.

According to a November survey of 2,042 e-book buyers, 86% bought e-books from only one retailer, most likely Kindle, IBooks and Nook, Codex Group's president Peter Hildick-Smith said.

What this data point implies is that the vast majority of e-book retail activity in the U. S. is happening in so-called "walled gardens"—digital content ecosystems run by companies like Amazon and Apple that keep consumers searching, discovering, buying and consuming all or most of their e-books, songs and movies in one place. If a reader has an Amazon account and has bought Kindle e-books, they are very likely to continue doing just that.

For the big retailers with significant market share in the U. S. , this is good news: Their current customers are mostly loyal.

The news isn't so good for the smaller e-book retail operations run by Sony, Google, Kobo, Samsung and others. The majority of these retailers' sales happened within the 14% of e-book buyers who bought from more than one retailer—and, even worse news for that group, 32% of unit sales among that group were Kindle e-books.

Customers of those smaller retailers were much more likely to go elsewhere to buy more e-books and the most likely place for them to go was Amazon.

For the big retailers, it pays to offer price promotions in select efforts to attract new customers but perhaps not to cater to old ones; that the price wars in the e-book world likely haven't done very much for the retailers engaging in them aside from help them lose a lot of money. Due to high customer loyalty, a returning reader is very likely to buy an e-book offered by Kindle, say, almost no matter the price—so why sell to them below cost?

The trick for these retailers over the next year or two will be to balance income-generating sales to loyal customers and money-losing efforts to attract new customers.

For the small retailers, the picture is fairly bleak. It's clear, though, that they need to think of ways to keep their small customer bases more loyal, perhaps through better sales and marketing of dedicated e-reading devices or promotions that reward loyalty.

Questions for Discussion

①What does "walled gardens" mean?

②How do the big e-book retailers retain their readers?

③What is the future customer relationship of the smaller e-book retailers? And what is your suggestion to the smaller e-book retailers?

4.1 OVERVIEW OF ONLINE CONSUMER BEHAVIOR AND CRM

Over 1.5 billion people across the world now regularly use the Internet. As a marketing media the Internet is eclipsing all comers. The phrase "online consumer behavior" describes the process of online shopping from a consumer's perspective. It is often described as the study of trends, including the influence of online advertising, consumer willingness to click on links, the prevalence of comparison shopping. The decision-making process of an online consumer is often very different from that of a consumer in a physical store. Companies are increasingly studying online consumer behavior in order to adapt their sales and marketing strategies to appeal to the Internet purchaser.

Online sales have increased all over the world, with more and more shoppers looking to the Internet before they head out to malls or other stores. In order to remain competitive, many companies are electing to devote at least some of their marketing capital to the online space. Companies decide many of the finer points of online sales, including advertising strategies, page layout, and ease of website searching by analyzing online consumer behavior.

Consumer behavior is primarily focused on consumer learning processes from internal phenomena—such as motivation, ritual phenomena, moods, personality, lifestyles, and attitudes—and from external factors—such as marketer endorsements and group behavior considering family, associative, and aspirational group influences. It also examines different demographic factors including social class, religion, household influences, and cultural attributes.

The field of online consumer behavior can be broad. Most of the time, theories in this field are posited by economists or market analysts who specialize in consumer analysis. Companies hire some consumer analysts on a contract basis to provide tailored advice. Others work for independent market analyst firms, for think tanks, or in academia.

In many respects, the study of online consumer behavior is the study of the intersection between online consumers and online businesses. Analysts look at how consumers respond to various aspects of an online business, and compare the factors that make a consumer either have a purchase or leave the website. The consumer psychology of making purchases online is usually a major part of an analyst's considerations, and analysts often conduct market segmentation studies based on gender, age, and relative sophistication.

Online consumer behavior can also be forward-looking. Behavior studies can tell businesses how consumers are responding to ads and site layouts, but they can also predict how consumers will respond to other future campaigns or Web features. Market analysis in the online space often leads to innovation. Businesses develop new advertising campaigns, and come up with different ways to reach potential purchasers based on behavioral statistics.

Sometimes, the way corporations use behavioral data are straightforward, such as sponsoring links on certain sites or optimizing home pages to appear more readily in search engines. Increasingly, however, market responses are more tailored to the consumer individually. Social networking promotions, interactive homepages, and special offers for subscribers of e-mail or messaging updates are all examples of ways in which online consumer behavior has influenced the modern retail world.

Customer relationship management (CRM) is a term that refers to practices, strategies and technologies that companies use to manage and analyze customer interactions and data throughout the customer lifecycle, with the goal of improving business relationships with customers, assisting in customer retention and driving sales growth. CRM systems are designed to compile information on customers across different channels—or points of contact between the customer and the company—which could include the company's website, telephone, live chat, direct mail, marketing materials and social media. CRM systems can also give customer-facing staff detailed information on customers' personal information, purchase history, buying preferences and concerns.

CRM software has been around for at least two decades. It was originally born in the age of desktop software and allowed companies to track all customer interactions in a single place. Historically, CRM applications have been complex, expensive and just out of the reach of small businesses. However, small businesses have the same needs as larger organizations, just on a smaller scale. Without CRM, small businesses risk missing opportunities at every stage of the sales process. There are five tasks universal to every small business: tracking prospects, managing customers, delivering products and services, sending invoices and getting paid. CRM tracks and improves each of these functions.

A report from HubSpot found unsuccessful sales teams are two times more likely to use Excel, Outlook or physical documents to store lead and customer data instead of a CRM solution that simplifies and integrates this information into one powerful tool.

4.2 TRAITS OF ONLINE CONSUMERS

◇Adventurous explorers (30% of online spending) are a small segment that presents a large opportunity. They require little special attention by Internet vendors because they believe online shopping is fun. They are likely the opinion leaders for all things online. Retailers should nurture and cultivate them to be online community builders and shopping advocates.

◇Shopping lovers (24% of online spending) enjoy buying online and do so frequently. They are competent computer users and will likely continue their shopping habits. They also spread the word to others about joys of online shopping whenever they have the opportunity. They represent an ideal target for retailers.

◇Business users (19% of online spending) are among the most computer literate. They use the Internet primarily for business purposes. They take a serious interest in what it can do for their professional life. They don't view online shopping as novel and aren't usually champions of the practice.

◇Suspicious learners (15% of online spending) comprise another small segment with growth potential. Their reluctance to purchase online more often hinges on their lack of computer training, but they are open to new ways of doing things. In contrast to more fearful segments, they don't have a problem giving a computer their credit card number. Further guidance and training would help coax them into online buying.

◇Fearful browsers (5% of online spending) are on the cusp of buying online. They are capable Internet and computer users, spending a good deal of time "window shopping". They could become a significant buying group if their fears about credit card security, shipping charges and buying products sight unseen were overcome.

◇Shopping avoiders (3% of online spending) have an appealing income level, but their values make them a poor target for online retailers. They don't like to wait for products to be shipped to them and they like seeing merchandise in person before buying. They have online shopping issues that retailers will not easily be able to overcome.

◇Technology meddlers (3% of online spending) face large computer literacy hurdles. They spend less time than any other segment online and show little excitement about increasing their online comfort level. They are not an attractive market for online retailers.

◇Fun seekers (2% of online spending) are the least wealthy and least educated market segment. They see entertainment value in the Internet, but buying things online frightens them. Although security and privacy issues might be overcome, the spending power of the segment suggests that only a marginal long-term payback would be possible.

4.3 DIFFERENT TYPES OF CONSUMER BEHAVIOR

The different types of consumer behavior determine how consumers make purchasing decisions. Though there are many influences on buyer behavior, four main categories are often cited as the primary factors in a purchasing decision. The four major types of consumer behavior are habitual, variety, complex, and dissonance-reduction. Each consumer behavior may be motivated by a variety of influences, including need, cultural influence, and psychological factors.

Habitual buying habits are the most common and the simplest purchasing decisions for most consumers. Choosing to buy a bunch of bananas rarely requires much extensive research on brands and product offering, and may be done on a regular or habitual basis. Since a bunch of bananas from one brand is likely to be quite similar to one from another brand, there is not a high level of distinction between product choices. Habitual buying behavior is most often found with low-cost products for which a consumer has a regular need; price, convenience, and brand loyalty may sometimes affect habitual purchasing decisions.

Varietal buying, also called limited decision making, involves a little more thought than habitual behavior. This type of behavior also requires little research on the part of the buyer, but may exist in markets where there is a high level of product variety. When buying ice cream, for instance, a consumer may have to choose among a hundred different flavors, often from different brands. Varietal buying is frequently motivated by the desire for a change from habits, or the search for a better product.

Complex or extensive decision making behavior requires research and significant difference exist between products. Dissonance-reduction decisions, by contrast, also may require research, but occur in markets where there is little difference between products. Both of the categories tend to apply to markets where products are high value and irregular purchases, such as houses or jewelry. Buying a car is often a complex decision, because there are many different brands and models that offer distinct features. Buying a one-carat pair of diamond earrings, however, might be a dissonance-reduction decision, since most one-carat earrings will be roughly similar, regardless of brand.

The motivating factors behind the different types of consumer behavior can be extremely complex. Need typically motivates most habitual purchases, such as food and gasoline. Cultural or social influence may affect decisions by giving a consumer a set frame of reference by which purchases are judged; for instance, a person may buy a certain style of jacket because it is said to be "in style" for the season. Personal and psychological attitudes or preconceptions may significantly alter some types of consumer behavior: a person who is against pesticides will likely buy only organic produce, for instance.

4.4 CONSUMER PURCHASE DECISION-MAKING

How do customers buy? Research suggests that customers go through a five-stage decision-making process in any purchase. This is summarized in the diagram below:

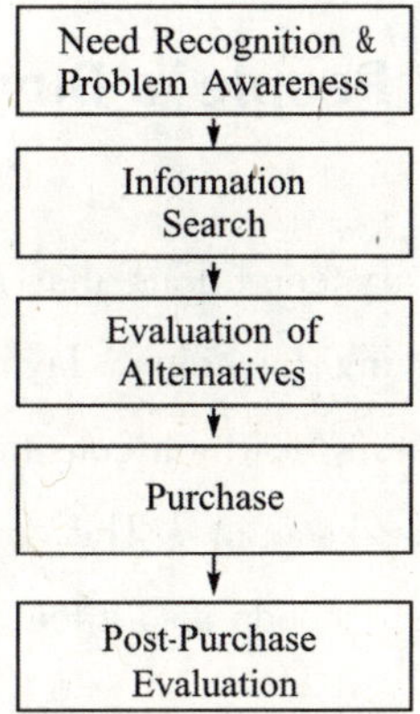

This model is important for anyone making marketing decisions. It forces the marketer to consider the whole buying process rather than just the purchase decision.

4.4.1 Purchase Decision-making Process and Support System

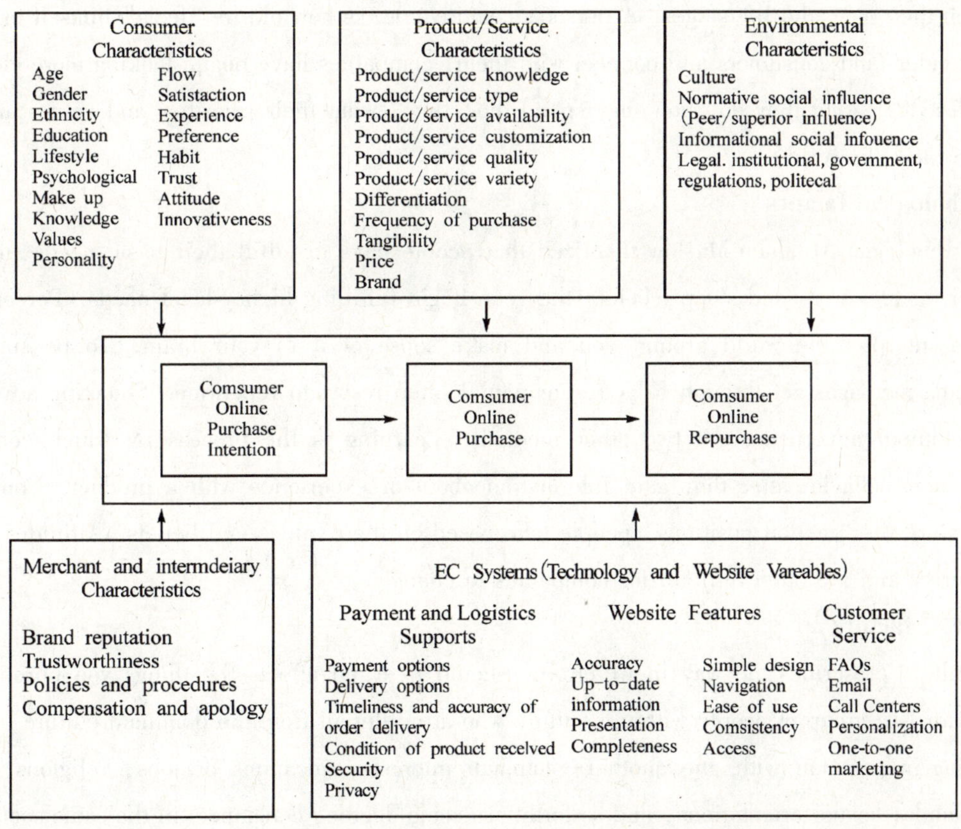

Source: O'keefe and McEachern (1998)

4.4.2 Factors That Affect People's Buying Behavior

◇**Situational factors**

Situational influences are temporary conditions that affect how buyers behave. They include physical factors such as a store's buying locations, layout, music, lighting, and even smells. Companies try to make the physical factors in which consumers shop as favorable as possible. If they can't, they utilize other tactics such as discounts. The consumer's social situation, time situation, the reason for their purchases, and their moods also affect their buying behavior.

◇**Personal factors**

Your personality describes your disposition as other people see it. Market researchers believe people buy products to enhance how they feel about themselves. Your gender also affects what you buy and how you shop. Women shop differently than men. However, there's some evidence that this is changing. Younger men and women are beginning to shop more alike. People buy different things based on their ages and life stages. A person's cognitive age is how old he "feels" himself to be. To further understand consumers and connect with them, companies have begun looking more closely at their lifestyles (what they do, how they spend their time, what their priorities and values are, and how they see the world).

◇**Psychological factors**

Psychologist Abraham Maslow theorized that people have to fulfill their basic needs—like the need for food, water, and sleep—before they can begin fulfilling higher-level needs. Perception is how you interpret the world around you and make sense of it in your brain. To be sure their advertising messages get through to you, companies often resort to repetition. Shocking advertising and subliminal advertising are two other methods. Learning is the process by which consumers change their behavior after they gain information about or experience with a product. Consumers' attitudes are the "mental positions" people take based on their values and beliefs. Attitudes tend to be enduring and are often difficult for companies to change.

◇**Societal factors**

Culture prescribes the way in which you should live and affects the things you purchase. A subculture is a group of people within a culture who are different from the dominant culture but have something in common with one another—common interests, vocations or jobs, religions, ethnic backgrounds, sexual orientations, and so forth. To some degree, consumers in the same social class exhibit similar purchasing behavior. Most market researchers consider a person's family to be one of the biggest determiners of buying behavior. Reference groups are groups that a consumer identifies with and wants to join. Companies often hire celebrities to endorse their products to appeal to people's reference groups. Opinion leaders are people with expertise in certain areas. Consumers respect these people and often ask their opinions before they buy goods and services.

4.4.3 Social Classes and Buying Patterns: An Example

Class	Type of Car	Definition of Class
Upper-Upper Class	Rolls-Royce	People with inherited wealth and aristocratic names (the Kennedys Rothschilds, Windsors, etc.)
Lower-Upper Class	Mercedes	Professionals such as CEOs, doctors, and lawyers
Upper-Middle Class	Lexus	College graduates and managers
Middle Class	Toyota	Both white-collar and blue-collar workers
Working Class	Pontiac	Blue-collar workers
Lower but Not the Lowest	Used vehicle	People who are working but not on welfare
Lowest Class	No vehicle	People on welfare

The aboue table shows seven classes of American consumers along with the types of car brands they might buy. The makers of upscale brands in particular walk a fine line in terms of marketing to customers. On the one hand, they want their customer bases to be as large as possible. This is especially tempting in a recession when luxury buyers are harder to come by. On the other hand, if the companies create products the middle class can better afford, they risk "cheapening" their brands. That's why, for example, Smart Cars, which are made by BMW, don't have the BMW label on them. For a time, Tiffany's sold a cheaper line of silver jewelry to a lot of customers. However, the company later worried that its reputation was being tarnished by the line. Keep in mind that a product's price is to some extent determined by supply and demand. Luxury brands therefore try to keep the supply of their products in check so their prices remain high.

4.5 SOCIAL MEDIA AND CRM

There's no denying that social media is changing businesses for good. It has opened up new avenues of marketing, sales and customer service which have never been imagined earlier. Many businesses have adopted Customer Relationship Management (CRM) as the preferred means to get closer to customers. Social Media has also played a key role in popularizing CRM with innovative apps and unique self-service models.

When it comes to deriving maximum gains for a business, a right combination of social media and CRM is the perfect tonic. Social media and CRM complement each other and it's fair to say that they are "made for each other". In fact, the use of social media and CRM in conjunction has gained phenomenal popularity over the last couple of years and is now coined as "Social CRM".

The Unique selling proposition/point(USP) of social media plus CRM combo is that it provides an intelligent community-based solution to bring customers closer by leveraging the unmatched power of social networks. A business can link its customer facing CRM app to Facebook/Twitter in order to make it a fun experience for its users. Or it could even tie its employee CRM module to use Twitter feeds for real time updates. Using YouTube channels to train your work staff on the latest CRM modules is another option. The possibilities are endless.

A business is all about customer experience and the social media CRM combo helps a business build great customer relationships. While CRM brings in the technology, social media brings in the required attitude.

Social CRM platforms are evolving fast and processes are being streamlined to gain maximum advantage from social media engagement. Social CRM is the new voice for online customers and it offers a win-win situation for enterprises as well as their customers.

With cloud Computing gaining grounds, a number of enterprises are looking at exploring cloud-based social CRM solutions in order to save costs on their customer management needs. Such solutions help improve an organization's overall efficiency by streamlining workflows, managing real-time responses, providing cross-reference social media content across various teams (e. g. sales, support, IT) and customers.

I'm office(IMO), Social CRM might be the next big game changer for social media adoption in the enterprise.

4.6 THE CRM TECHNOLOGY MARKET

The four main vendors of CRM systems are Salesforce. com, Microsoft, SAP and Oracle. Other providers are popular among small- to mid-market businesses, but these four tend to be the choice of large corporations.

On-premise CRM puts the onus of administration, control, security and maintenance of the database and information on the company itself. With this approach the company purchases licenses up front instead of buying yearly subscriptions. The software resides on the company's own servers and the user assumes the cost of any upgrades and usually requires a prolonged installation process to fully integrate a company's data. Companies with complex CRM needs might benefit more from an on-premises deployment.

With cloud-based CRM—also known as SaaS (software-as-a-service) or on-demand CRM—data is stored on an external, remote network that employees can access anytime, anywhere is an Internet connection, sometimes with a third-party service provider overseeing installation and maintenance. The cloud's quick, relatively easy deployment capabilities appeals to companies with limited technological expertise or resources.

Companies might consider cloud-based CRM as a more cost-effective option. Vendors such as Salesforce. com charge by the user on a subscription basis and give the option of monthly or yearly payments.

Data security is a primary concern for companies using a cloud-based system since the company doesn't physically control the storage and maintenance of its data. If the cloud provider goes out of business or is acquired by another company, a company's data can be compromised or lost. Compatibility issues can also arise when data is initially migrated from a company's previous system to the cloud. Finally, cost may be a concern, since paying subscription fees for software can be more costly than on-premises-based models.

4.6.1 Trends

Traditionally, data intake practices for CRM systems have been the responsibility of sales and marketing departments as well as contact center agents. Sales and marketing teams procure leads and update the system with information throughout the customer lifecycle and contact centers gather data and revise customer history records through service call and technical support interactions.

The advent of social media and the proliferation of mobile devices have caused CRM providers to upgrade their offerings to include new features that cater to customers who use these technologies.

Social CRM is engaging customers directly through social media platforms such as Facebook, Twitter and LinkedIn. Social media presents an open forum for customers to share experiences with a brand, whether they're airing grievances or promoting products.

To add value to customer interactions on social media, businesses use various tools that monitor social conversations, from specific mentions of a brand to the frequency of keywords used, to determine their target audience and which platforms they use. Other tools are designed to analyze social media feedback and address customer queries and issues. Companies are interested in capturing sentiments such as a customer's likelihood of recommending their products and the customer's overall satisfaction in order to develop marketing and service strategies. Companies try to integrate social CRM data with other customer data obtained from sales or marketing departments in order to get a single view of the customer.

Another way in which social CRM is adding value for companies and customers is customer communities, where customers post reviews of products and can engage with other customers to troubleshoot issues or research products in real time. Customer communities can provide low-level customer service for certain kinds of problems and reduce the number of contact center calls. Customer communities can also benefit companies by providing new product ideas or feedback without requiring companies to enlist feedback groups.

Mobile CRM—or the CRM applications built for smartphones and tablets—is becoming a must-have for sales representatives and marketing professionals who want to access customer information and perform tasks when they are not physically in their offices. Mobile CRM apps take advantage of features that are unique to mobile devices, such as GPS and voice-recognition capabilities, in order to better serve customers by giving employees access to this information on the go.

4.6.2 Challenges

For all of the advancements in CRM technology, without the proper management, a CRM system can become little more than a glorified database where customer information is stored. Data sets need to be connected, distributed and organized so that users can easily access the information they need.

Companies also struggle to achieve a "single view of the customer," where many different data sets can be seamlessly accessed and organized in a single dashboard or interface to create one view of a customer's account and relevant information. Challenges arise when customer data is silted in several separate systems or when data is complicated by duplicate or outdated information that slows down and hampers the business process. These problems can lead to a decline in customer experience due to long wait times during phone calls, improper handling of technical support cases and other issues.

Studies show that customers, particularly Millennials, are increasingly dissatisfied with the contact center experience. They demand multiple avenues of communication with a company and expect a seamless interaction across many different channels, the most popular of which tend to be web chat, mobile apps and social media. The main challenge of a CRM system is delivering a cross-channel customer experience that is consistent and reliable.

Social media, for example, has been touted as a more efficient channel by which customers can reach companies and get problems resolved or queries answered, rather than enduring the traditional method of waiting in a phone queue or awaiting an email response. In some cases, particularly in high-touch customer service scenarios, social platforms can fall short for customer service.

Companies also continue to struggle to identify real sales prospects with their data. New lead-generation technologies that combine CRM data with third-party data from companies like Dunn & Bradstreet and social streams have also been emerging to provide sales and marketing teams with better sales prospects. These methods work best, however, when companies spend time cleaning up their existing data to eliminate duplicate and incomplete records before they supplement CRM data with external sources of information.

SUMMARY

Over the past year, consumers have demanded an even better customer service experience from their favorite brands both in-store and online. In response, retailers have used social media platforms and personalization as a way to improve their customer's experience. Now, retailers are planning their next move in order to fine-tune their customer service. Here's some predictions on the trends that will shape the customer service trends in the new year:

IoT (Internet of Things)—Just like the omnichannel trend, IoT is here to stay and will be a game changer over the next year. Soon, all of your devices will be connected whether you like it or not. Spinn Coffee is already using IoT to connect their coffee makers to the devices. Doesn't it sound nice to wake up, check your emails and social media and brew your coffee all from the comfort of your bed? IoT will create more opportunity for personalization in the coming year and also make consumers lives much easier with improved customer experiences.

Leverage customer data—CRMs hold so much data on customers, but many retailers are failing to take advantage of the information they have access to. Over the next year, expect retailers to start to get smarter about how they leverage their customer data to improve both online and in-person experiences. For example, some brands are already focused on implementing facial recognition cameras within their stores. Not only are they hoping it will help provide a better customer experience, but it will give associates a better idea of product recommendations for customers based on past purchases. Time will tell how privacy laws will impact this technology.

Eligibility verification—In order to remain competitive, brands can no longer limit exclusive offers to their brick and mortar stores. If the deals aren't available and easy to find online, business owners risk lost sales and a decrease in brand loyalty. Eligibility verification gives retailers the ability to offer exclusive promotions through their websites, in-store POS systems, call centers, and on mobile devices without worrying about fraud. With just a few simple, non-sensitive pieces of information, eligibility verification technology verifies against live data sources within seconds. Eligibility verification creates a quick, easy customer experience and gives businesses peace of mind when offering these types of deals. It's a win-win for both retailers and consumers.

Internet marketing is always evolving, so being flexible in your approach is important. However, having a mobile-responsive website, active social media engagement, an eye on SEO and a consistent presence on all of your local directories will position you well to compete in the 21st century.

Words and Expressions

①**associative**: characterized by or causing or resulting from the process of bringing ideas or events together in memory or imagination 联合的

②**cloud computing**: Storing and accessing data and programs over the Internet instead of your computer's hard drive. The cloud is just a metaphor for the Internet. 云计算

③**coax**: influence or urge by gentle urging, caressing, or flattering 劝诱;哄

④**cross-reference**: a reference at one place in a work to information at another place in the same work 参见项;相互参照

⑤**cusp**: point formed by two intersecting arcs (as from the intrados of a Gothic arch) 介于两个状态之间的

⑥**dashboard**: instrument panel on an automobile or airplane containing dials and controls 仪表板

⑦**deploy**: to distribute systematically or strategically 部署

⑧**eclipse**: be greater in significance than 盖过;使相形见绌

⑨**hinge on**: be contingent on 有赖于;取决于

⑩**homepage**: the opening page of a web site 网站首页

⑪**onus**: an onerous or difficult concern 义务;责任

⑫**optimize**: modify to achieve maximum efficiency in storage capacity or time or cost 使最优化;使最有效率

⑬**page layout**: the part of graphic design that deals in the arrangement of visual elements on a page 页面

⑭**posit**: to take as a given; to put before 假定;设想

⑮**preconception**: an opinion formed beforehand without adequate evidence 事先形成的看法;先入之见

⑯**proliferation**: growth by the rapid multiplication of parts 激增;剧增

⑰**subliminal advertising**: promotional messages the recipient is not aware of 隐性广告

⑱**think tank**: a company that does research for hire and issues reports on the implications 智囊团;智库

⑲**tarnish**: discoloration of metal surface caused by oxidation 玷污;损害(名誉或形象)

⑳**tout**: someone who advertises for customers in an especially brazen way 兜售;吹嘘

Exercises

Ⅰ. **Key Terms**(Explain the following terms.)

①group behavior

②USP

③decision-making

④social CRM platform

⑤omnichannel

Ⅱ. Multiple Choice Exercises (Choose the correct answer to the following questions from A, B, C and D. There is only one correct answer.)

①Practices, strategies and technologies that companies use to manage and analyze customer interactions and data throughout the customer lifecycle refers to ________.

A. social media B. customer profitability C. CRM D. SEO

②About "adventurous explorers", which of the following statements is incorrect?

A. They require little special attention by Internet vendors because they believe online shopping is fun.

B. They are likely the opinion leaders for all things online.

C. Retailers should nurture and cultivate them to be online community builders and shopping advocates.

D. They enjoy buying online and do so frequently.

③Which of the following statements does not belong to the Consumer's Decision-making Process?

A. Realizing the need or want something.

B. Searching for information about the item.

C. Using and evaluating the product before buying the purchase.

D. Disposing of the product.

④The major types of consumer behavior include the following statements except ________.

A. habitual buying habits

B. varietal buying

C. complex or extensive decision making behavior

D. impulse buying

⑤Which of the following statements is not the factors that affect people's buying behavior?

A. Distance factors. B. Personal factors.

C. Psychological factors. D. Societal factors.

⑥Which of the following words has a different meaning from others?

A. Client. B. Patron. C. Purchaser. D. Vendor.

⑦Which might be the next big game changer for social media adoption in the enterprise?

A. USP. B. Social CRM. C. Apps. D. SaaS.

⑧Which of the following statements is about the customer service trend?

A. IoT (Internet of Things).
B. Leverage customer data.
C. Eligibility verification.
D. All of the above.

Ⅲ. Review Questions

①What is consumer behavior? Why do companies study it?

②What stages do people go through in the buying process?

③Which system will be useful when managing a company's interactions with customers, clients, and sales prospects? And how does it work with social media?

Ⅳ. Online Practice

①Go to the website of Hospreypacks. Does the site make you more or less inclined to purchase an Osprey backpack?

②Visit the website of Tesco and analyze the success of Tesco's loyalty plan and it's enlightenment.

③Visit the websites of Gap and Oldnavy and discuss the following questions: Who is most likely to buy from these sites? What is the difference between the two sites? Do the sites appeal to different age cohorts? What kind of experience do they bring to customers?

Ⅴ. Case Study

Since 1996, Bizrate has been the leading resource for shoppers and retailers. Bizrate began as a business school assignment in the mind of founder Farhad Mohit, who felt that customers needed a way to navigate the growing landscape of online retailers. To provide customers with a way to assess the quality of different online stores, Bizrate launched the very first online customer feedback and ratings platform. With Bizrate, customers could rate their store experiences and retailers could learn about how they were performing. In October 1999, Bizrate integrated product search into the site to provide a holistic shopping experience.

Today, Bizrate continues to help shoppers find the best value for all the products they are looking to buy. Bizrate also remains true to its roots, allowing shoppers to provide candid opinions on their experiences with different online retailers and allowing retailers to find shoppers as well as discover insights on how to provide the best customer service to those shoppers.

Find the best value with Bizrate

Bizrate is the trusted shopping resource, linking shoppers with over a million products, brands, and stores with one click. Bizrate enables shoppers to search for virtually every product, store, brand, and deal on the web. Shop the biggest names you know to the small but trustworthy stores just waiting to be found. Compare across products, prices, and store information. Quickly access all the ratings and reviews you need to make a confident buying decision. With Bizrate, shoppers can find the right product, at the right price, every time.

Grow customer loyalty and satisfaction with Bizrate Insights

Bizrate Insights is the customer feedback and ratings platform of Bizrate, providing tools and reports to over 6,000 retailers worldwide and empowering retailers to achieve their end goal of growing sales and customer loyalty. Bizrate Insights assists retailers in listening to their customers in way that is fast and measurable, resulting in insights, action, conversation, and customer loyalty.

Questions for Discussion

①What value does Bizrate provide consumers?

②In what ways is Bizrate "the antidote to Amazon"? What are the differences in web site loyalty for Bizrate vs. Amazon?

Chapter 5 B2B Electronic Commerce

本章导读

B2B 指的是商家(泛指企业)对商家的电子商务,即企业与企业之间通过互联网进行产品、服务及信息的交换。通俗的说法是指进行电子商务交易的供需双方都是商家(或企业、公司),他们使用了 Internet 技术或各种商务网络平台来完成商务交易。B2B 模式是电子商务中历史最长、发展最完善的商业模式,能迅速地带来利润和回报。它的贸易金额是消费者直接购买的 10 倍,同时也意味着企业间的电子商务是电子商务的重头。

成本控制、差异化和创新一直被公认是企业竞争力的三大核心要素。传统的企业一直都在尝试各种途径来降低成本,例如:早期通过标准化生产流程、机械化生产和流水线生产来提高生产效率。后期通过在采购、物流运输、管理等方面减少浪费来改善其内部的经营管理等。互联网和电子商务的诞生给企业带来了新的机遇来削减其成本。通过 B2B 的交易方式,买卖双方能够在网上完成整个业务流程:从建立最初印象,到货比三家,再到讨价还价、签单和交货,最后到客户服务。B2B 使企业之间的交易减少了许多事务性的工作流程和管理费用,其主要优势体现在:降低采购成本、降低库存成本、节省周转时间、扩大市场机会等,它的利润来源于相对低廉的信息成本带来的各种费用的下降,以及供应链和价值链整合而产生的利益。本章将对 B2B 电子商务进行介绍,包括 B2B 的概念、种类、商业模式等。同时,本章将讨论中国在线批发市场的发展情况,如:中国 B2B 电子商务的现状,发展趋势及前景等。此外,本章将简要介绍中国 B2B 电子商务的支付形式。最后,本章将讨论中国 B2B 电子商务发展中所面临的问题和挑战,这些挑战给 B2B 平台提出了新的要求,他们应当不断更新和转换经营理念,应用新媒体来改善客户体验。

Business Terms

①**EDI**: an electronic communication method that provides standards for exchanging data via any electronic means. By adhering to the same standard, two different companies or organizations, even in two different countries, can electronically exchange documents (such as purchase orders, invoices, shipping notices, and many others)

②**purchasing activities**: activities such as identifying and evaluating vendors, selecting specific products, placing orders. The resolving any issues that arise after receiving the ordered goods or services. These issues might include late deliveries, incorrect quantities, incorrect items, and defective items.

③**business process**: a collection of related, structured activities or tasks that produce a specific service or product (serve a particular goal) for a particular customer or customers.

④**business support activities**: activities that support all of a business' processes include finance and administration tasks, the operation of human resources, and technology development activities.

Introductory Case

The Alibaba B2B Strategy: What Wholesalers & Distributors Need to Know

Alibaba, China's eCommerce giant, handles billions of dollars a year in transactions, increasingly acting as a bridge between mainland China, North America, Europe, and the rest of the world. Alibaba follows the supplier aggregator model (much like many B2B marketplaces of the 90s) working to ease the pain of global sourcing.

Just how exactly will the Alibaba B2B juggernaut affect business around the world? What do wholesalers, distributors, and manufacturers around the world need to know?

According to David Moth of Econsultancy, Alibaba has 231 million active buyers, and over 11.3 billion orders flowed through the company's eCommerce platforms in 2013. An average buyer makes about 49 purchases a year, and the total gross merchandise volume of Alibaba's three main consumer retail marketplaces is roughly $248 billion. Alibaba has B2B and B2C suppliers in more than 20 countries.

The scene continues to play out in US markets as well. Alibaba's global IPO was the world's largest ever at $25 billion. The United States has more than 7 billion B2B customers on Alibaba, and about 1.5 million in the U.K. Ben Popper of *The Verge* writes that in 2013, Alibaba recorded $240 billion in sales—more than Amazon and eBay combined.

Alibaba's meteoric rise can be attributed to its focus on growing its enormous supplier base, which targets Chinese and other Asian sellers that Amazon and other marketplaces don't. In other words, Alibaba's B2B marketplace has acted like a gateway to China and the growing economy's enormous capacity to produce goods that the world wants. To cater to this global demand, Alibaba does everything it can to build more trust, opening the gates wider to the world. This is evidenced in initiatives like business verification, factory inspections, and stringent demands on quality of products.

Alibaba is only the beginning of the future of B2B e-commerce. There are still lots of opportunity for e-commerce stores, wholesalers, distributors, and retailers. Broadly, there's opportunity for:

- Adopting, embracing, and deploying modern technologies using matching algorithms, intuitive UX/UI, personalization, and big data.
- Supporting mobile transactions. Mobile accounts for almost half of China's retail e-commerce sales, according to e-marketer. Mobile B2B e-commerce is a priority. Face-to-face transactions must also pave way to mobile order writing, seamless integration between order taking and enterprise resource planning systems, and mobile-first workflows.
- Competing with Alibaba's broad marketplace model with more focused direct models that engender stronger relationships between suppliers/brands and customers/retail buyers.

  Alibaba's B2B stance is such that it has also led to offshoot opportunities for many wholesalers and distributors. For some wholesalers and manufacturers, it may be beneficial to take advantage of this resource to access to global marketplaces across the world.

Questions for Discussion

①How can Alibaba make these Asian suppliers and buyers part of its own supply chain strategy?

②What do you think of Alibaba's B2B strategy?

③For wholesalers and distributors in the era of e-commerce, do you see any opportunity or threat?

5.1 OVERVIEW OF B2B

Business-to-business (B2B) refers to a situation where one business makes a commercial transaction with another. This typically occurs when: A business is sourcing materials for their production process (e. g. a food manufacturer purchasing salt).

In most cases, the overall volume of B2B transactions is much higher than the volume of B2C transactions. The primary reason for this is that in a typical supply chain there will be many B2B transactions involving subcomponents or raw materials, and only one B2C transaction, specifically sale of the finished product to the end customer. For example, an automobile manufacturer makes several B2B transactions such as buying tires, glass for windscreens, and rubber hoses for its vehicles. The final transaction, a finished vehicle sold to the consumer, is a single (B2C) transaction.

However, in certain cases, for example a toothbrush manufacturer may make lesser B2B transactions of raw materials than the number of B2C transactions of toothbrush units that are sold.

The top 5 B2B Marketplaces worldwide (2015) are:

Alibaba; Indiamart; DHgate; Global Sources; Trade India.

5.2 B2B BUSINESS MODELS

A business model describes who in the market segment are served in which goods/services, how these goods/services being produced and how the business plan to make revenue. B2B e-businesses adopt various models to benefit its procurement/acquisition functions, effectively manage its supply chain and customer relationship. From this perspective, B2B e-commerce can be classified according to the nature of the goods/services in transaction, the procurement policy, and the nature of the supply chain.

5.2.1 Classification by Ownership

Depending on who is controlling the marketplace and initiating the transactions, B2B e-commerce can be classified as a company-centric model operating in a private e-marketplace or an exchange model operating in a public marketplace.

A company-centric model, representing a one-to-many business relationship, involves one business party initiating transactions and deals with many other parties interested in buying or selling its goods and services. In these models, the initiative company has complete control over the supportive information systems. However, a third party may serve as an intermediary to introduce buyers to sellers and vice versa, and to provide them with a platform and other added-value services for transaction.

An exchange or trading model, representing a many-to-many business relationship, involves many buyers and many suppliers who meet simultaneously over the Internet to trade with one another. Usually there is a market maker who provides a platform for transactions, aggregates the buyers and sellers, and then provides the framework for the negotiation of prices and terms.

Direct selling. This is a company-centric B2B model focusing on selling, in which a supplier displays goods and services in a catalog at its host site for disposal. The seller could be a manufacturer or a distributor selling to many wholesalers, retailers, and businesses. In the B2B direct selling, the involved parties may benefit from speeding up the ordering cycle and reducing errors processing. They also benefit from reducing order processing costs, logistics costs, and paperwork, especially the reduction of buyers' search costs in finding sellers and competitive prices and the reduction of sellers' search costs in advertising to interested buyers.

Most major manufacturers have conducted B2B e-commerce with their business partners. For example, Dell. com, Cisco. com, and among others, have special secured sites for registered partners to provide them with information on products. At this kind of site, business customers can browse the whole catalog, customize it, create and save a shopping list/shopping cart for internal approval before placing orders. The sites have the tracking facility for customers to follow up on the status of their orders and also have links to shipper's web site (UPS, FedEx, TNT etc.) to help customers keep track of delivery.

Direct buying. This is a company-centric B2B model focusing on buying, in which a company posts project specifications/requirements for goods and services in need and invites interested suppliers to bid on the project. In this model, a buyer provides a directory of open request for quotation (RFQ) accessible to a large group of suppliers on a secured site. The buying company doesn't have to prepare requests and specifications for each of these potential tenders. Suppliers could be notified automatically with an announcement of available RFQ, or even the RFQ sent directly from the buyer site.

This model streamlines and automates the traditional manual processes of requisition, RFQ, invitation to tender, issue of purchase orders, receipt of goods, and payment. The model makes the procurement process simple and fast. In some cases, it increases productivity by authorizing purchases from the units/departments where the goods/services are needed and therefore bypassing some paperwork at the procurement departments. The model helps in reducing the administrative processing costs per order and lowering purchase prices through product standardization and consolidation of orders.

Exchange/trading mall. The exchange model involves many suppliers and buyers meeting at the marketplace for transactions. The marketplace could be a dedicated site or a trading mall open to the public. Transactions in this marketplace involve spot buying as well as negotiation for a long-term buying/selling contract. In spot buying, a deal is concluded at a price based on supply and demand at any given time at the marketplace. In systematic sourcing, the exchange aggregates the buyers and sellers and provides them with a platform for the negotiation of prices and terms.

The exchange provides an open marketplace so that buyer and seller can conclude/negotiate the transaction at a competitive price resulting from the supply/demand mechanism. It has the characteristics and benefits of a competitive market in terms of classic economics. A buyer may benefit from lower costs due to a large volume of goods/services being transacted. A supplier may benefit from reaching a larger pool of new buyers than is possible when conducting business in a traditional market. Using this business model, Alibaba has more than 3.6 million registered members in more than 200 countries and regions exchanging millions of product and supplier listings in over 5,000 product categories and 30 industry categories.

5.2.2 Classification by Transaction Methods

B2B business models could be classified by the transaction methods a buying/selling company uses to conduct business with its partners in the e-marketplace. A company may use one or many transaction models suitable for its transactions.

Electronic catalogs

Using this model, a supplier posts an electronic version of its catalog in a web site for free access from interested parties. The company benefits from exposure to a large pool of potential buyers over the Internet without the costly creation and distribution of voluminous catalogs. The electronic catalog can be updated in a timely manner.

In this passive and low-cost business model, a supplier could inform potential buyers of the existence of the catalogs via regular mail or e-mail. The supplier may also register the web site in the directories of some exchanges or intermediaries. Using a search engine, interested buyers may discover the competitive offer and then contact the supplier directly for further information about products and services.

Automated RFQ

In this model, RFQ are automatically distributed from the buying company to its business partners via a private communication network. The sourcing department receives requisitions electronically from other departments. It sends off RFQ containing specifications for the requisitions to a pool of approved suppliers in the network via the Internet. Potential suppliers around the world are notified of incoming RFQ almost immediately. Suppliers have a few days to prepare bids and to send them back over the extranet to the buying company. The bids are then routed over the intranet to the appropriate purchasing agents and a contract could be awarded on the same day. Because the transactions are handled electronically, invoices are automatically reconciled with purchase orders and human errors in data entries/processing are minimized accordingly.

Having automated RFQ, sourcing cycle time in the acquisition process is reduced significantly, with the distribution of information and specifications to many business partners simultaneously. It allows purchasing agents to spend more time negotiating for the best deal and less time on administrative procedures. A company also consolidates a partnership with suppliers by buying only from approved sources and awarding business based on performance. Consequently, it allows the company to acquire quality goods and services from a large pool of competitive suppliers around the world.

Metacatalogs/Directories

In this model, catalogs of approved suppliers are aggregated, indexed so that buyers will have the opportunity to deal with a large pool of suppliers of goods/services. These metacatalogs are usually kept in a central site for ease of access to potential buyers. Using this model, a global company may maintain a metacatalog of suppliers for the internal use of its branches. Or a trading mall can keep a metacatalog for the wide public access. For the internal use of a global company, the model aggregates items of all approved suppliers from their catalogs into one source. Buyers from affiliated firms or branches can find the items in need, check their availability and delivery time, and complete an electronic requisition form and forward it to the selected supplier. In this transaction, prices could be negotiated in advance. Potential suppliers tend to offer competitive prices, as they would be exposed to a larger pool of buyers, in this case the world-wide affiliations/branches of the buying company. In addition, suppliers may become involved in a long-term relationship with a global company and its affiliations/branches. The listing in the metacatalog is free to the suppliers as a result of the negotiation of terms and prices for the goods/services to be provided to the buying company.

Order aggregation

In this model, RFQ from buyers are aggregated and sent to a pool of suppliers as invitations to tender. The order aggregation could be internal or external. In an internal aggregation, company-wide orders are aggregated to gain volume discounts and save administrative costs. In an external aggregation, a third party aggregates orders from small businesses and then negotiates with suppliers or conducts reverse auctions to reach a deal for the group. Usually, an intermediary will aggregate RFQ of participant buyers and match then with RFPs from participant suppliers.

In order aggregation, small buyers benefit from the volume discount through aggregation that could not be realized otherwise. Similarly, suppliers benefit from providing a large volume of goods/services to a pool of buyers and save the transaction costs incurred from dealing with many, fragmented buyers. Order aggregation works well, with defined indirect production materials and services having relative stable prices. In this model, if the order aggregation is undertaken by an intermediary, then involved business parties may have to pay a flat fee and/or a commission on the transaction value.

Auction

To reach a deal, business partners involved in B2B could use auction and/or matching mechanisms. A forward auction involves one seller and many potential buyers. A reverse auction involves one buyer and many potential sellers. In double auction, buyers and sellers bid and offer simultaneously. In matching, related price, quantity, quality, and delivery terms from the bid and ask are matched. The auction can be in real time or last for a predetermined period.

In a buying-side marketplace, a buyer opens an electronic market on its own server, lists items in need, and invites potential suppliers to bid. The trading mechanism is a reverse auction, in which suppliers compete with one another to offer the lowest price. The bidder who offers the lowest price wins the order from the buyer.

In a selling-side marketplace, a seller posts the information for the goods/services to be disposed and invites potential buyers to bid. The trading mechanism is a forward auction, in which participating buyers compete to offer the highest price to acquire goods/services in need.

The transaction can also take place at an intermediary site, at which buyers post their RFQ and suppliers post their RFPs. Depending on the regulations of the auction site, bidders can bid either only once or many times. In the latter case, bidders can view current supply and demand for the goods/services and change their bids accordingly. The transaction concludes when bidding prices and asking prices are matched. The involved business parties may have to pay an access fee. In addition, sellers may have to pay a commission on transaction value.

5.3 B2B E-COMMERCE IN CHINA

Currently in China, B2B e-commerce mode is of the largest market share, highest operability and easiest to succeed.

5.3.1 Understanding the B2B Marketplace in China

Over the past two decades, the Chinese government has strongly promoted globalization as it strives to become a world leader in global trade. During this rise, small and medium enterprises (SMEs) have contributed more than half of the value of China's exports. About 96 percent of the more than 50 million enterprises in China were SMEs as of 2011, and that number is expected to grow 8 percent every year. Despite their growing economic importance, Chinese SMEs typically have not invested heavily in IT, creating a significant gap in their technical sophistication compared to their Western counterparts.

5.3.2 How the B2B Landscape in China Is Changing?

China's role as the largest US exporter and major global exporter has been consistently growing. Prior to the 2008 global financial crisis, Chinese manufacturers had sufficient purchase orders from multinational companies (MNCs), so neither joint-venture companies nor local service providers had urgent reasons to focus on supply chain management and build a robust B2B infrastructure. Companies relied on manual processes, purposely overstocked items for buffering, relied on educated guessing for resource planning and required long lead times to respond to deviations from the initial orders. Although MNCs understood the benefits of supply chain efficiency, they were unable to convince manufacturers to focus on supply chain reforms. These issues contributed to the high logistics costs Chinese companies face today.

Chinese manufacturers are facing pressure from decreasing export volumes and increasing competition from other developing countries. To remain competitive, Chinese companies must keep their logistics costs low by establishing better supply chain visibility and real-time forecasting. Chinese companies are now more willing to work or comply with MNCs for better supply chain strategies and recognize that supply chain reform is integral to increased competitiveness.

Supply chain reforms such as vendor managed inventory (VMI), just in time (JIT) and collaboration planning forecasting replenishment (CPFR) require the use of information logistics to deliver the right information to the right people or systems at the right time. Electronic Data Interchange (EDI) is a fundamental solution to increase the efficiency of information logistics, with capabilities to rapidly deliver information to the right people or processes. EDI helps minimize lead times and data errors, improve supply chain visibility and reduce costs through streamlined, harmonized business processes. Information logistics has been so critical to supply chain management that the Chinese government has included it as one of the key initiatives in its 12th five-year plan. Key supply chain and information management initiatives include:

- Streamline supply chain efficiency, including B2B, B2G, B2C, B2G2B and B2B2C, with the help of government support
- Reduce the cost of import and export trade to sustain competitiveness

- Promote information logistics to be in sync with physical logistics

Official government support on supply chain management through the 12th five-year plan makes it easier to conduct B2B integration and B2B trading as a foundation of supply chain reforms.

5.3.3 China's SME B2B Platforms Are Growing Steadily

According to iResearch, the revenue of China's small and medium-sized enterprises B2B platforms attained 21.59 billion Yuan in 2015 with a growth rate of 14.6%. iResearch predicted that its growth would remain more than 10% in the following years and its revenue is expected to exceed 30 billion Yuan in 2018. iResearch believes there are four factors affecting the revenue. Firstly, the economic downturn in China cast negative effect on the development of B2B platforms. Besides, the decrease of China exports and imports, which reflected the trend of SME export and import, has also influenced SME's online trading. However, the value-added services of B2B platforms including the advertising service, information service, trading service and other financing services allowed the stable development of B2B platforms. Also, the preferential policies from the government provided B2B platforms with favorable development environment.

Revenue of SME B2B Platforms in China 2011-2018

Note: The revenue of China's SME B2B platforms 2011-2018 is estimated; 2. From Q1 2015, iResearch only calculated the revenue of China's SME B2B e-commerce platforms, including membership fee, transanction commission and advertisement revenue, excluding revenue from operators' direct sales; 3. Since Q1 2015, revenue of JQW. com has been counted in the revenue of China's B2B platforms.

Source: The data were calculated and estimated in line with the financial results published by enterprises and interviews with experts in iResearch statistical model. It is for reference only, not financial advice.

Among all the China's SME B2B platforms, Alibaba still had absolute advantages over others in 2015 with a market share of 50.1%. Top 9 platforms altogether accounted for 73.0% of the market. The top 3 platforms were Alibaba, Global Sources and JQW, with market shares of 50.1%, 5.1% and 4.6% separately.

Share of China's Main SME B2B E-commerce Platforms by Revenue 2012-2015

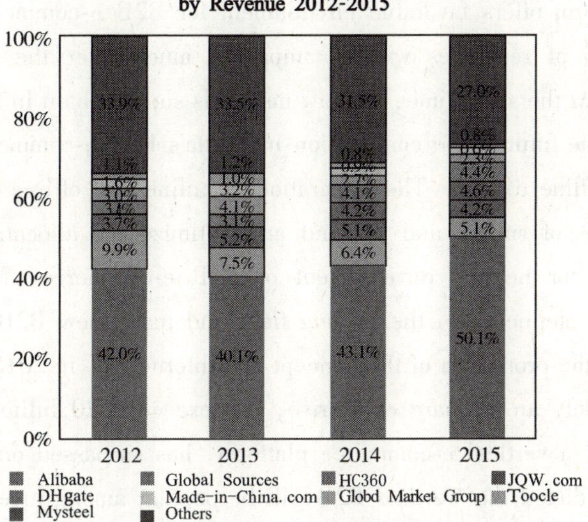

Note: 1. From Q1 2015, iResearch only calculates the revenue of SME B2B e-commerce platforms in China, including membership fee, transanction commission, advertisement revenue and etc., excluding revenue from operators' direct sales; 2. Since Q1 2015, revenue of JQW. com has been counted in the revenue of China's B2B platforms.

Source: The data were calculated and estimated in line with the financial results published by enterprises and interviews with experts in iResearch statistical model. It is for reference only, not financial advice.

In 2015, the supply-side structural reform offered new opportunities to B2B e-commerce and capital market fueled its rapid development. Due to the domestic economic downturn, China's exports continued to decline hand in hand with China's CPI index and PPI index. Under the conditions, the government promoted the supply-side reform and encouraged traditional companies to explore the business through Internet. Therefore, "Internet + Traditional Business" is believed to boom up in B2B e-commerce sector. The preferential policies on supply-side reformation will motivate the increasing usage of cloud computing, big data analysis and the Internet of Things(iot) in productive service industries, improve the services of the enterprises and strengthen the combination of B2B e-commerce and enterprise service. The supply-side structural reforms aim to deliver five key tasks: ①reduce overcapacity; ②reduce inventories; ③de-leverage; ④lower costs and ⑤shore up weak growth areas. These five tasks are interconnected and mutually reinforcing. Therefore, it will help the economy gain speed in the future. Pushed by the reforms, B2B companies are required to optimize the industrial structure and business modes. For B2B e-commerce platforms, they are expected to break the limits of traditional industrial structure with their technology and big data, to find out their sales channels and increase their profit. The two challenges upstream companies in B2B e-commerce sector face are overcapacity and low resource utilization ratio. However, with the supply-side structural reform, those companies will have chances to adjust their structure and reach a high level balance of demand and supply. iResearch believes that the supply-side reform offers favorable environment for B2B e-commerce upstream companies and the utilization ratio of resources will be improved much after the structure adjustment of traditional enterprises. At the same time, the raw materials supply chain in the sector will also enjoy great development. In the future, the competition in China's B2B e-commerce industry will extend from online market to offline market. The integration of online and offline market will improve the transparency of resources of supply and demand and optimize the allocation of resources, which provides the possibility for healthy development of B2B e-commerce. Moreover, a number of traditional B2B websites stepped into the trading field and many new B2B companies focusing on vertical fields rose with the promotion of the concept of "Internet +" in 2015. Recently, the market value of Shanghai Mysteel, an A share enterprise, has exceeded 20 billion Yuan and the market value of Zhaogang. com, a vertical e-commerce platform, has surpassed one billion Yuan as well. Therefore, it can be predicted that vertical B2B will be popular among investors in the future.

5.3.4 B2B Payments in China

B2B electronic payments will reach US $47 billion in 2013, accounting for 5. 1% of B2B e-commerce transactions. Celent estimates that the total transaction volumes of e-commerce, B2B e-commerce, and B2B electronic payments will amount to US $1. 8 trillion, US $1. 4 trillion, and US $140 billion, respectively, in 2015. B2B payment providers have developed individualized strategies to stay competitive in the marketplace. 99 Bill Corporation has positioned itself as an "electronic financial service provider" and plans to provide mutual fund management solutions for more traditional industries. The international payment giant PayPal, a subsidiary of eBay, has expressed its intention to become the first foreign enterprise to obtain China's electronic payment license. Gopay is China's only state-owned payment platform for ministries and their subordinate institutions, and is able to provide adequate security for funds transfers by customers. China

B2B Payment Market Size in China

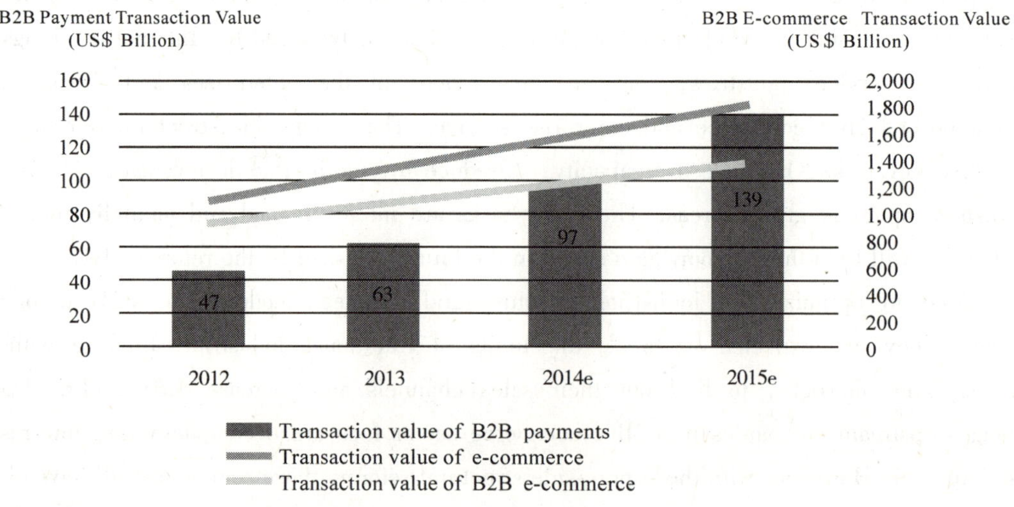

UnionPay has launched a B2B online payment service for the public sector via its public payment platform. "B2B payment vendors have focused on strengthening their services in the areas of cross-border payments, foreign exchange settlement, foreign exchange risk management, and collaboration with more foreign partners."

5.3.5 B2B E-commerce Growing; Becoming More Like B2C

While B2C-gets the most media attention, B2B e-commerce is the bigger revenue generator. The entry of e-commerce giants such as Alibaba and Amazon into B2B has accelerated the trend of B2B websites becoming more like B2C. Online B2B sellers now recognize that the customer experience in a B2B environment is just as important as the customer experience for B2C.

Consequently, expectations have grown and more B2B buyers require a simple e-commerce experience that mimics the consumer purchase model. Detailed specifications and product descriptions are crucial. Amazon Supply—the company's B2B portal—offers free two-day shipping on orders above $50, detailed specifications, and an underutilized, but available, customer review section.

Recently, Alibaba announced that the boundary between B2B and B2C will be broken through to realize the overall transformation and upgrading of Alibaba B2B e-commerce. Jingdong Mall will also join in the B2B field soon, confided by Liu Qiangdong at early time. With these measures of top runners in the field of e-commerce, the B2B industry transformation and upgrading certainly will be accelerated and driven, thus promoting the industry development.

In stark contrast to the previous status of B2B which was collectively badmouthed, in 2013, nearly all the top-ranked websites in B2B industry took efforts to strengthen their construction. Being far ahead, Alibaba announced to divide its structural adjustment into 25 business units, and then its sub-website AliExpress built the "international Taobao" platform, which aims to fully transform the previously small online-trade wholesale into an overseas-oriented shopping platform; both focusing on B2B, HC network and CMSB worked together to create Internet inclusive finance, which intends to offer service and build a bridge for the financing of small enterprises; "Yigang online" also acquired equity investment of RMB100 million from Softbank China Venture Capital (SBCVC), which is really rare in steel B2B e-commerce industry. However, considering the present situation, China B2B e-commerce websites is far from popular compared with B2C, its decreasing market share also casts a shadow over the entire industry. But in the meantime, many traditional enterprises join in the B2B field for exploration. According to statistics, the total quantity of B2B industry websites is over 7 000, making an increase of over 700 compared with that in 2011.

At this time, the leading enterprises come to lead the trend once again with the emergence of new media and technology. The release of news that Alibaba bought stake in Sina microblog for US $586 million became the "heavy bomb" of global IT field, which brought fresh blood for B2B field. The Sina microblog, whether being used as microblog for media or for communication, will become the B2B marketing platform. Participating enterprises, including industries such as logistics, tourism, telemedicine, steel and manufacturing, are mostly keen on the development of mobile e-commerce. If the 46 million active users of Sina microblog and 300 million "listeners" of micro-letter can be used properly, believed by entrepreneurs, the enterprise is bound to gain the benefit of "ten-thousand fold profit without any investment". For example, product marketing of Xiaomi phone was conducted through "Mi fans", and its application of media also increases the service efficiency of Xiaomi, thus attracting plenty of customers to follow Xiaomi.

5.4 B2B E-COMMERCE ISSUES

5.4.1 Merits and Limitations of B2B E-commerce

Merits

B2B e-commerce in general exposes a selling/buying company to a larger pool of suppliers and corporate buyers. Transactions over the Internet help overcome the geographical barrier, bringing business partners from all over the world to the e-marketplace. A company may benefit from transactions with business partners beyond the local market. The Web-based technology of e-commerce helps minimize the human error found in the paper-based activities and supports timely, if not real-time, communication between and among partners. Different from traditional, costly telecommunications networks, Web-based technology makes transactions over the Internet affordable to most businesses involved in the e-marketplace. Also, the existence of many intermediaries also provides interested businesses with low-cost solutions for implementing a B2B e-commerce model. B2B e-commerce models address the concerns about the effectiveness and efficiency of the supply chain management of business partners—suppliers as well as company buyers. Supply chain management coordinates business activities from order generation, order taking to order distribution of goods/services for individual as well as corporate customers. Interdependencies in the supply chain create an extended boundary that goes far beyond an individual firm, so that individual firms can no longer maximize their own competitive advantageand therefore profit from cutting costs/prices. Material suppliers and distribution-channel partners, such as wholesalers, distributors, and retailers, all play important roles in supply chain management. B2B e-commerce models address the creation of partnerships with other parties along the supply chain, upstream as well as downstream, to share information of mutual benefit about the need of final customers. The key issue is that all upstream and downstream business activities should be coordinated to meet effectively the demand of final customers. Each partner in the stream should coordinate its own production/business plans (order fulfillment, procurement, production, and distribution) with those of the other partners so that sufficient streams of goods/services will reach customers in the right place at the right time. B2B business models also address issues of customer relationship management, the front-end function of a supply chain. An effective business model helps in creating more loyal customers who are not inclined to shop for lower prices but rather who pay for quality and service, in retaining valued customers, and in developing new customers by providing them with new quality products and services. The customer base could be segmented on history of performance in sales/purchases. This information will serve as a basis for promotion and discount, promoting the loyalty of current customers.

Limitations and possible solutions

Some limitations of B2B e-commerce have been identified, such as conflicts with the existing distributing channel, cost/benefit justification for the venture, integration with business partners, and trust among business partners. Most suppliers have existing distributing networks of wholesalers, distributors and dealers. If a company decides to do business over the Internet directly with interested partners, it may cause conflict in terms of territory agreement and pricing policies on product lines. A possible solution could be redirecting these potential customers to the appropriate distributors and having the company handle only new customers outside the current sales territories of these distributors. Another alternative could be the company handling specific products/services not available within the traditional distribution channel. Or orders could be taken at the central site, with a distributor providing downstream added-value services (delivery, maintenance, support) to the new customers of the company. Another limitation is the number of potential business partners, and sales volume must be large enough to justify the implementation of a Web-based B2B system. Selling-side marketplaces for B2B e-commerce is promising if the supplier has a sufficient number of loyal business customers, if the product is well known, and if the price is not the critical purchasing criteria. For the buying side, the volume of transactions should be large enough to cover the investments and costs in the B2B e-commerce venture. In many cases, the interested business could participate in an exchange by paying a fixed fee or a commission on the volume of transactions. Using an intermediary could be feasible, as the company would not need to invest and maintain the expensive and sophisticated infrastructure of B2B e-commerce systems. On a technical perspective, unless a B2B e-commerce site has implemented comprehensive network/system architecture, integration with a variety of business partners systems may cause an operational problem. These business partners should be able to transact on compatible network platforms and protocols of communication. Sometimes the conversion implies additional investments and requires an extra cost/benefit analysis for the project. Also the technology should handle global transactions, such as multiple currencies and multiple languages from multiple countries, multiple terms of contract, and multiple product quality standards. Most current service providers in B2B e-commerce offer solutions to address these issues. Because transactions over Internet are not face-to-face, most business partners are unknown to each other. Consequently, the issue of trust in B2B is the same as in B2C e-commerce transactions. Many B2B exchanges have failed because they did not assure the creditability of the involved business partners. Trust in e-commerce could be enhanced with some quality assurance services and warranty seal programs. In these programs, a third party (such as a CPA) audits the e-commerce transactions and infrastructure of a company to assure that it implements and follows some procedures and policies to guarantee privacy, security, processing integrity, availability, and confidentiality of online transactions and its obligation toward its business partners. Once the company meets some prescribed criteria, it is awarded with a warranty seal to post on its Web-site to inform the potential business partners on the security and quality of its online transactions. Some service providers in B2B e-commerce, such as ariba. com, have been awarded with the seals.

5.4.2 B2B E-commerce, the Road Ahead

B2B e-commerce framework could expand to cover activities beyond than just selling and buying. B2B e-commerce partners in an extended value chain could involve in collaborative commerce (c-commerce) and product life cycle maintenance in a Web-based system to meet final consumer demand by sharing information on product design, production planning, and marketing forecasting/coordination. Once consumer demand is identified, the quantity on hand of the raw material and semifinished and finished products of one partner will be made visible to others, avoiding bottlenecks along the value chain and supply chain. In this type of business, some partners act as value chain integrators while others are value chain service providers. This business model assures the production of goods/services that effectively meet consumer demand with the collaboration between manufacturers and retailers. Then the product design and production cycle will be efficiently shortened with the collaboration between manufacturers and upstream suppliers. It also helps in just-in-time (JIT) sourcing to lower transportation and inventory costs, and to reduce stock-outs.

SUMMARY

This chapter mainly discusses issues regarding B2B electronic commerce. B2B, or "business to business", means that by using computers and network, different enterprises make the trade activities through e-commerce platform. B2B business models can be classified into various types based on different classification standards. The most common classification is based on the classification by the ownership. Then, depending on who is controlling the marketplace and initiating the transactions, B2B e-commerce can be classified as a company-centric model operating in a private e-marketplace or an exchange model operating in a public marketplace. In addition, it can be classified by the transaction methods a buying/selling company uses to conduct business with its partners in the e-marketplace including electronic catalogues, automated RFQ, order aggregation and etc. Different from that of B2C, the value of B2B lies in the features of rapidity, low-cost and low-consumption. Once there were industry experts said: "The development of our manufacturing can't be separated from B2B information platform, the platform itself is also credited for the cost reduction, which is more valuable than cheap labor force." So we can see that B2B e-commerce has a good chance of development. However, owing to the competitions among B2B counterparts, lots of problems have been brought about, such as the assimilation of products and service, lack of new breakthrough in technical means, low efficiency of supply chains, as well as the degradation of external environment and reduction of enterprise orders, etc. which lead to the bad operation of many domestic B2B small and medium enterprises. Businesses need to update and transform by taking advantage of the new media thus improving the customer's experience and generating more revenue.

Words and Expressions

①**aggregation**: the act or process of gathering 聚集

②**AliExpress**: an online retail service made up of mostly small Chinese businesses offering products to international online buyers 速卖通

③**competitive advantage**: the attribute that allows an organization to outperform its competitors. 竞争优势

④**equity investment**: money that is invested in a firm by its owner(s) or holder(s) of common stock (ordinary shares) but which is not returned in the normal course of the business. Investors recover it only when they sell their shareholdings to other investors, or when the assets of the firm are liquidated and proceeds distributed among them after satisfying the firm's obligations. Also called equity contribution. 股权投资

⑤**financing**: the act of providing funds for business activities, making purchases or investing 融资

⑥**integration**: the act of combining into an integral whole 集成;整合

⑦**JIT inventory**: just-in-time inventory 即时库存

⑧**PayPal**: an American company operating a worldwide online payments system that supports online money transfers and serves as an electronic alternative to traditional paper methods like checks and money orders 贝宝

⑨**reverse auction**: a type of auction in which the roles of buyer and seller are reversed. In an ordinary auction (also known as a forward auction), buyers compete to obtain a good or service by offering increasingly higher prices. In a reverse auction, the sellers compete to obtain business from the buyer and prices will typically decrease as the sellers underbid each other. 逆拍卖

⑩**sourcing**: a number of procurement practices, aimed at finding, evaluating and engaging suppliers for acquiring goods and services 采购

⑪**supply-side reform**: As China strives to sustain growth, supply-side reform is the latest tool to be taken from the box and sharpened. Viewed as a whole, these measures can also be considered structural reform. 供给侧改革

⑫**value chain**: a set of activities that a firm operating in a specific industry performs in order to deliver a valuable product or service for the market 价值链条

⑬**venture capital**: a type of private equity, a form of financing that is provided by firms or funds to small, early-stage, emerging firms that are deemed to have high growth potential, or which have demonstrated high growth (in terms of number of employees, annual revenue, or both) 风险投资

Exercises

Ⅰ. **Key Terms** (Explain the following terms.)

①sourcing

②procurement

③JIT inventory

④supply side management

⑤logistics

Ⅱ. **Multiple Choice Exercises** (Choose the correct answer to the following questions from A, B, C and D. There is only one correct answer.)

①B2B e-commerce can be classified according to ________.

A. the nature of the goods/services in transaction

B. the procurement policy

C. the nature of the supply chain

D. all of the above

②Which of the following benefits regarding Direct Selling is not true?

A. Reduction of buyer's search cost. B. Speeding up the ordering cycle.

C. Increase of productivity. D. Reducing logistic costs.

③Direct buying streamlines and automates the traditional manual processes of ________.

A. requisition, RFQ, invitation to tender

B. issue of purchase orders, receipt of goods, and payment

C. both A and B

D. posting product catalogue

④Which of the following statements regarding forward auction is not true?

A. A forward auction involves one seller and many potential buyers.

B. The bidder who offers the lowest price wins the order from the buyer.

C. The auction can be in real time or last for a predetermined period.

D. Participating buyers compete to offer the highest price to acquire goods/services in need.

⑤Which of the following areas is not viewed as part of supply chain reforms?

A. JIT. B. EDI. C. MNC. D. Information logistic.

⑥Among all the China's SME B2B platforms, ________ still had absolute advantages over others.

A. AliExpress B. Tmall C. Alibaba D. Jingdong

⑦________ is China's only state-owned payment platform for ministries and their subordinate institutions.

A. UnionPay B. Alipay C. PayPal D. Gopay

⑧The value of B2B e-commerce lies in ________.

A. cheap labor force B. the use of new media

C. low cost and low consumption D. none of the above

Ⅲ. Review Questions

①Which sector of Chinese economy turns out to be the focus of B2B e-commerce?

②What are the most important values of B2B e-commerce?

③What are the most common B2B e-commerce business models?

Ⅳ. Online Practice

①Using your library or your favorite search engine, identify the main reasons a medium-sized manufacturing company might want to utilize a B2B platform for its operation. Summarize your findings in two or three paragraphs.

②Please visit one B2B platform, such as Alibaba, DHgate, and then analyze their business models.

③Summarize the benefits and barriers of B2B e-commerce in your own words. Identify some critical factors and make suggestions on the future development of B2B e-commerce.

Ⅴ. Case Study

Alibaba Revamps Struggling B2B Efforts in India

Alibaba is ramping up its B2B e-commerce efforts in India just over a year after the conglomerate introduced its most recent SME-serving platform in the nation.

Reports said China-based Alibaba is strengthening its B2B efforts in India by partnering with logistics companies DHL and Delhivery to provide solutions to online suppliers. The company will also be collaborating with local banks to provide financing to its online sellers.

These solutions will target Alibaba's B2B platform in India, and will provide both domestic and international support for suppliers. IDFC Bank, Aditya Birla Finance and Kotak Mahindra have inked agreements with Alibaba to provide financing to sellers using Alibaba's B2B e-commerce platform, with a focus on SMEs and startups.

Speaking to reporters in India, an unnamed source with information on Alibaba's plans said that the company is looking to finally get its B2B services off the ground. "Their B2B platform has been around for years, but they haven't been able to make much progress scaling it," the source said. "Now, it seems, they are seriously looking to focus on the B2B side by helping sellers with working capital and logistics. They'll also bring in Chinese vendors onto the site as they have great depth in the merchant ecosystem back home."

Alibaba has had a presence in India for several years, but last year, the company introduced its most recent B2B service in the country, a trade facilitation center that provides a digital platform for suppliers and SMEs to link with logistics and financial services.

Questions for Discussion

①What does Alibaba attempt to achieve in India?

②Why do the company's efforts focusing on SMEs?

Chapter 6 Innovative EC Systems

本章导读

电子商务系统是保证以电子商务为基础的网上交易实现的体系。市场交易是由参与交易的双方在平等、自由、互利的基础上进行的基于价值的交换。网上交易同样遵循上述原则。作为交易中的两个有机组成部分,一是交易双方信息沟通,二是双方进行等价交换。在网上交易,其信息沟通是通过数字化的信息沟通渠道而实现的,一个首要条件是交易双方必须拥有相应的信息技术工具,才有可能利用基于信息技术的沟通渠道进行沟通。例如要保证能通过Internet进行交易,必须要求企业、组织和消费者连接到Internet,否则无法利用Internet进行交易。在网上进行交易,交易双方在空间上是分离的,为保证交易双方进行等价交换,必须提供相应货物配送手段和支付结算手段。货物配送仍然依赖传统物流渠道,对于支付结算既可以利用传统手段,也可以利用先进的网上支付手段。此外,为保证企业、组织和消费者能够利用数字化沟通渠道,保证交易顺利进行的配送和支付,需要由专门提供这方面服务的中间商参与,即电子商务服务商。本章将对创新电子商务进行介绍,主要包括:创新电子商务系统概要、格式、信用机制、在线支付、物流以及移动电子商务。

Business Terms

①**EC format**: the business operation mode and profit model based on a certain technical basis in the network environment and large data environment

②**O2O**: Offline to Online, the combination of offline business opportunity and the Internet, making the Internet an offline trading platform.

③**EC credit mechanism**: The credit system refers to the system arrangement of the relationship between credit and creditor. It is the standard and guarantee of credit behavior and relationship, and the behavior rules of people's credit activities and relationships.

④**fingerprint identification**: Fingerprint identification refers to the identification of minutiae by comparing the minutiae of different fingerprints.

⑤**facial recognition**: using a video camera or camera to capture the image or video stream containing human face, and automatically detect and track human face in the image, and then to detect the face of a series of related technologies.

⑥**third party e-commerce platform**: It refers to the provider and the demander of the product or service, through the network service platform, according to the transaction and service specification, to provide services for buyers and sellers.

⑦**5A theroy of ecnomics**: anytime, anywhere, anything, anyone, anyhow

Introductory Case

China's E-commerce Emperor

As numerous e-tailors fold under highly competitive market pressures and others battle it out with nasty price wars, through all of this, one company—the Alibaba Group has risen to become the undisputed leader of e-commerce in China.

The Alibaba Group is now China's second biggest Internet company in terms of revenue. Combined, the Group's web sites cover the entire spectrum of e-commerce and related services in China and cater to all business and consumer needs.

For any fashion company or foreign brand with ambitions of doing business in China, understanding the Alibaba e-commerce network is fundamental knowledge. This is true even for brands not intending to sell online, as Alibaba's shopping portal Taobao. com has become so big that it influences the entire retail ecosystem in China.

Alibaba was founded by Jack Ma in 1999 in Hangzhou—an enchanting city 200kms south west of Shanghai. Once an English-speaking tour guide, over the last decade the charismatic Ma has grown Alibaba into China's leading Internet company and earned himself nationwide admiration as a business figure and CEO.

By definition, Alibaba is not an online retailer because it doesn't own or trade any of its own merchandise, nor manage inventory or warehouses. Instead, Alibaba acts like a shopping mall developer, owning Internet real estate that allows buyers and sellers to congregate online. Alibaba then makes revenue through online advertising and subscription fees.

Below is a brief introduction to each of Alibaba Group's main websites and services.

Alibaba. com and Aliexpress. com

Alibaba. com is an English language B2B marketplace that offers a platform for importers and exporters to connect and source products from over 2.5 million storefronts (many of which are Chinese manufacturers). Products are sold wholesale and orders are usually for thousands of pieces at a time. According to the company, as of June 2012, Alibaba had 29. 4 million registered users from more than 240 countries.

Aliexpress. com is similar to Alibaba. com in that it is primarily a B2B operation, but it allows transactions of much smaller order sizes while still at wholesale prices.

A basic understanding of Alibaba. com and Aliexpress. com is enough for fashion brands operating in China as these sites don't influence consumer's individual purchases in China very much.

Taobao. com

In a nutshell Taobao is the eBay of China and primarily a C2C platform, but with one striking difference—most products traded are brand new. Taobao. com was launched in 2003 and has now grown to account for around 80% of online transaction volume in China.

According the Alibaba's website, as of June 2012, Taobao can boast more than 800 million product listings and more than 500 million registered users. Google ranks Taobao as one of the top 20 most visited websites in the world.

Understanding what Taobao is, how it works and how it influences retail and your brand image etc. in China is absolutely vital knowledge.

Tmall. com

Tmall opened for business in 2008 and is Alibaba's B2C platform dedicated to individual brands across all categories including fashion, home furnishings and books etc.

Tmall. com allows brands to create their own pages on the Tmall platform and now claims to feature over 50,000 international and Chinese brands. Many fashion brands including Gap, Ray-Ban, Nike and L'Oreal etc. operate part, if not all, of their online retail in China through Tmall.

Whereas many counterfeit products can be found on Taobao, brands operating on Tmall are all verified by Alibaba to be genuine. So proper brand retailers should only consider opening their brand pages on Tmall and never Taobao.

Etao. com

Etao is a comparison-shopping service with information about prices, special offers and promotions from a host of e-commerce operators in China, including Taobao, Tmall, Amazon China, Dangdang, Nike China and Vancl etc.

Alibaba hopes etao will become a one-stop shopping engine for all China, however, some disputes have arisen between Alibaba and other e-tailers regarding conflicts of interest and fairness with the price comparisons.

Currently in the beta phase etao has recently launched "Discover etao"—a Pinterest like social network and social commerce site that links to Taobao and Alibaba's other e-commerce portals.

Juhuasuan. com

Juhuasuan is Alibaba's group shopping platform and not so relevant to the majority of multinational fashion brands in China.

Alipay. com

Through Alipay, Alibaba solved their own online payments issues early on and also provided payment system solutions for millions of Internet merchants in China.

Questions for Discussion

①What are Alibaba Group's main websites and service?

②Why is it important to know about Taobao?

6.1 OVERVIEW OF INNOVATIVE EC SYSTEMS

A new round of technological and Industrial Revolution gave birth to the electronic commerce, created a new consumer demand, triggered a new wave of investment, opened up new channels to increase employment, and provided sufficient space and stage for public's entrepreneurship and innovation. E-commerce has become an important way for China to promote entrepreneurship and employment.

At the same time, along with the development of urbanization in China, the new growth of urban and rural economy is an urgent need to make great strides in the development and innovation of electronic commerce. E-commerce innovation in Alibaba and other leading enterprises as the representative of the financial industry, retail, consumer goods, agriculture, manufacturing and logistics industry and other traditional industries formed a transformative impact. Its spillover effect is very significant. Through the promotion of innovative social forces, it is possible to become the next step to deepen the reform of a breakthrough. Making full use of the flow, seizing the transformation and upgrading of the economic structure becomes particularly important.

According to the different depth of the consumer in the e-commerce, the innovation of electronic commerce can be summed up in three aspects.

6.1.1 Trading Technology

Mainly in order to reduce the cost of technology, simplify the payment and optimization experience to promote the mass of users of frequent transactions, activate the incremental market.

6.1.2 Transaction Structure

E-commerce provides B2B, B2C, C2C and C2B and other rich trading channels, not only covers the traditional wholesale and retail, but also includes a new type of buy, personal and collective custom pre-sale. Diversified trading channels formed diversified trade structure, which brings the full right to choose for the consumer, effectively prevents the monopoly of individual business products and channels and ensures that different levels of needs of consumers can be effective and affordable to meet.

6.1.3 Power Contract

Consumer status reversal (or the rise of consumer sovereignty). In the e-commerce environment, the consumer has the right to evaluate the goods and services, which directly affect the reputation of the business and sales of goods. In particular, the emergence of group buying and C2B mode, the user has a certain right to speak for the design and production of products. In other words, the power of producers and sellers is shared by users, and the latter is an equal contract with the former in order to purchase, evaluate and participate in the former. Before this equal contract, producers and sellers of the mandatory power monopoly difficult place for.

Different levels of innovation did not change the logic of business. But the business is more close to the nature of the business services—docking producers and consumers. Its core lies not only in the Internet technology, but also lies in the Internet logic.

The innovation logic of e-commerce is likely to reflect the typical characteristics of the Internet economy: it does not change the industry itself but logic. It makes all industries closer to its original essence. E-commerce is the logic of the Internet and the spirit of the Internet in the field of business, financial industry and other aspects of innovation.

6.2 INNOVATIVE EC FORMAT

EC format refers to the business operation mode and profit model based on a certain technical basis in the network environment and large data environment. With the continuous expansion of the application field of EC format and the uninterrupted innovation of information service, the format of e-commerce is also emerging. It can be mainly divided into the following several types: B2C, B2B, C2C, C2B, O2O, B2Q. This section will focus on O2O.

6.2.1 Definition of O2O

O2O refers to "Online To Offline". It combines the offline business opportunities with the Internet and makes the Internet the platform of offline transaction. In other words, online stores push offline store messages to online users to complete orders and payments. After that, the user can use the order voucher to pick up the goods or enjoy the service from the offline stores. The value of online and offline fusion is staggering. And its data analysis provides a steady stream of momentum for the development of O2O.

O2O e-business models need to have five elements: an independent online store, the trusted websites certified by national authority certification, online advertising, social media interaction with customers, integration of the affiliate marketing system online and offline.

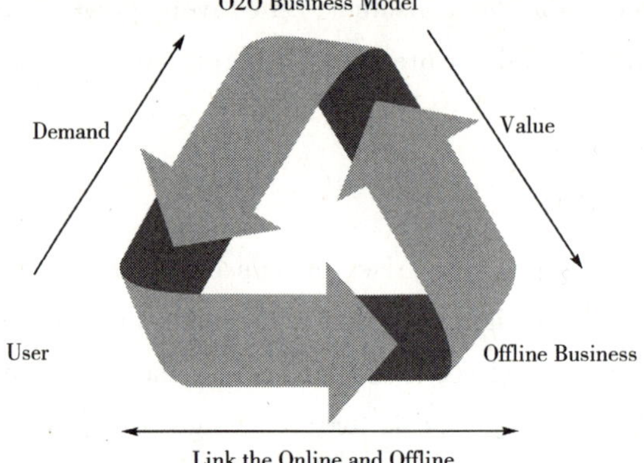

6.2.2 Analysis of O2O's Advantages and Disadvantages

<table>
<tr><th></th><th>Advantage</th><th>Disadvantage</th></tr>
<tr><td rowspan="5">Consumer</td><td>a large amount of reference information</td><td rowspan="3">The quality of goods or services may be lower than expected.</td></tr>
<tr><td>the cheaper price</td></tr>
<tr><td>easy to search</td></tr>
<tr><td>Online consultation is usable.</td><td rowspan="2">After-sale problem is difficult to solve.</td></tr>
<tr><td>high reliability of information</td></tr>
<tr><td rowspan="5">Seller</td><td>more publicity and display opportunities</td><td rowspan="2">serious homogenization competition</td></tr>
<tr><td>Promotion effect can be checked.</td></tr>
<tr><td>tracking user data for precise impact</td><td rowspan="2">The effective duration of the information is restricted by the O2O web site.</td></tr>
<tr><td>Reasonable arrangement saves the cost.</td></tr>
<tr><td>decreased reliance on store location</td><td>low customer loyalty</td></tr>
<tr><td rowspan="5">O2O</td><td>a large number of highly viscous customers</td><td rowspan="2">Honesty is hard to guarantee.</td></tr>
<tr><td>a large number of offline living service providers</td></tr>
<tr><td>more cash flow than B2B and C2C</td><td rowspan="2">Seller's qualification need inspection.</td></tr>
<tr><td>huge advertising revenue</td></tr>
<tr><td>more profitable ways after a certain scale</td><td>lack of creative ability</td></tr>
</table>

6.2.3 Suggestions for the Development of O2O

- Establish a more perfect credit system.
- Further subdividing the market.

- Attract more traditional industries to participate.
- Seize the development opportunities of mobile commerce.
- Explore better profit models.

6.3 INNOVATIVE EC ONLINE-PAY

Innovative EC online-pay means combining the latest and most advanced technology with online-pay on the premise of ensuring safety. This section will introduce several high-tech online-pay ways.

6.3.1 Fingerprint Payment

Fingerprint identification is one of the most frequently used biometric identification techniques. As early as the Tang and Song Dynasties, fingerprint had already used in the judicial trial and contracts. Modern fingerprint identification has experienced many years of accumulation. It becomes very mature and widely used in the judicature, public security and entrance guard.

Fingerprint payment uses mature fingerprint system for consumer certification. Customers use fingerprint registration to become a fingerprint consumer discount alliance platform member. After that consumer payment can be completed by fingerprint identification. And customer can enjoy the lowest discount business.

6.3.2 Acoustic Wave Payment

This is aimed to complete the identification between two equipments through the transmission of acoustic. Many people think they need to speak to the vending machine to complete the payment. That's not really true. Actually its specific process is when you pay for something you can open this function, and then align your phone's microphone with payee. Your phone will play an audio like "Xiu Xiu Xiu". Maybe you will wonder whether it is safety enough. Don't be afraid. Every acoustic wave audio has quality guarantee period. And it's very short, about a few minutes. So if somebody else record and decipher it, he will be disappointed. Because he can only get a string of code and it is overdue.

6.3.3 Shaking Payment

Alipay launched a new client function which contains Near Field Communication (NFC) and Location Based Service (LBS). Both users can touch or shake the phone at the same time to automatically fill in the Alipay account number. It improves the speed of payment and makes the business between two strangers much easier. The function is the fusion of NFC, acceleration transducer, LBS and other technologies. It can double the speed of payment between strangers.

6.3.4 Face Scan Payment

On March 16, 2015, Hannover IT exhibition with the theme of "digital economy" opened in Germany. During the opening ceremony, Alibaba's founder Jack Ma showed a new face scan payment technology called "Smile to Pay" at the fair.

Face scan payment uses facial recognition. It is understood that the face scan payment used by Jack Ma is developed by Alipay and "face ++". It will take the place of traditional password payment. So far this technology is still in the testing phase. Its accuracy rate may achieve 97%, which is beyond recognition of human.

6.4 INNOVATIVE EC CREDIT MECHANISM

Credit system is the lifeline of electricity suppliers. Social credit system and its related laws and regulations are the foundation of China's e-commerce market. If we only pay attention to e-commerce logistics, online payment and other "hardware" factors, but ignore the hidden credit system, a small number of online fraud will produce "bad money drives out good" effect, then the integrity problems will become a bottleneck in the development of electronic commerce.

Credit in electronic commerce seems to be dynamic and changing in the majority of online consumers. Credit is based on the purchase experience slowly formed. For each shopping site, online consumers are from the initial stage of cognition, to the early stage of understanding, and then to the middle of the purchase attempt, and finally to form a successful purchase of the basic trust. This trust will gradually increase with the increase in the success of purchase experience, that is, online shopping businesses in the eyes of consumers with their success and stability of the purchase experience synchronized formation and stability. In the process of credit formation, the initial attempt is the most important step in the consumer decision to trust the site. Therefore, the online consumer credit to businesses is accompanied by the consumption process.

Next, we will learn several aspects of the credit system's construction.

6.4.1 Electronic Commerce Platform's Credit

The electronic commerce industry in China is in a crucial period of development. It is critial to strengthen the construction of network integrity. Credit evaluation is a comprehensive evaluation of the ability and willingness to fulfill corporate social responsibility and commercial contracts. Credit level can reflect the overall credit status of enterprises and provide decision reference for trading partners. It not only can help honest enterprise gain more business opportunities, but also is a valuable intangible assets of enterprises.

- Credit rating is divided into nine grades (AAA, AA, A, BBB, BB, B, CCC, CC, C). Enterprises above the level of a credit will be accepted. The evaluation results are valid for three years.

- Evaluation indicators: the basic quality of the enterprise, the financial situation, management level, competitiveness and social credit records, etc.
- The SASAC will award a unified credit rating of bronze medal.
- Award website credit electronic sign and electronic certificate. Click on the electronic identification, it will display the credit rating, website identity information, customer service phone, user's privacy information protection, etc.
- Reporting time: Credit rating accepts the declaration of the enterprise throughout the year. March and September each year to review and publish.
- Evaluation process: ①Fill in the application form. ②Get the "acceptance notification letter". ③Submit "evaluation report" and pay. ④Reference check. ⑤Assess credit rating. ⑥Make it public. ⑦Award website credit electronic sign, electronic certificate and bronze medal.

6.4.2 Commodity Credit Certification

The significance of commodity quality certification system:

- Promote the improvement of product quality.
- Improve the reputation and competitiveness of goods.
- Provide customers with quality information of products.
- Reduce the cost of social repeat inspection and evaluation.

6.4.3 Electronic Commerce Management Main Body Credit Certification

The electronic commerce management main body credit certification refers to an independent third party, according to the independent, impartial and objective principle, to evaluate enterprise's authenticity and credit status from the perspective of business credit. Let's take Taobao as an example.

Credit evaluation system

It is composed by heart, diamond and crown. The purpose is to provide a reference for the integrity of the transaction and protect the interests of buyers. Once the seller gets a "good", it is able to accumulate one point. Less than 250 points, the seller gets a heart. The yellow diamond is used to represent 250 to 10,000 points and the blue crown to represent 10,000 to 500,000 points. 500,000 points above, the credit rating is shown by a golden crown.

Deposit

In order to protect the consumer and enhance the service level and product quality of the seller, Taobao stipulates some goods need to pay the deposit according to "consumer protection service agreement". Deposit is the money saved in the seller's Taobao account when setting up the shop to ensure the integrity of the seller and prevent him/her from selling fake goods. When there is a consumer dispute, it is also a part of the protection for the consumer.

6.4.4 Consumer Credit

Buyer credit rating

Both trading sides can obtain a corresponding evaluation once the business is completed. After the success of the order transaction, the seller can make an evaluation to the buyer according to the transaction process. Evaluation is divided into three categories: "praise", "middle" and "poor". "Praise" can get one point; "middle" has not extra points; "poor" lose one point.

Black list system

Sometimes there are bad buyers who usually give a malicious negative evaluation to the seller, which makes the seller miserable. To solve this problem, Taobao launched the "black list" function. With this function, the seller can ban the customer who is in the blacklist to do transactions in the seller's shop.

6.5 INNOVATIVE EC LOGISTICS

Simplifying the business processes and reducing the cost of business is one of the electronic commerce's advantages. This advantage must depend on a credible and efficient logistics system, which is the key of modern enterprise competition.

6.5.1 The EC Logistics

The use of EMS services logistics model

The enterprise obtains the consumer's shopping list and home address from the website or the hypothesized website, then goes through the special delivery formalities to the nearby post office to mail out the cargo, then the customer receives the notice to go to the local post office to get the cargo, or the cargo can be delivered directly by an mailman to the customer. The use of EMS services is convenient and fast.

Corporate self-distribution logistics model

The enterprise establishes its own cargo allocation spot in the customer-crowded area, and delivers goods to the customer's doorstep by allocation personnel after obtaining the shopping information. This kind of physical distribution pattern may satisfy the customer's shopping psychology demand "namely to buy namely results in". But it also has problems: to determine an allocation layout, the population equipment, the commodity reserve and so on.

The third party physical distribution company pattern

The third party physical distribution company itself does not have the commodity, but it forms the cooperation alliance with the enterprise and provides the service for the customer. This physical distribution method is the specialized, multi-purposed and omni-directional.

6.5.2 Problems of EC Logistics

- The theoretical study of the logistics system isn't in-depth enough. The researchers on physical distribution management in China are studying new theories, whose applications need time.
- Lacking of infrastructure, high-tech technologies and equipments, the logistics industry in China is relatively backward. The transportation system can not meet the needs of commerce development.
- Laws and regulations related to EC logistics need to be improved.
- The logistics management should be strengthened. Lacking of the physical distribution talents, there isn't enough intellectual support for a new physical distribution system.

6.5.3 Trends of EC Logistics

Multi-faceted

In the electronic commerce era, the integrated allocation center should not only provide the warehousing and transportation service, but also distribute orders and so on to make added-value to the service. The enterprise pursues the system's comprehensive effect more and more. In this aspect, logistics should be multi-faceted.

First-class service

Nowadays, how to provide high quality service has become the core issue of the management and development of logistics enterprises. Only those who has the first-class service can promote the development of e-commerce.

Informatization

In the era of electronic commerce, to provide the best service, logistics system must have a good information processing and transmission system. When the cargo is being transported, the customer can get the shipping information and the arrival time. And the warehousing and the transport company can also raise the service level greatly, thus the logistics can reduce the cost and enhance the competitive power.

6.6 INNOVATIVE MOBILE EC

According to the statistic of China Internet Network Information Center, the number of China netizens connecting to the Internet through desktop computers has achieved 380 million, and the number of mobile phone has reached 388 million. The Mobile Internet Storm is coming. Nowadays it is the world of mobile EC, but why? It should start from the 5A theory of economics.

6.6.1 5A Theory of Economics

5A theory of economics means anytime, anywhere, anything, anyone and anyhow. People have sought for the achievement of 5A theory for a long time. Finally it is realized in the mobile Internet's era. Mobile EC reduces the costs of transaction, improves transaction's efficiency and achieves the optimal state of resource allocation.

6.6.2 Innovative Technology of Mobile EC

NFC

Near-field communication (NFC) is a set of communication protocols that enable two electronic devices, one of which is usually a portable device such as a smartphone, to establish communication by bringing them within 4 cm of each other.

NFC devices are used in contactless payment systems, similar to those used in credit cards and electronic ticket smartcards and allow mobile payment to replace/supplement these systems. NFC is used for social networking, for sharing contacts, photos, videos or files. NFC-enabled devices can act as electronic identity documents and keycards. NFC offers a low-speed connection with simple setup that can be used to bootstrap more capable wireless connections.

This technology evolved from non-contact radio frequency identification (RFID). NFC is a short-range high frequency radio technology. When it combines with retailing, it will enhance the shopping experience by the combination of wireless coupons and membership card. Through scanning NFC tag of goods by the personal application, consumers can get more merchandise's information. For example, if you are allergic to the nut, through scanning the product, your NFC device can automatically detect whether the product contains nuts or not. You can get not only the information of wares but also other useful things such as coupons and discounts by this way. All those functions will have an increasing impact on retailing.

ETC

ETC (Electronic Toll Collection) is an international automatic toll collection system for highways, bridges and tunnels, which is being developed and promoted internationally. There are ETC lanes for vehicles equipped with ETC vehicles.

It is a microwave dedicated short range communication between the on-board electronic tag mounted on the windshield of the vehicle and the microwave antenna on the ETC lane of the toll station. Using computer networking technology and bank settlement in the background, it makes the vehicle go through the Luqiao toll station without parking. In China, IC card and magnetic card are used as the medium, and the road toll collection mode, which is mainly based on manual toll collection, is undoubtedly affected by this trend.

Alipay Wallet

Alipay Wallet is a leading mobile payment platform. It not only contains the civilian financial artifact—YuEBao but also includes services of paying off credit cards, transferring, charging calls, paying utilities, etc. With Alipay Wallet you can get a cheaper taxi, go shopping to the convenience stores, buy drinks from vending machines and get many other intimate services. Here are some advantages of Alipay Wallet: ① Consumers needn't to run around and the online payment is convenient and simple. ②The transaction fee is free and it is economical and practical. ③After the successful payment, the seller will deliver goods immediately. To a certain extent, Alipay Wallet realizes the 5A theory of economics.

Alipay also provides an escrow service, in which consumers can verify whether they are happy with the goods they bought before releasing money to the seller. This service greatly improves the consumer's confidence in C2C and even B2C quality control.

SUMMARY

This chapter mainly discusses issues related to innovative electronic commerce. Along with the development of urbanization in China, the new growth of urban and rural economy is an urgent need to make great strides in the development and innovation of electronic commerce. The innovation of electronic commerce has three aspects according to the different depth of the consumer in the e-commerce. They are trading technology, transaction structure and power contract. The fundamental reason why people innovate electronic business is the pursuit of 5A theory. The purpose is to reduce transaction costs, improve transaction efficiency, and achieve the optimal state of resource allocation.

A broader environment: people are not subject to time constraints and not limited by the space. There are little restrictions on online shopping and it can be done anywhere. To get a broader market: the world will become very small on the Internet. A merchant can face global consumers, while a consumer can shop in any place of the world. To get a more rapid circulation and low price, e-commerce is to reduce the intermediate link in the circulation of goods, saving a lot of expenses, thus greatly reducing the cost of commodity circulation and transaction.

Nowadays more and more people pursue fashion and pay attention to personality. Electronic commerce is closely combined with this personalized shopping process. Mobile payment's development is the most mature and has achieved full coverage of urban life. It includes medical, traffic, public security household, entry and exit of the country, payment, education, accumulation fund and other 16 public service. China is now in the world's leading position in the aspect of mobile payment.

Words and Expressions

①**acoustic wave**: a mechanical wave and a form of sound transmission 声波

②**added-value**: the new value created by the production process of the resident units and the transfer value of the fixed assets 附加值;增加值

③**contactless payment**: a bank card/client terminal that generates a wireless signal connection through the built-in chip and the receiving end machine 非接触支付

④**convenience store**: a small retail store or online store that takes the convenience of demand as its first purpose 便利店

⑤**diversification**: a combination of different characteristics, and business diversification refers to non-related, cross industry and multi category business combinations 多样化

⑥**downstream industry**: the end of the whole industry chain, processing raw materials and components, manufacturing finished products and engaged in production and service industries. 下游产业

⑦**electronic tag**: Electronic tags are also called radio frequency tags, transponders and data carriers 电子标签

⑧**guarantee period**: the time period when the manufacturer sells the goods to the consumer and provides free maintenance if the product is faulty due to quality problems 保修期

⑨**highway bridge expense**: a general term for tolls 路桥费

⑩**Industrial Revolution**: a revolution in production and science and technology, which replaced the manpower with machines instead of individual workshops 工业革命

⑪**industry chain**: It is a chain related relation formed by certain industrial sectors based on certain technical and economic relations, and based on specific logical relations and temporal and spatial layout 产业链

⑫**Internet Network Information Center**: One mechanism which is responsible for the operation, management and service of the national network basic resources, and undertakes the technical research and development of the basic resources of the national network and safeguards the safety. 互联网信息中心

⑬**logistics industry**: the flow of goods from the supply place to the receiving place 物流业

⑭**marketing promotion**: The industry and commerce organizations advertise their products to customers in various ways to stimulate their purchasing desire and behavior. It is a kind of business activity to enlarge the sales volume of products. 促销

⑮**online fraud**: the act of using the Internet to make use of the fictitious facts or concealing the truth to defraud the larger amount of public and private property 网络欺诈

⑯**radio frequency identification**: a communication technology that identifies specific targets and reads and writes related data via radio signals 射频识别

⑰**social division of labor**: It is the activity that shortens the average social labor time and improves the production efficiency remarkably. 社会分工

⑱**spillover effect**: It refers to an organization in carrying out an activity that will not only produce the desired effect, but also affect people or society outside the organization. 溢出效应

⑲**vending machine**: a machine that automatically delivers goods according to input coins 自动贩卖机

Exercises

Ⅰ. **Key Terms** (Explain the following terms.)

①O2O

②5A theroy

③acoustic wave payment

④black list system

⑤electronic commerce format

Ⅱ. Multiple Choice Exercises (Choose the correct answer to the following questions from A, B, C and D. There is only one correct answer.)

①Which of the following innovations has not been mentioned in Section 6.1?

A. Power contract. B. Transaction structure.

C. Trading technology. D. Commodity innovation.

②Which of the following is not the ingredient of O2O commerce?

A. Independent online mall.

B. Online advertising marketing promotion.

C. Online interaction between social media and customers.

D. Offline experience store.

③How can the seller get one point of credit mechanism?

A. Complete transaction. B. Get a "good".

C. With the increase of time. D. Give judges money.

④Which of the following is not the security assurance of acoustic wave payment?

A. We can't understand its meaning. B. Its expiry date is very short.

C. It can't be heard by us. D. It can't be recoded.

⑤Which is not the problem of logistics in China?

A. Staff quality needs to be strengthened.

B. Laws and regulations need to be improved.

C. The logistics management should be strengthened.

D. Lacking of infrastructure, high-tech technologies and equipments, the logistics industry is relatively backward.

⑥Which of the following is not included in the evaluation process?

A. Fill in the application form. B. Reference check.

C. On-the-spot investigation. D. Assess credit rating.

⑦Which one is the significance of commodity quality certification system?

A. Reduce the cost of social repeat inspection and evaluation.

B. Confuse consumers and increase sales.

C. Simplify commodity circulation.

D. Regulate the market.

⑧Which of the following is not a trend in the logistics industry?

A. Multi-faceted. B. First-class service.

C. Artificialization. D. Informatization.

Ⅲ. Review Questions

①What is a business model?

②What are the categories of business models?

③How to innovate the mode of e-commerce?

Ⅳ. Online Practice

①Please visit one electronic commerce platform, such as Taobao. com, Tmall. com, and analyze its revenue models.

②Please visit several online travel businesses, such as Ctrip, Tuniu, and analyze their services and operating features.

③Try to buy or sell an item on the website of XianYu, and then make a evaluation of this experience.

Ⅴ. Case Study

Thanks to the hyper-growth of e-commerce in China, bicycles, scooters, pedicabs, and pedestrians increasingly have to compete with a new breed of guided human missile—the e-commerce delivery man. Led by Taobao, the surge in e-commerce in China has caused exponential growth to the country's domestic logistics sector. In the Blue Book study on the e-commerce in China, CSLA reports that private logistics companies are doubling their size every year to keep up with demand.

While speedy delivery times can be expected in the big first tier cities like Beijing and Guangzhou, ensuring efficient, safe and secure product delivery across the entire country is a monumental challenge for any e-tailers in China. Delivering to office towers in Shanghai's CBD is one thing, delivering the far reaches of Tibet, completely another.

This Technode article delves into the issues logistics companies are facing and the delivery impediments to growth for e-commerce in China. However, the situation described is still the same today and there is no real solution on the horizon.

Luckily, the Chinese Government sees e-commerce as a key to boosting domestic consumption and stimulating growth as China transitions away from being an export-led economy. The Chinese Government has already spent billions Yuan to upgrade the nation's highway system, and within a few years the bullet train network will be completed and criss-cross the entire country.

This action is encouraging, yet China's logistics sector is still largely closed to foreign operators who may have the expertise to alleviate the problems. According to the Global Times, China's State Postal Bureau just recently granted FedEx and UPS access to up to eight more cities in China.

Although an important step, in the scheme of things, eight cities is a pittance considering China has hundreds of cities with populations of millions.

International logistics company DHL did attempt operations in China and through worldwide fashion event partner IMG even sponsored China Fashion Week's Young Designer Award. Yet after incurring massive losses DHL ceased their Chinese domestic operations in 2011 and now only focuses on international shipments in and out of China.

As infrastructure and access improves, efforts also should be focused on improving the additional services included with e-commerce deliveries. International fashion e-tailer Yoox has been leading such initiatives in China and provides a wait-while-you-try-on service that permits customers to return orders if they aren't right.

Fashion companies may wish to take note of KFC's delivery service in China that apparently caters to customers requests for handsome delivery boys.

The quickest solution for many e-tailers in China may be to invest and build their own logistics companies, yet covering every mile of China will always be a challenge. The reverse is occurring too and Chinese logistics operators including Shun Feng have opened their own e-commerce platforms to tap into the growing appetite for online purchasing.

Questions for Discussion

①What is the problem of the logistics industry in China?

②How to solve these problems?

Chapter 7 E-supply Chains

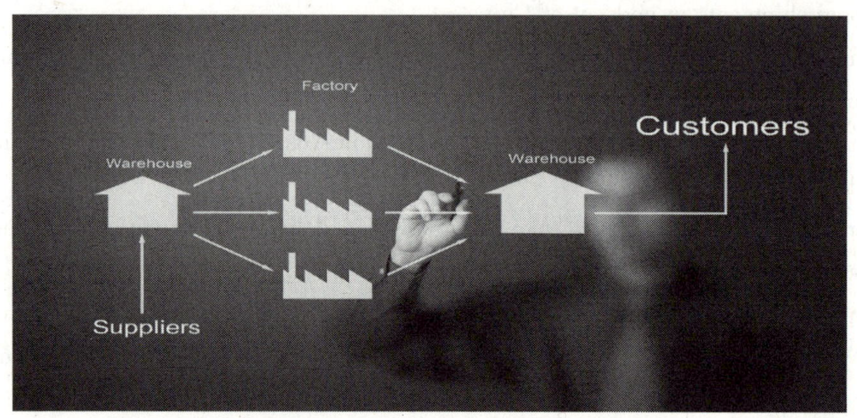

本章导读

作为21世纪企业管理的一种新模式,供应链管理(SCM)围绕核心企业,通过对物流、信息流和资金流的控制,对供应链上各业务伙伴的业务流程进行集成和整合,从而有效地管理从原材料采购、生产制造、经销,到将产品交付给最终用户的全过程。这个过程将供应商、制造商、分销商、零售商、终端用户连接为一个整体,既提高了客户满意度,也降低了企业成本,提高了效率。基于互联网的电子供应链(e-SCM)通过集中协调不同企业的关键数据,实现供应链上的信息集成,为各业务伙伴之间创建了一个无缝的、自动的供应链,实时共享各类信息。电子供应链能够整合企业的业务流程,节约交易成本,降低库存水平,降低采购成本,增加企业收入和利润。本章首先将对电子供应链进行整体介绍,包括电子供应链的概念、内容、优势和意义等;然后将深入讨论电子供应链的实施过程,例如实施前的准备和计划、实施的步骤和要求等;此外,还将讨论电子供应链实施所面临的问题和挑战。这将有助于企业对其现行及即将部署的电子供应链管理系统有一个清晰的认识,从而采取恰当策略,不断提高企业供应链系统的性能,增强业务竞争力。

Business Terms

①**e-procurement**: The use of web-based technology to support the key procurement processes, including requisitioning, sourcing, contracting, ordering, and payment.

②**supply chain management**(SCM): A set of approaches utilized to efficiently integrate suppliers, manufacturers, warehouses and stores, so that merchandise is produced and distributed at the right quantities, to the right locations, and at the right time, in order to minimize system-wide costs while satisfying service level requirements.

③**third party logistics** (TPL): the use of an outside company to perform all or part of the firm's materials management and product distribution function

④**business process reengineer** (BPR): the analysis and redesign of workflows within and between enterprises in order to optimize end-to-end processes and automate non-value-added tasks

Introductory Case

Dell's Distribution and Supply Chain Innovation

In 1983, 18-year-old Michael Dell left college to work full-time for the company he founded as a freshman, providing hard-drive upgrades to corporate customers. In a year's time, Dell's venture had $6 million in annual sales. In 1985, Dell changed his strategy to begin offering built-to-order computers. That year, the company generated $70 million in sales. Five years later, revenues had climbed to $500 million, and by the end of 2000, Dell's revenues had topped an astounding $25 billion. The meteoric rise of Dell Computers was largely due to innovations in supply chain and manufacturing, but also due to the implementation of a novel distribution strategy. By carefully analyzing and making strategic changes in the personal computer value chain, and by seizing on emerging market trends, Dell Inc. grew to dominate the PC market in less time than it takes many companies to launch their first product.

No more middleman

Dell started out as a direct seller, first using a mail-order system, and then taking advantage of the Internet to develop an online sales platform. Well before the use of the Internet went mainstream, Dell had begun integrating online order status updates and technical support into their customer-facing operations. By 1997, Dell's Internet sales had reached an average of $4 million per day. While most other PCs were sold preconfigured and pre-assembled in retail stores, Dell offered superior customer choice in system configuration at a deeply discounted price, due to the cost-savings associated with cutting out the retail middleman. This move away from the traditional distribution model for PC sales played a large role in Dell's formidable early growth. Additionally, an important side-benefit of the Internet-based direct sales model was that it generated a wealth of market data the company used to efficiently forecast demand trends and carry out effective segmentation strategies. This data drove the company's product development efforts and allowed Dell to profit from information on the value drivers in each of its key customer segments.

Virtual integration

On the manufacturing side, the company pursued an aggressive strategy of "virtual integration." Dell required a highly reliable supply of top-quality PC components, but management did not want to integrate backward to become its own parts manufacturer. Instead, the company sought to develop long-term relationships with select, name-brand PC component manufacturers. Dell also required its key suppliers to establish inventory hubs near its own assembly plants. This allowed the company to communicate with supplier inventory hubs in real time for the delivery of a precise number of required components on short notice. This "just-in-time", low-inventory strategy reduced the time it took for Dell to bring new PC models to market and resulted in significant cost advantages over the traditional stored-inventory method. This was particularly powerful in a market where old inventory quickly fell into obsolescence. Dell openly shared its production schedules, sales forecasts and plans for new products with its suppliers. This strategic closeness with supplier partners allowed Dell to reap the benefits of vertical integration, without requiring the company to invest billions setting up its own manufacturing operations in-house.

Innovation on the assembly floor

In 1997, Dell reorganized its assembly processes. Rather than having long assembly lines with each worker repeatedly performing a single task, Dell instituted "manufacturing cells". These "cells" grouped workers together around a workstation where they assembled entire PCs according to customer specifications. Cell manufacturing doubled the company's manufacturing productivity per square foot of assembly space, and reduced assembly times by 75%.

Dell combined operational and process innovation with a revolutionary distribution model to generate tremendous cost-savings and unprecedented customer value in the PC market.

Questions for Discussion

①What is the distribution model of Dell?

②What is the virtual integration strategy of Dell?

③What can we learn from the story of Dell's incredible rise?

7.1 OVERVIEW OF SUPPLY CHAINS

7.1.1 Definition of Supply Chains

Supply chain refers to the series of links and shared processes that exist between suppliers and customers. These links and processes involve all activities from the acquisition of raw materials to the delivery of finished goods to the end consumer. For example, a company that makes vehicles would need to purchase spare parts such as automobile engine. The automobile engine company would need to purchase materials to produce them, including cylinder block and pistons. All of these materials and components form part of the company's supply chain of materials needed to produce the end result of a working vehicle. Once the car is made, a trucking company may take it to a wholesaler warehouse, and then it may be delivered to a retail store for sale or shipped directly to an end user. Every step—from sourcing of raw materials to final delivery to the customer—is considered part of the supply chain of the vehicle.

A supply chain should have a focal company, which is the dominant company in the chain, control and manage the information flow, material flow and capital flow, and then combine the suppliers, manufacturers, distributors, retailers and end users into an integrated network.

The product flow includes the movement of goods from a supplier to a customer, as well as any customer returns or service needs. The information flow involves transmitting orders and updating the status of delivery. The financial flow consists of credit terms, payment schedules, and consignment and title ownership arrangements.

7.1.2 Characteristics of Supply Chains

To understand the nature of supply chains, one should be clear about the following characteristics:

- The supply chain includes all activities and processes to supply a product or service to a final customer.
- Any number of companies can be linked in the supply chain. In a supply chain, there should be a focal company.
- A customer can be a supplier to another customer so the total chain can have a number of supplier-customer relationships.
- While the distribution system can be direct from supplier to customer, depending on the products and markets, it can contain a number of distributors such as wholesalers, warehouses, and retailers.
- Products or services usually flow from supplier to customer. Likewise, design and demand information usually flows from customer to supplier. (Physical products move "downstream", while demand information flows "upstream".)
- The information flow, material flow and capital flow play a key role in supply Chains.

7.1.3 Supply Chain Management

According to APICS Dictionary, supply chain management (SCM) refers to "the design, planning, execution, control, and monitoring of supply chain activities with the objective of creating net value, building a competitive infrastructure, leveraging worldwide logistics, synchronizing supply with demand and measuring performance globally". It includes the management of the material flow, information flow and capital flow involved in the production and logistic processes, and the reasonable regulation of business process.

According to Institute for Supply Management, SCM means "The design and management of seamless, value-added process across organizational boundaries to meet the real needs of the end customer". While, as per The Supply Chain Council, SCM indicates "managing supply and demand, sourcing raw materials and parts, manufacturing and assembly, warehousing and inventory tracking, order entry and order management, distribution across all channels, and delivery to the customer". In conclusion, SCM is the process of planning, implementing and controlling supply chain operations in an optimized manner.

The management of supply chains should obey following principles:

- It should be the customer-centric management. Customers' wants and needs should be the starting point and be satisfied through the efficient supply chain management.
- The relevant enterprises should share profits and risks. Supply chain management values the overall integration and cooperation among members, thus the relevant profits and risks should be shared by all members.
- The modern information technology should be applied to realize the management objectives. To realize the high-efficient supply chain management, one should have the fast material flow and capital flow, especially the fast information flow, which can guarantee the quick response of the whole supply to the market demand. The development and application of Internet technology and e-commerce makes the fast transmission of information available.

7.2 INTRODUCTION TO E-SUPPLY CHAINS

The essence of SCM is effective material and information flow among all the members in the chain. E-supply chain originates in 2004, encompassing only procurement management originally. With the development in past years, it has evolved into covering all the procedures and members in the whole supply chains. E-supply chain includes the coordination between supply and demand, delivery management, procurement management, suppliers' management, logistics of the finished goods, warehousing management, e-commerce platform, etc.

7.2.1 Definition of E-supply Chain

E-supply chain means a supply chain that is managed electronically, usually with Web technologies. Taking the focal company as the center, Internet as the platform, e-commerce as the method, based on the integration and controlling of material flow, capital flow and information flow, e-supply chain starts from the procurement of raw material, makes semi-products and finished products, and finally delivers the products to customers through the sales network. It can have suppliers and customers seamlessly linked together in the world, exchanging information almost instantly.

To have a clear understanding of e-supply chain, following points should be emphasized:

- Taking focal company as the center, it establishes its overall supply chain network through the focal company.
- It integrates the supply chain by means of Internet and e-commerce.
- It should go with the Internet structure and model.
- Each node enterprise in the chain is independent of each other in terms of property rights.

The Structure of Supply Chains

The upside of suppliers ← Suppliers — Customers → Ultimate users

Flows on supply side — Focal company — Flows on demand side

Material flow, information flow

Capital flow, information flow

7.2.2 Advantages of E-supply Chains

In traditional supply chains, the finished products should be transferred through various wholesalers and retailers before they finally come to the end users. However, in the e-commerce era, customers can purchase products directly from the manufacturers' online stores, thus many intermediaries in the downstream of the supply chains can be cut out. The distance between manufactures and customers can be greatly shortened.

Generally speaking, e-supply chains can bring about the following benefits:

- Lowering the transaction cost. With the help of Internet, the integrated supply chain can substantially shorten transaction time, improve the transaction efficiency and eliminate lots of paperwork, and therefore lower the transaction cost.
- Reducing the inventory. Through the instant information transmission, suppliers can always keep the inventory information on hand, procuring raw materials only when needed, thus it is not necessary for them to have a high inventory level.
- Reducing procurement cost and managing suppliers efficiently. Since suppliers can get inventory and procurement information with less effort, the low-value added time of manual processing can instead be devoted to higher-value added work.
- Shortening cycle time. With the automation of supply chain, the accuracy of prediction can be greatly improved, which can help enterprises to make needed products, reduce producing time and increase customers' satisfaction.
- Increase revenues and profits. Through the expansion of organization's boundary, enterprises can fulfill their contract, increase revenues, sustain and expand market share.

7.3 E-SUPPLY CHAIN MANAGEMENT

Internet has offered great opportunities to improve supply chain management by lowering costs and shortening cycle time, thus it is really a good method to have highly competitive e-supply chain capabilities. E-supply chain management (e-SCM) refers to the collaborative use of technology to improve the operations of supply chain activities as well as the management of supply chains.

7.3.1 Methods of E-supply Chain Management

Just in time (JIT)

Being an inventory strategy, just in time(JIT) refers to delivering the right materials and parts with right quantities at right time to the specific production line to make appropriate products. In short, it means producing right products at right time with right quantity.

Following is a good example. A computer manufacturer, operating with very low inventory levels, relies on its supply chain to deliver the parts it needs to build computers. The parts needed to make the computers do not arrive before or after they are needed; instead, they arrive just as they are needed.

JIT has lots of advantages. This method can improve efficiency and shorten production cycle time, which makes production runs remain short. It can also reduce costs by eliminating warehouse storage needs. Companies also spend less money on raw materials and decrease waste by receiving goods only as they are needed in the production process, thereby reducing inventory costs.

Quick response (QR)

Developed under the influence of JIT, quick response(QR) is an management concept to manufacturing which aims at reducing internal and external lead time to increase consumer satisfaction and then survive in the serious competition. As a production and distribution system for QR to the market, it intends to shorten the lead time from receiving an order to the product delivery and to increase the cash flow.

QR can improve quality, increase logistic speed, reduce cost and eliminate non-value-added waste within the organization. It can also increase the organization's competitiveness and market share by serving customers better and faster.

Efficient consumer response (ECR)

Efficient consumer response (ECR) is a supply chain management strategy that requires the whole distribution system more responsive to consumer demand and then to promote the removal of unnecessary costs from the supply chain.

The objective of ECR is to bring more benefits to customers by reducing unnecessary costs and charges in the supply chain. It stresses providing customers with better products, better inventory service and more convenience. ECR makes use of standardized working procedures and revenue systems, which can improve the efficiency of the whole system through the identification of potential revenues and the availability of fair sharing of returns. ECR should make use of accurate and timely information to support the efficient market production and logistics, which will be freely transmitted among trade members. Another key point of ECR is to ensure that customers can obtain the required goods at any time.

Enterprise resource planning (ERP)

Enterprise resource planning (ERP) is an integrated system based on the supply chain management within the enterprise, which can help enterprises to collect, manage and utilize data from all the business activities.

ERP makes full use of common database of the enterprise to integrate core business processes. It leads departments in the enterprise to share data with other departments (purchasing, manufacturing, marketing, accounting, etc.), which greatly improves the efficiency of information flow in the organization and thus gains more customers and markets. ERP can also improve enterprise's adaptability to changes in the market, reduce the operating cost, strengthen the supervision and improve the market share.

ERP system generally includes the following features:

- Making uses of databases of various departments in the enterprise;
- Integrating in (or near) real time various functions of the enterprise, avoiding the periodic updating of the information;
- Installing the relevant software, with the close cooperation with the Information Technology (IT) department.

7.3.2 The Design of E-supply Chain

The design of e-SCM mainly constitutes the application of following systems:

- Electronic ordering system
- E-procurement system
- Advanced planning and scheduling system
- Electronic logistic system
- Inventory management system
- Customer service system
- E-payment system

Electronic ordering system (EOS)

Electronic ordering system inputs the ordering data needed by wholesalers and retailers into the computer, and then transmits them through the commercial value-added network center to the headquarter, wholesalers, suppliers or manufacturers, who will arrange delivery in time based on the information received. EOS covers all the business procedures, capable of dealing with the overall transaction from gaining commodity information to accounting.

To retailers, EOS can lower the inventory, reduce delivery errors, improve ordering efficiency and set up shop integrated management system. While to wholesalers, EOS can improve the service, establish efficient logistics system, raise working efficiency and systemize the sales management system.

E-procurement system

The word "procurement" means purchasing something, which stresses "five rights": deliver at the right time, with the right price, of the right quality and right quantity, from the right source. Thus electronic procurement (e-procurement) refers to the electronic integration and management of all procurement activities, including purchase request, ordering, delivery and payment between purchasers and suppliers, together with other information and networking systems, such as electronic data interchange and enterprise resource planning. In simple words, e-procurement is simply making use of various forms of electronic communication to perform the procurement function.

E-procurement can bring lots of benefits for the company. It can reduce purchasing cycle time and staff time spent in procurement, lower inventory level and decrease transaction costs. It can also facilitate the tracking and predicting of procurement spending through information automation. In general, e-procurement can improve the enterprise's efficiency and save a lot of cost.

The application of e-procurement may have the following models:

- Sell-side system. The supplier establish their own website to sell the products or services, and the buyer directly procures from the website. It is typically not integrated with the buyer's system.
- Buy-side system. The system is controlled by the buyer, which is generally connected to the buyer's intranet or the extranet with buyers' other partners, integrating the sellers' catalogs with the buyer's procurement system.
- Third-party system/portals. Portal refers to various marketplaces on the Internet. There exist two types of basic portals: vertical portal and horizontal portals. The former refers to the specialized website that serves as an entry point to a specific market or industry niche or subject area, such as some specialized energy websites, steel websites or chemical sites; while the latter refers to the specialized website that serves as an entry point to several firms or suppliers in different industries, such as Free Markets, Commerce One, Ariba, etc.

Advanced planning and scheduling system

Advanced planning and scheduling (APS), also known as advanced manufacturing, refers to a manufacturing management process by which raw materials and production capacity are optimally allocated to meet demand.

Traditional production planning and scheduling systems utilize a stepwise procedure to allocate material and production capacity, which cannot readily adapt to changes in demand, resource capacity or material availability. Materials and capacity are planned separately, and many systems do not consider limited material availability or capacity constraints. Thus, this approach often results in plans that cannot be executed. Unlike previous systems, APS simultaneously plans and schedules production based on available materials, labor and plant capacity.

APS enables customers' orders to be connected directly with workshops' orders, reflects the resource capacity and material availability with vivid figures, and thus responds customers' demands quickly with the accurate allocation of manufacturing resources.

Advanced planning and scheduling software makes manufacturing scheduling and advanced scheduling optimized. Currently, the widely accepted APS softwares in Chinese market include Yongkai APS, Asprova, etc.

Electronic logistic system

In e-commerce, a complete purchasing process involves information flow, capital flow and material flow. Without efficient material flow system, the convenience of e-commerce cannot be achieved. The present logistic system in modern e-commerce society includes two forms:

The self-established logistic system. Some enterprises prefer to solve the logistic distribution through the establishment of their own logistic company. This method can facilitate them to monitor the whole process, get the relevant information immediately, deliver the goods to customers with the least time and thus improve customers' experience.

The third party logistics (TPL) or even fourth party logistics (FPL). The company contracts out its distribution and logistic business to the professional logistic company, namely the third party logistics provider. In this way, the company can save much time and cost and concentrate on the improvement of their core competency. Fourth party logistics is the further step of TPL, which means after outsourcing its logistical operations to the third party logistics, the company may hire another specialist firm (the fourth party) to coordinate the activities of the third parties.

Inventory management system

Inventory management refers to the ongoing process of moving parts and products into and out of a company's location(s). It can be applied on a daily basis when companies place new orders for products and ship orders out to customers. It is made up of many key components, which include:

Order management. If inventory is going to be in shortage, the inventory management system can be programmed to tell managers to reorder that product. This helps companies avoid running out of products or tying up too much capital in inventory.

Asset tracking. When a product is in a warehouse or store, it can be tracked via its barcode and/or other tracking criteria, such as serial number, lot number or revision number. Nowadays, inventory management software often utilizes barcode, radio-frequency identification (RFID), and wireless tracking technology.

Service management. For service-oriented companies, they can use this system to track the cost of the materials they use to provide services, by which they can attach prices to their services that reflect the total cost of performing them.

Product identification. This can be achieved through barcodes, which is read by a barcode reader to look up information on the products they represent. RFID tags and wireless methods of product identification are also growing in popularity. Modern inventory software programs may use QR codes or NFC tags to identify inventory items and smartphones as scanners.

Inventory optimization. It is a fully automated demand forecasting and inventory optimization system, which can be measured by reorder point, order quantity, lead demand, stock cover and accuracy.

Customer service system

It is a configuration of people, business procedures, technology and strategies connected via value propositions and shared information. Taking customer satisfaction and loyalty as core values, customer service system is designed to deliver services that satisfy the needs, wants, or aspirations of customers to increase sales and revenues. Customer service system consists of the following parts:

Automatic voice response (IVR). It can liberate the customer service staff from a lot of repetitive work and offer more professional services for customers with least cost.

Automatic call distribution (ACD). It is responsible for equally distributing calls to present operators or professional representatives, which can improve the efficiency, save cost and also better use customer resources.

Progress editing. Customers can make any combinations of the controls offered by the system to generate the needed business conveniently and quickly. Also, they can visit the business application system through the external service controls of the system.

Recording management. The system can record and monitor multi-channel telephone simultaneously with advanced digital recording technology and powerful software. It is much better than traditional telephone recording.

Automatic receiving and dispatching of SMS and its management. Through this, operators can send the latest information or promotion information of the company to various customers by clicking a mouse. In addition, they can store customers' messages for future management.

Receiving and dispatching of emails. As an important communication method, email can facilitate a lot of customers, showing the care to customers. The usage is quite similar to that of SMS.

Operators' response. Based on customers' requirements, the calls on IVR road can be transferred to operators, who will communicate individually with customers, receive their orders, answer their questions, input their information or tell query results to customers through automatic voice. Besides, the system can display the caller's ID and automatically pop customer data, which can improve operators' efficiency and make customers more satisfied.

E-payment system

Electronic payment refers to that the participants of e-commerce, including consumers, manufacturers and financing institutes, complete the payment or financial transaction through the Internet by secure e-payment methods. It is based on the advanced technology to transfer information digitally, making use of the Internet and other advanced communication means, thus it has the advantages of convenience, fastness and high efficiency.

An e-commerce payment system is a comprehensive system, integrating the following parts together: consumers, businesses, security authentication center, payment gateway, customers' bank, businesses' bank and special financial network.

The common e-payment instruments include Internet bank, credit cards, third-party payment, digital cash/e-cash, e-check, e-wallet, mobile payment, etc.

7.4 BUSINESS PROCESS RE-ENGINEERING OF E-COMMERCE BUSINESS

The successful e-SCM scheme means the optimization and improvement of all supply activities, which cannot be realized without the redesign and re-engineering of the business process. Therefore, it is necessary to discuss the business process re-engineering here.

7.4.1 General Introduction to BPR

Also known as business process redesign, business transformation, or business process change management, business process re-engineering (BPR) means the radical rethinking and ground-up redesign of a company's business processes, with the purpose of dramatically improving cost, quality, service and efficiency, to make the organization adapt to the modern management.

Focusing on the analysis and restructuring of workflows and business processes within an organization, BPR emphasizes the concepts of process and re-engineering with the integration of technology and process. It starts from the identification of organization's core business process, organizes the business around the optimized core process, requires streamlining or merging then on-value adding process and eliminating the waste caused by repeated and unnecessary steps. It also stresses the customer-centered service, demanding all the work should meet customers' needs and wants. Therefore, BPR can make the organization more adaptable to the market, dramatically decrease the production cost, greatly improve products and service quality.

7.4.2 The Application of BPR

The "restructure" in BPR means the redesign and rearranging the whole process of production, service and operation, making them optimal. In practice, it can be completed through following procedures:

Analyzing existing problems

To ensure the success of BPR, the organization should conduct a thorough analysis of the function and efficiency of the original process and identify existing problems.

With the development of market demands and technology, the existing business process may be failed to adapt to the new situation, thus it is necessary to analyze the current problems from following aspects:

Functional barriers. The development of technology can generate inseparable team work and thus affect personal efficiency, which may increase management costs through the fragmentation of the original operating process or result in separation of power and responsibility of the organization.

In all, it will lead to unreasonable organizational design, forming the bottleneck of enterprise development.

Importance. Different operating process has different effects on enterprises. With the development of the market and the changes of customers' needs towards products and services, the key links in the operation process and the importance of each link are also changing.

Feasibility. Based on the changing of market and technology, the organization should be clear about the order of importance and emergency and find out the breakthrough point of process re-engineering. To make it more targeted, the management should conduct thorough fieldwork and specific observation to analyze the function, constraints and key issues of the existing business process.

Designing and evaluating of new process

In order to design a more scientific and reasonable operation process, the management must work together, discuss collectively and encourage innovation. When designing new process, following factors can be included:

- Merging several current business or work combinations into one;
- Each step of the workflow being performed in its natural order;
- Enabling employees to participate in decision-making;
- Setting up several kinds of methods for the same workflow;
- Making work go beyond the boundaries of the organization and putting it in the most appropriate place;
- Minimizing the management work, such as inspection, control and adjustment;
- Setting case manager.

The one hard-and-fast rule about the designing of new process is that there is no universal rule. The practical forms vary by the company's specific situation.

Making restructuring plan

The application of business process should be supported by corresponding organizational structure, human resources allocation, business norms, communication channels and even corporate culture. Therefore, to achieve the desired purpose, the organization should take the process improvement as the core to form a systematic re-engineering plan.

Implementing and continuously improving the plan

The implementation of re-engineering program will inevitably influence the original interests' pattern. Therefore, careful organization is necessary. In order to ensure the smooth development of re-engineering plan, the management should overcome resistances with firm attitude, and also actively promote the plan to reach a consensus.

In addition, the implementation of new plan does not mean the ending of re-engineering. In the era with rapid development, enterprises are constantly facing new challenges, which requires continuous improvement of re-engineering programs to adapt to the needs of the new situation.

7.5 CHALLENGES OF E-SUPPLY CHAINS

The efficient integration of logistics and information flow is the primary goal of supply chain management(SCM); however, there are still many misunderstandings about SCM. One significant misunderstanding is that some organizations just focus on logistics in a supply chain, which can provide customers with high quality products and minimize inventory. They fail to pay enough attention to information flow, which can provide timely information. In fact, while the electronic supply chain fundamentally changes the business processing model, SCM model must also make corresponding changes on the basis of the principle of serving the market.

The biggest challenge for SCM is how to reasonably determine the priority and locate the resources needed to achieve the best target benefits. In this respect, the risks and challenges faced by manufacturers also include that they cannot follow the changes in the market, losing customers and market share, thereby affecting profits and revenues. Although Internet technology can effectively improve efficiency and reduce costs, solely relying on the addition of software is not the right solution to SCM. In e-SCM, software system is necessary, but the efficient integration of material flow and information flow is the essence of SCM.

Due to the fact that the market and relevant technology change rapidly, and E-SCM system is just a relatively new thing, many enterprises still have no clear idea on how to keep the system's competitiveness, as well as how to apply and improve the system. For this point, considering following questions carefully can help them have a better understanding about E-SCM system to improve the efficiency and enterprises' competitiveness.

- Whether the enterprise has set appropriate objectives for SCM? Whether these objectives are in the leading position in the industry, or have clarified the primary task of SCM? the advantages and disadvantages of the existing system? How to effectively make use of the existing system to strengthen the communication between customers and suppliers?
- Whether the existing SCM system facilitates the decision-making of senior management? Whether E-SCM system is building on the basis of real-time planning, execution and control techniques? Whether it is supported by the information technology system, aiming at meeting the needs of various links of the SCM system?
- Has enterprise's E-SCM system effectively taken advantage of e-commerce technology to sell products and make B2B transactions? What are the disadvantages of existing E-SCM system? Can the system offer efficient information flow service for inventory management, material flow and business decision? What barriers does the enterprise possess to the integration of material flow and information flow in SCM?
- Have the responsibilities of each link in the supply chain been clearly defined? Have the relevant personnel been specially trained? Have other business partners made corresponding SCM strategies? Can all the links in the supply chain, including external suppliers of the

enterprise, adapt to requirements of the fast and efficient logistics and decision making?

- Whether the system can shorten product life cycle and decrease costs through the constant improvement of the efficiency of logistics and information flow? Can it improve the efficiency of product distribution and logistics, reduce operation costs and improve customer service quality?

In all, the application of electronic supply chain should start from the actual situation of the enterprise, from the clear understanding of what it can do for the solution of existing problems in the enterprise.

SUMMARY

This chapter mainly discusses issues related to e-supply chains. The series of links and shared processes existing between suppliers and customers are called supply chains, while a supply chain that is managed electronically is e-supply chain. E-supply chains can lower the transaction cost, reduce the inventory, reduce procurement cost, shorten cycle time, and increase revenues and profits. E-supply chain management is based on just in time, quick response, efficient consumer response and enterprise resource planning. The design of e-supply chain mainly constitutes electronic ordering system, e-procurement system, advanced planning and scheduling system, electronic logistic system, inventory management system, customer service system and e-payment system. The success of e-supply chain management cannot be realized without the redesign and re-engineering of the business process. Thus BPR is a necessity in e-supply chain management.

Words and Expressions

①**allocate**: to give something to someone as their share of a total amount, to use in a particular way 分配;划拨

②**collaborative**: involving two or more people working together for a special purpose 合作的,协作的

③**coordination**: the organization of people or things so that they work together well 协作

④**feasibility**: the possibility that can be made, done, or achieved, or is reasonable 可行性

⑤**lead time**: the time between the design of a product and its production, or between ordering a product and receiving it 提前期(新产品之前所需的设计时间)

⑥**life cycle**: the series of changes that a living thing goes through from the beginning of itslife until death 生命周期

⑦**upstream**: (moving) on a river or stream towards its origin 向上游(的)

⑧**value-added**: value-added products or services have an increased value because work has been done on them, they have been combined with other products etc 增值的

⑨**warehouse**: a large building for storing things before they are sold, used, or sent out to shops 仓库

⑩**workflow**: the way that a particular type of work is organized, or the order of the stages in a particular work process 工作流程

Exercises

Ⅰ. **Key Terms**(Explain the following terms.)

①e-supply chain

②ERP

③BPR

Ⅱ. **Multiple Choice Exercises** (Choose the correct answer to the following questions from A, B, C and D. There is only one correct answer.)

①Which of the following is not a stage within a typical supply chain?

A. Customers and Retailers.

B. Wholesalers/Distributors.

C. Manufacturers.

D. All of the above are stages within a typical supply chain.

②Which of the following decision phases are required by successful supply chain management?

A. Supply chain strategy/design. B. Supply chain planning.

C. Supply chain operation. D. All of the above.

③A company's supply chain strategy ________.

A. defines the set of customer needs that it seeks to satisfy through its products and services

B. specifies the portfolio of new products that it will try to develop

C. specifies how the market will be segmented and how the product will be positioned, priced, and promoted

D. determines the nature of procurement and transportation of materials as well as manufacture and distribution of the product

④A supply chain strategy includes ________.

A. supplier strategy B. operations strategy

C. logistics strategy D. all of the above

⑤The process by which a firm decides how much to charge customers for its goods and services is ________.

A. supply chain coordination B. forecasting

C. revenue management D. pricing

⑥Which of the following is not a measure of customer service that is influenced by the structure of the distribution network?

A. Returnability. B. Customer experience.

C. Customer maturity. D. Product availability.

⑦Activities involved in the Customer Relationship Management (CRM) macro process include all of the following except ________.

A. demand planning
B. marketing and sales
C. order management
D. call center management

⑧As the number of facilities in a supply chain network increases, total logistics costs will ________.

A. decrease
B. decrease at first and then increase
C. increase
D. increase at first and then decrease

Ⅲ. Review Questions

①What principles should supply chain management obey?

②What should be included in the design of e-supply chains?

③What are the challenges in the application of e-SCM?

Ⅳ. Online Practice

①The following are some notable global companies with high-efficient supply chains: Dell Inc., P&G, IBM, Walmart Stores, Inc., Toyota Motor Corporation, Johnson & Johnson. Please visit one of their websites, and then learn its design of supply chain and analyze its reason for success.

②Choose the supply chain models of two successful companies in the world and compare their differences.

③Find a product or business which is familiar to you in the line of home appliance, clothing or food, learning the components, process and inventory level of its supply chain. Suppose it is going to implement e-supply chain management, please design an e-SCM plan for it.

Ⅴ. Case Study

When Groupthink Is Good

The Internet and intranet phenomenon that has revolutionized the way people communicate, shop, and read the news is also reshaping the way companies manage the supply chain process. Savvy, progressive companies are tying together their suppliers, distributors, and customers via the Internet or intranets so that all the players can share information and build supple and production plans collaboratively.

Heineken USA has reaped great benefits from collaborative planning. As competition intensified from regional and local microbreweries in the late 1980s and the early 1990s, the then-family-owned Heineken USA was slow to react. As a result, Heineken USA's market share eroded and Heineken NV, the parent company in the Netherlands, decided to take over its American distribution and marketing operations. Heineken USA in its current form began operation in 1995 and set about overhauling its demand and production forecasting process.

Heineken's old forecast and ordering mechanisms involved face-to-face meetings with distributors and several steps of faxing orders among Heineken USA district offices, its headquarters, and the world headquarters in Amsterdam. Consequently, it took an average of 10 to 12 weeks for distributors to receive shipments.

To resolve the problem, Heineken USA implemented a private network connecting the company to its suppliers, distributors, and customers through Internet technology. Distributors log onto customized Heineken USA web pages using a standard Internet browser and connection. By simply entering their ID and password, they can view their sales forecast and modify and submit their orders.

Heineken USA reassessed the company's entire strategy of getting product from the factory to the distributors. The company assembled a cross-functional team including representatives from the marketing, sales, finance, ordering, and shipping departments of the company. For collaborative planning to work and enhance the efficiency of the supply chain, each department had to embrace the process and make it work in its sector. The new collaborative planning program has reduced order cycle times from 3 months to 4 weeks and simplified planning for Heineken USA's distributor customers. The results are reduced inventory levels and fresher product to consumers.

Questions for Discussion

①What were the problems of Heineken's old forecast and ordering mechanisms?

②How did Heineken solve the problem?

Chapter 8 E-commerce Security

本章导读

随着我国综合实力的不断增强，国际地位的不断提高，我国各项事业都在与国际接轨。电子商务应运而生，近些年在我国迅速发展，网上购物已经成为时下较为流行的购物方式，深受广大消费者的欢迎。然而，随着我国网络技术的进一步发展和广泛应用，电子商务的安全问题逐渐凸显出来，逐渐成为困扰我国电子商务工作人员的重要难题，如何应对电子商务安全问题值得我们进行深入思考。根据调查可知，我国计算机受到木马攻击、病毒侵染的数量和频率正在逐年增加，新病毒的种类层出不穷，防不胜防，这些都为我们的电子商务安全问题敲响了警钟，解决电子商务的安全问题迫在眉睫。

Business Terms

①**encryption**: It is a very effective and practical way to safeguard the data being transmitted over the network. The sender of the information encrypts the data using a secret code and specified receiver only can decrypt the data using the same or different secret code.

②**digital signature**: An e-signature authenticated through encryption and password

③**security certificate**: a unique digital ID used to verify identity of an individual website or user

④**firewall**: a technological barrier designed to prevent unauthorized or unwanted communications between computer networks or hosts

⑤**application-level gateway**: It consists of a security component that augments a firewall or NAT employed in a computer network. It allows customized NAT traversal filters to be plugged into the gateway to support address and port translation for certain application layer "control/data" protocols such as FTP, Bit Torrent, SIP, RTSP, file transfer in IM applications, etc.

⑥**HTTP**: an application protocol for distributed, collaborative, hypermedia information systems

⑦**public key infrastructure (PKI)**: a set of roles, policies, and procedures needed to create, manage, distribute, use, store, and revoke digital certificates and manage public-key encryption

⑧**intrusion detection system (IDS)**: a device or software application that monitors a network or systems for malicious activity or policy violations

Introductory Case

Report: Cyber Security Awareness and Implementation

Cyberattacks are becoming more and more frequent, and continue to be a source of headaches for businesses. The sheer number of cyberattacks increased by 48% from 2013 to 2014, and the AV-Test Institute currently registers over 390,000 new pieces of malware every day. Protecting company data is becoming an increasingly essential and significant cyber security issue for organizations.

F-Secure conducted an online study in 2015 within France, Germany, the UK, Poland, and the Nordics. The over 1700 respondents were all IT decision makers in various roles and in different sized companies. The key of the report focuses on how companies are adjusting to a threat landscape populated by increasingly sophisticated threats.

Current security priorities. For most companies, getting the basic rights is still the first priority. Ensuring smooth IT operations and performance without disruptions, as well as anti-virus protection and protecting against malware infection, are still the top priorities. But, to achieve this in today's world, companies need to focus on different aspects of IT security.

In the study, IT decision makers also clearly confirm that protecting the confidentiality of their company data (personnel data, customer data, intellectual property and financial data) is a security priority for their company.

Most respondents agree that cyber threats are something that every company needs to be wary of.

However, this knowledge does not translate very widely into concrete actions—the more advanced protection methods and tools are still not widely used, even amongst bigger companies.

Challenge with implementation. The study found that while many companies appreciate the security challenges facing them, many of them are unaware of how to meet these challenges using their current approach to security. Furthermore, the study found that companies are mainly concerned with data protection rather than a more holistic approach to cyber security. While this is unsurprising given the current discussions on the new data protection regulations being ushered in within Europe, it does indicate that the emphasis on data protection has yet to translate into businesses adopting comprehensive cyber security solutions designed to prevent data breaches.

Awareness of security and cyber security is strong in European companies. In most cases, awareness is also reflected in attitudes, and even the language used. However, awareness and attitudes is not always apparent in the behavior of the respondents.

Questions for Discussion

①What is a cyberattack? Please give a few examples.

②How can we prevent or control a cyberattack?

③If you suffer from cyberattacks, what will you do?

8.1 OVERVIEW OF COMMERCIAL ACTIVITIES AND PROCESSES IN ONLINE BUSINESS

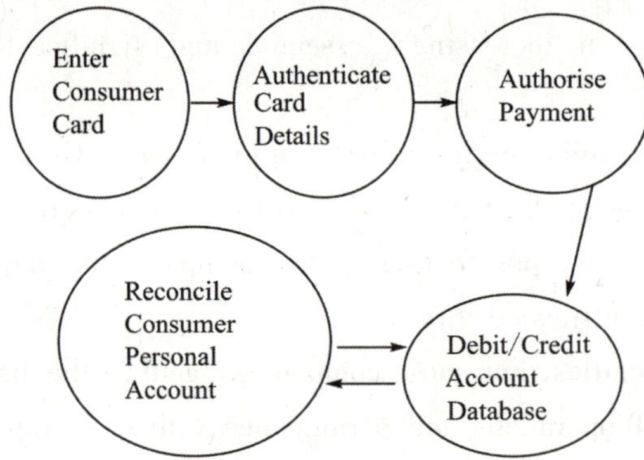

Internet Based Activities

In this activity, the consumer enters their debit or credit card details on the web. The details entered are verified for authenticity. The system authorizes payment made by the card holder. The card holder's personal bank account or credit card account is debited. There is a reconciliation of consumer's accounts regardless of the payment method. The reconciliation is part of a synchronization process between a holding account and the consumer's actual account. An electronic data processing specialist will classify this account as a transaction file.

8.2 SECURITY THREATS OF E-COMMERCE

8.2.1 Security Threat of E-commerce Network System

Communication through the network has great blindness and uncertainty, and e-commerce also brings risk to the user: Users need to connect the host or intranet to the Internet; Data and information need to be sent/received via the Internet; Transfering money to the user's bank account is through the network.

All these activities will prompt all parties of electronic transactions to consider security issues.

Interception and stealing of information

In the process of electronic commerce, an attacker can steal useful information through the Internet, such as consumers' bank account passwords, and business secrets.

Tampering of information

In the electronic commerce transaction, an attacker can tamper or delete the information for the sake of hislher own benefit.

Counterfeiting of information

An attacker may fake legal users or businesses or build fake websites or send false information to deceive consumers, businesses and banks.

Repudiation of information

Some pelple may deny the presence of sending information, such as the purchase orders submitted due to price changes.

Malicious attack

After invading the website by illegal means, the attacker modifies or deletes the information in the website, grasps the confidential information on the Internet, and even attacks the internal network, causing serious consequences.

8.2.2 Main Reasons for Security Threats

Due to the lack of strict management systems for hardware, software, databases, passwords and user rights, there may be security accidents.

Security problems in computer software system

No matter what operating system you use, there are some security issues under default installation. Only when the security of the operating system is strictly configured can a certain degree of security be achieved. Network software vulnerabilities and "back door" are the first targets of cyber attacks.

Improper use of network security products

Although many websites have adopted some network security products, they have not played a proper role because of the problem of the product itself or the use of the product.

Even though the business initially gives the user right installation configuration, once the system changes, the user still need to adjust the configuration of the relevant security film, or it is prone to security problems.

The lack of strict network security management system

For network security, the most important thing is to attach great importance to the security of the network or intranet. It needs to be protected with a complete security system. The establishment and implementation of strict computer network security management system is the basis to ensure network security.

8.3 SECURITY STANDARDS AND PROTOCOLS

A standard is a document established by consensus and approved by a recognized body which provides, for common and repeated use, rules, guidelines or characteristics for activities or their results, aimed at the achievement of optimum degree of order in a given context.

It is also a document that ensures uniformity, consistency, openness and global participation in the advancement of technology through set rules and guidelines. While standards ensure uniformity, openness and global participation, protocols serve as rules that govern the implementation of standards.

The subject of online payment technology is paramount and central to electronic commerce and business applications. The role of credit cards, such as its applications in mail and telephone ordering, face to face exchange and the role of the Internet in online transactions are pivotal to the current climate of freedom economy. Security standards and protocols including SSL, SET and IPSEC contribute to the drivers of cyber commerce. These technologies are central to the security and success of credit card payments. The other forms of e-payment systems central to cyber commerce and online businesses include digital cash and cheque, debit cards, smart cards, store and loyalty cards, prepaid, telephone and micro payments systems.

Although there have been much emphasis on online payment systems and security methods, vulnerability assessment is not adequately performed on these systems. Security is important to clients who use payment technologies and systems, although most users and consumers of these online systems are quite naive about the value of information and associated asset being protected. It is also true that they are not fully aware of their state of vulnerability. More recently, mobile payments and wireless systems are also beginning to play a key role in online businesses.

It is also becoming a subject of critical importance to on-going technological agenda within academia and industry. Software agents are also growing in popularity within the online auction market, for example, eBay uses agent applications for searching bargains on the Internet for customers. Software agents, in lay terms, perform useful services on behalf of customers who surf the Internet or search online auction market generic services. Examples of such services are naming and directory services. For instance, Google search engine applies efficient and intelligent techniques in data search and retrieval which is tailored to respond to customer and client needs.

In general security protocols deployed as part of the TCP/IP protocol suite, include IPsec, SSL and SET. IPsec is implemented at the network layer. Although contents are usually protected, there are issues with traceability of source and destination data. This could be a form of vulnerability. IPsec can also encrypt a standard message and subsequently place this message in a disguised header. This technique is known as tunnel mode. This permits users to set up private groups over networks, usually in the form of VPNs (Virtual Private Networks). There are also difficulties in authenticating individual users, since IP addresses could be shared on a network. Even though Secure Socket Layer(SSL) has its strengths, recent developments reveal key vulnerabilities. This is because it provides only transport level security. SSL lacks effective mutual authentication which is critical to security of electronic commerce transactions.

Most security vulnerabilities originate from the network layer. This might serve as a loop hole if there is no robust security at the network layer. Complimenting this is application layer security. Secure electronic transactions(SET) is a form of application layer security standard that relies more on digital certificates. Certificates sometimes have trust issues with them. Robustness is a key strength of SET, it however has performance related problems.

8.4 MANAGING THE IMPLEMENTATION OF STANDARDS

Domain Areas of ISO 17799—2005

No.	Domain Name	Sub Domain
1	Security policy	N/A
2	Organizational information security	• Information security infrastructure • Security of third party access • Outsourcing
3	Asset management	• Accountability of assets • Information classification
4	Personnel security & Human resources security	• Security in job definition and resource management • User training • Responding to security incidents/malfunctions
5	Physical and environment security	• Secure areas • Equipment security • General control

(Continued)

No.	Domain Name	Sub Domain
6	Communications and operations management	• Operational procedures and responsibilities • System planning and acceptance • Protection against malicious programs • House keeping • Network management • Media handling and security • Exchange of information and software
7	Access control	• Business requirement for access control • User access management • User responsibilities • Network access control • Operating system access control • Application access control • Monitoring system access and use • Mobile computing and tele-working
8	Information system development, acquisition and maintenance	• Security requirement of systems • Security in application systems • Cryptography controls • Security of system files • Security development and support processes
9	Information security incident management	N/A
10	Business continuity management	N/A
11	Compliance	• Compliance with legal requirements • Review of security policy and compliance

The above table is an outline of 11 domain areas that provide the framework for best code of practice for information security management. It is highly recommended that any information security system implemented should be bench marked against this standard. There are other forms of standards that ensure other aspects of system requirements are addressed at the appropriate level. These standards include:

- COBIT—Effective for ICT governance and control framework. While COBIT3 focuses on how to implement controls, COBIT4 focuses on what to do of control. There is emphasis on good practice, which revolves on standards.
- ISO 21188—A public key infrastructure (PKI) standard that ensures security of financial transactions on the Internet. It is designed to protect online transactions from identity theft, intrusion attacks and cyber crime. It provides a set of guidelines designed to assist security and audit managers, business directors in the financial sector.
- ITIL—This is the Information Technology Infrastructure Library (ITIL) developed by the UK

office of Government Commerce. It is a source of reference for IT service management. It is effective for ICT auditing and can be mapped unto other best practice standards such as COBIT, ISO 17799 and BS 1500.

- ISO/IEC TR-13335—Guidelines for the management of ICT security (technical guidelines).
- NIST 800-14—Accepted principles and practices for securing ICT systems.
- COSO—Applied for internal control that is mapped unto COBIT.
- CMMI—Capability Maturity Model Integration (CMMI), best practice for improving processes.
- FIPS—USA federal information processing standards, minimum security requirement for federal information systems.

Adopting best practice standards have several benefits in online businesses, such as:

- Increase in confidence and trust among customers.
- Effective security implementation.
- Sustenance of business operations and processes.
- Long term cost reduction in training and modalities for exceptional control.
- Benchmark for companies' performance.
- Improvement in auditing of information systems by meeting basic industry requirements.

8.5 SECURITY SYSTEMS AND TECHNOLOGIES

8.5.1 Secure Electronic Transactions (SET)

SET is a system for ensuring security of financial transactions on the Internet. It is also a standard designed to support the security of credit and electronic card transactions on public networks such as the Internet. Transactions are verified using digital certificates. SET uses SSL, Microsoft Secure Transaction Technology (MSTT), and Secure Hypertext Transfer Protocol (SHTTP). It also applies some aspects of Public Key Infrastructure (PKI) discussed in subsequent sections.

8.5.2 Virtual Private Network (VPN)

VPN is a tunnel created through a public network (Internet) that carries encrypted data via the network. B2B communications usually uses this form of network to ensure that integrity and confidentiality of data sent across the businesses involved in the transaction and commercial activity is protected. Businesses use VPN due to its cost effectiveness. Prior to VPN two or more organizations who wanted to do business had to setup a wide area network (WAN) as a means of ensuring security of data sent to the respective locations of these organization. The common attacks that VPN attempts to prevent include spoofing, session hijacking of a network device such as the firewall. Some other attacks are eavesdropping or sniffing, man-in-the-middle attack and brute force attack. The main requirements of a VPN implementation is a VPN client and server and a tunnel that connects the client and server in front of a firewall.

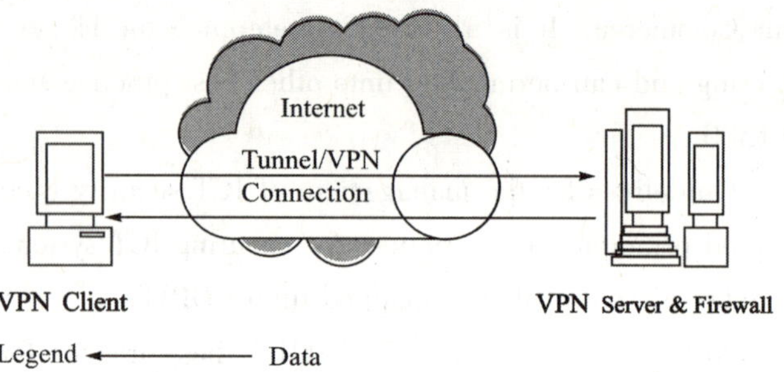

VPN Server in Front of Firewall

The encryption of the tunnel could be implemented by using protocols such as IPSEC, PPP and SSL.

8.5.3 IP Security (IPSec)

IP security commonly known as IPSec is a protocol designed to primarily provide security at the network layer of the TCP/IP protocol suite. It is used to enable private communication and data transfer on public networks such as the Internet with the sole aim of making the communication secure. It is an open standard that could be deployed in conjunction with other open standards. It is usually used to create a virtual private network (VPN). VPN implementation improves authentication and the prevention of denial of service (DOS) and replay attacks. This is because the connection is secured and insulated from the public domain. IPsec consist of the following elements:

- A set of two security protocols, known as Authentication Header (AH) and Encapsulating Security Payload (ESP).
- The Internet Key Exchange (IKE) protocol. IPsec uses IKE to negotiate Tunnel/VPN IPsec connection configuration. It provides end point authentication, sets up security parameters, manages key distribution and communication channels.
- IP Payload compression protocol for packet compression prior to encryption.

8.5.4 Secure Socket Layer (SSL)

SSL is a protocol applied to secure the transport layer of the TCP/IP protocol. Its application supports inter and intra-website communication. SSL uses asymmetric cryptography to encrypt data transferred across a network. One key is used to encrypt while another is used to decrypt. These keys are known as private and public keys. The public key encrypts while the private key decrypts. Keys are deployed in the form of digital certificates for purposes of key exchange and authentication. Authentication is at client and server levels. Although SSL intends to provide confidentiality and integrity services using Data Encryption Standard (DES) algorithm, it has its own embedded weaknesses.

8.6 ENCRYPTION AND ONLINE SECURITY

It is vital to note that the art and science of cryptography provide support to data confidentiality, integrity and availability. There is significance placed on the common algorithms applied in business and commerce world that employ cryptography based systems. This intricacy is relevant for understanding the issues associated in ensuring that data which traverse across networks that support electronic commerce and business are secured. Most common algorithms include DES, 3DES, AES, RSA and Diffie Hellman public key distribution scheme. These form the caucus of technologies required for ensuring privacy and protection of data.

8.6.1 DES, 3DES and AES

DES is an acronym for Data Encryption Standard. It is a crypto algorithm and standard that uses symmetric or same encryption and distribution keys for converting plaintext to cipher-text. The key length of DES is 56 bit. In the mid 90's, DES became weak and unreliable as a crypto algorithm. It was broken using a computer with reasonable computational strength. The technique for breaking the key is known as brute force or in-depth key search.

3DES also known as triple DES. It is a derivative of DES. It uses double encryption and single decryption. It has embedded weakness which was inherited from DES. New developments in encryption standard have led to AES (Advanced Encryption Standard). Although there are a number of algorithms considered to be AES, Rijndael algorithm is a federal information processing standard for AES. Rijndael has key length ranging from 128, 192 and 256 bits. One of the main reasons why Rijndael has become an AES defacto standard is its capability to handle nonlinearity among bits and efficiency of computer memory use.

8.6.2 Encryption and Authentication

Authentication is crucial and essential in online businesses. Issues related to authentication of e-commerce activities could enlighten both technical and non-technical people respectively regardless of their interest in the subject matter. This could serve as a catalyst in transforming their understanding and appreciation of the issues involved. This is based on the notion that end users seem to lack interest in technical intricacies, although this could vary from one case to another.

Server security is equally important in online business security modeling, a view shared by researchers in this field. Confidentiality, Integrity, Availability, Non-repudiation, Authentication, Audit and third party systems are required to facilitate electronic commerce transactions.

Trust, access control and corporate security ensure some level of integrity, although that was not the original purpose of the science and art. The different forms of crypt-analysis provide useful insights to the meaning of cipher text and protected data and the problems caused when confidentiality of data becomes compromised. Attacks such as plain text attacks, chosen plain text attack, known plaintext attack, man-in-the-middle attack, correlation against hardware and faults in crypto-systems are issues that need to be addressed. Quantum computing is a research area related to polynomials and discrete logarithms that could contribute solutions to online business problems. It is, however, not in a matured stage. DNA computing is also being developed to address crypto systems implemented globally on online business systems.

8.6.3 Authentication Methods and Online Business

This section classifies authentication into three categories, namely human to human, human to system and system to system. The reason for these three categories is based on the premise that authentication is a multidirectional or multidimensional activity.

Human to human authentications

Human in this context refers to person, group of people and organizations. It discusses mutual authentication and digital certificates as aspects of human to human authentication.

Human to system authentication (**HSA**)

A system here refers to the hardware, software and process components of a computer and its processing environment. It discusses the use of user identification and names, passwords, profiling and biometrics as methods of authentication.

System to system authentication (**SSA**)

◇ **Challenge handshake authentication protocol** (CHAP)

CHAP is a Point to Point Protocol (PPP). The objective of CHAP is to ensure that end to end systems that communicate with each other are legitimate. The main object of CHAP is to ensure that a user's computer has authorization to access resources from another computer providing a service.

CHAP can be described as a system that authenticates a user's computer using a technique known as "challenge response". CHAP generates a key transmitted to the user for encrypting the user's password. Passwords stored in the server table do not have to be encrypted. The main end systems involved in this challenge are CHAP server and a user's computer. Responses to the server's challenge are without human involvement. It uses a technique known as session management. This means that a request made by a user's computer to gain access to resources of the other end system has to be authenticated when the request is being made. This duration is what is known as a session.

◇ **Kerberos authentication process**

Kerberos uses a ticket granting system for authenticating processes. The system consists of an authentication server, main server and user's computer. A user's request is assigned a ticket. A user also known as a client sends a message containing a password and user ID to an authentication server. The authentication server verifies both the password and user's access rights correctness on the main server. If the verification process is successful, the main server releases a ticket to the authentication server. This ticket is encrypted. It consists of user's identification, network address of user's computer and main server's identification. The authentication server sends a ticket back to user's computer. The user's computer requests access to the main server using the ticket. The main server decrypts ticket and verifies whether user's identification matches with the plaintext in the message. If it does, access is granted.

◇ **Authentication and global online business**

Successful authentication of a transaction from platforms and networks with poor standards cannot be guaranteed. The mindsets of certification bodies and authorities show that the underlying design concept for designing a certificate is usually based on how systems are perceived in advanced economies. Regardless of this, most businesses and standard organizations expect businesses with poor standards to trust the certificates issued to them. This usually occurs due to the trading policies adopted by leading IT companies in advanced economies. Online business will be more effective and secured if advanced economies strongly engage IT companies in developing economies during development of certificates meant for the global market. The lack of joint system of development explains why EU and other advanced economies legislative framework prohibit persons and businesses from engaging poor nations in electronic business.

◇ **Public key infrastructure (PKI)**

A public key infrastructure (PKI) combines software, encryption technologies and services that enable corporations and enterprises to protect communication infrastructure, business forecasting and the Internet. PKI uses a holistic approach by integrating digital certificates, public key cryptograph, certification, enterprise wide area network architecture. This is cherished from a theoretical point of view. There are however problems associated with certification authorities and bodies, which sometimes cause the conceptual foundations of PKI to shake. There are issues related to trust, law and inconsistencies with existing regulatory frameworks. There is the need for a comprehensive assessment of the role of certification, design and issuing methods among enterprises.

◇ **Biometric system**

A biometric system is a system that uses measurements of physical attributes to authenticate consumers and customers. The principle underlying biometric suggests a form of authentication based on who you are rather than something you know. The attributes are usually captured from fingerprints, facial geometry, iris pattern, retina, hand and finger geometry, vein structure, the structure of the ear, voice, DNA, odour, etc. The attributes are captured by computer program. The program creates a template for storage in a database. The database could be integrated with an immigration control system, smart card for access control to systems and buildings. In order to authenticate a person, a life scan of the information describing the physical attributes captured have to be matched to the attributes stored in the computer database. The system derives a score which matches the criterion specified for identification and authentication. An audit trail is occasionally generated as an exceptional control measure to check the reliability of the system. Another method of implementing a biometric system is to generate biometric key. This implementation involves a signal component of a physical measurement separated from the noise that comes along the capturing of such data; process the signal resulting in an exact number (key). This should be based on factors such as ambiguity resolution, error correction and noise reduction. Although this method improves security and privacy as a result of the crypto-transformation it is not widely adopted and used in the commercial environment.

◇ **Smart card applications**

A smart card uses an electronic chip to store details about a person, a set of processes or set of authorisation and authentication keys. The information could be stored in infrared format.

The makeup and architectural constitution of smart cards and its genesis was in 1974. Architecture and the operating systems supporting smart card technology are not as robust of the operating systems supporting desktops. There is a connection between TCP/IP reference model and smart card readers. Examples of some smart cards are the Java and Octopus smart cards. The introduction and application of Octopus smart card in the transport system in Hong Kong many years ago seem to have had some bearing on the Oyster transport card introduced a few years for Londoners. These cards serve as useful sources of information for homeland security, control and monitoring of road and rail transport systems.

◇ **Firewall**

A firewall is a software or hardware that filters packets that travels across a network. A packet is the name given to information sent across computer networks. Firewalls therefore allow and disallow (non-) authorized packets across networks. Firewalls are generally classified as restrictive based or connective oriented (permissive or service oriented). In general firewalls are meant to implement some aspects of an organization's information security policy.

SUMMARY

This chapter mainly discusses e-commerce security. There is an overview of standards and protocols that govern security technologies. Protocols, Standards and technologies such as SET, SSL and IPSEC are evaluated. The chapter studies the role of VPN in B2B transactions. There is also an overview of crypto-systems and explanation of their role in security. New trends in authentication are introduced, while common models such as PPP, CHAP and Kerberos are also reexamined. There is a discussion on problems associated with authentication, the role of browsers in mention of biometric systems and Public Key Infrastructure (PKI). Descriptions of firewalls centre on types of firewalls and configuration setups.

Words and Expressions

①**back door**: a secret or underhand means of access 后门,秘密途径

②**blindness**: the state of being blind or lacking sight 盲目;无知;轻率

③**CA**: Certificate Authority, the authority responsible for issuing and managing digital certificates and is responsible for the legality test of public key in the public key system as the trusted third party in the e-commerce transaction. 电子商务认证授权机构

④**configuration**: the particular arrangement or pattern of a group of related things 配置;布局,构造

⑤**consensus**: agreement in the judgment or opinion reached by a group as a whole 一致;舆论;一致同意,合意

⑥**counterfeit**: to make a copy of with the intent to deceive 仿制,造假;假装,伪装

⑦**cyberattack**: an illegal attempt to harm someone's computer system or the information on it, using the Internet 网络攻击

⑧**implementation**: the act of putting a plan into action or of starting to use something 贯彻;成就;安装启用

⑨**improper**: not appropriate for a purpose or occasion 不合适的,非正常的;不正确的;不正派的,不合礼仪的;不道德的

⑩**inbound**: travelling towards a particular point 到达的;入境的;归航的;回程的

⑪**infinite**: the unlimited expanse in which everything is located 无限的,无穷的;无数的;极大的

⑫**interception**: the act of catching a ball intended for someone on the opposing team 中途夺取,拦截,侦听;阻留;定方位;断球

⑬**optimum**: most favorable conditions or greatest degree or amount possible under given circumstances 最适宜的

⑭**paramount**: having superior power and influence 最高的,至上的;最重要的,主要的;卓越的;有最高权力的

⑮**reconciliation**: a situation in which two people or groups of people become friendly again after they have argued 和解;调停

⑯**synchronization**: to (cause to) happen at the same time 同步;同一时刻;使时间互相一致;同时性

⑰**tamper**: to play around with or alter or falsify, usually secretively or dishonestly 篡改;(用不正当手段)影响,干预;瞎摆弄;贿赂

⑱**via**: going through or stopping at a place on the way to another place 经过;通过,凭借;取道

⑲**VPN**: Virtual Private Network extends a private network across a public network, and enables users to send and receive data across shared or public networks as if their computing devices were directly connected to the private network. 虚拟专用网络

⑳**vulnerability**: susceptibility to injury or attack 脆弱性;弱点,攻击;易伤性;致命性

Exercises

Ⅰ. **Key Terms**(Explain the following terms.)

①SSL

②software agent

③e-payment system

④PKI

⑤software and hardware

Ⅱ. **Multiple Choice Exercises** (Choose the correct answer to the following questions from A, B, C and D. There is only one correct answer.)

1. EC security technology includes ________.

A. encryption technology　　B. authentication technology

C. firewall technology　　D. A, B and C

2. Tasks that ensure the realization of secure e-commerce are not included ________.

A. data integrity　　B. confidentiality of information

C. correctness of operation　　D. authenticity of identity authentication

3. The phenomenon ________ may be caused by viral infection.

A. messy code　　B. hard disk damage

C. printer jam　　D. case overheating

4. Nowadays, the most critical problem that influences the development of electronic payment is ________.

A. technical problem　　B. cost problem

C. security problem　　D. conceptual problem

5. Which of the following methods can be used to provide protection for the publication of electronic documents online?

A. Digital signature.　　B. Digital certificate.

C. Message digest.　　D. Digital time stamp.

6. Which company did the SSL protocol come out with?

A. Netscape.　　B. IBM.

C. Microsoft.　　D. VISA.

7. The most famous public key encryption algorithm is ________.

A. DES　　B. Triple DES

C. SET　　D. RSA

8. Which of the following is not a firewall technique?

A. Condition monitoring.　　B. PKI.

C. Packet filtering firewall.　　D. Application-level gateways.

Ⅲ. **Review Questions**

①What security risks are associated with Business-to-Business e-commerce?

②Give some examples of e-commerce security technologies.

③What are common disruptions to website stability?

Ⅳ. Online Practice

①What are the security threats faced by enterprises in the process of e-commerce transactions? In real life, find an e-commerce enterprise and study the security threats it has received. How does it deal with the threats?

②What aspects of e-commerce security protection measures should be included? Why is it not comprehensive to consider only technical factors?

③Collect and think about what security technologies an enterprise can use to determine the identity of an electronic message received, or how to respond to the information sent by a party and then deny it.

Ⅴ. Case Study

Business Security as a Way to Increase Productivity

A growing economy and a fast rising Internet population make India one of the most attractive targets for cyber criminals. In the global cyber security scale, India is the third most vulnerable country and the easiest target for cyber criminals.

Sanjay Khera, Head of Marketing for F-Secure in India, shares some facts of the Indian security space:

- Even today majority of small size companies don't have the right security in place to protect their business against online threats. They think they're very small and would not be an attractive target for hackers, but the fact is that attackers generally don't discriminate based on the size and it's the lax security and vulnerability that make them a fit target.
- Email still remains to be the top threat vector—whether it's spam mails containing links to malicious websites, phishing attempts, or spreading infected documents through attachments. The sub-standard security solutions are not able to stop, detect, or clean new threats. Low awareness, use of freeware solutions, and unpatched software give rise to new threats fast-spreading across networks. The cleaning process may involve formatting hard disks, which is time consuming and laborious task. This has become a big challenge for the small companies who usually have limited IT resources.
- Security is no more a matter of choice but an absolute need to remain in the business. One has to look for security only from reputed and trusted vendors. A multi-layer security solution that protects at all levels—gateway to endpoint and cloud is the best choice to safeguard against modern day threats which are more advanced and sophisticated in nature.

India Glycols Ltd(IGL) is a manufacturing conglomerate in India with multiple locations across the country. They have used F-Secure Business Suite to secure their IT infrastructure for 650 + IT users with a wide range of operating systems and across multiple locations. And achieved an increase of 20% in employee productivity.

Atul Govil, the CIO of IGL explains:

"*Besides the corporate network becoming more secure, the key visible metric was an approx. 40% reduction in incidents of hard disk formats and approx. 15% less calls landing on our IT help desk. Virus-related issues have also reduced by 50% after installing F-Secure products. Before, our help desk team very often cleaned viruses by formatting hard disks since it clears all the data on the drive including the operating system and any viruses. This would be an involved and time consuming process requiring review of back up data, other user content in specific machines. Such outages also caused loss of productivity since machine was not available for use to users during this 5—6 hours cycle.*"

IGL had professional malware protection software of good reputation in use earlier as well, so cutting the incidents down to half was considered a success. In India, which is the number one host country of botnet-related malware in Asia, cutting down the number of incidents is critical. To give some concrete figures to the botnet problem, India was on top of the list with the Ramnit botnet, which infected about 3 million computers before finally being taken down by Europol. In general, the Indian market is a challenging one: a 136-percent increase in cyber threats and attacks against Indian government organizations and a 126-percent spike in attacks targeting financial services organizations.

The operations at all plants of IGL are closely monitored through distributed control systems (DCS), which facilitate a high degree of control over the quality of products. Protecting confidential data according to industry compliance standards and government regulations, as well as protecting their own and customers' data are of prime importance to the company.

In 2014, IGL needed to upgrade security across their multi-location corporate network. Their existing security solution was weak in several key areas, such as policy management and software updating. There were no automatic updates. Employee productivity was a serious concern, as most of the IT team's time was spent on patch management, formatting hard disks, and other manual activities with the existing software. In addition, the most important consideration was that the new security solution had to be future-proof.

Implementation was done through a trusted partner—Aarna Global Infotech provided implementation support, and was involved throughout the whole project to add value to the solution. Govil explains:

"*Security is of paramount importance for any organization, and a good, proven security technology acts as a fundamental catalyst. To establish a business edge through competitive advantages and brand loyalty, data and related transactions have to be secure and confidential at all times. Security cannot be compromised at any point.*"

IGL needed a solution that provided strong security while having a minimal impact on performance. Email and web traffic scanning, as well as centralized management, were important security requirements. It also had to be easy to set up and maintain.

One key improvement was in the protection of physical servers, desktops, and laptops. According to Govil, the automatic deployment of security updates (with the possibility of exclusions and manual deployment) greatly reduced the amount of time the IT staff had to dedicate to maintaining endpoint security. IGL has found the protection of physical servers, desktop computers, and laptops in the same solution to be one of the key benefits. All this helps the IT team to dedicate their time to other projects, and therefore, improves productivity.

Questions for Discussion

①Why has India become one of the most attractive targets for cyber criminals?

②If you are a network security officer in a company in India, what will you do to protect your network?

Chapter 9 E-commerce Payment System, Order Fulfillment and Other Support Service

本章导读

随着计算机、网络、信息技术三大领域的发展以及它们的日益融合，社会生活的各个领域和各个环节已经离不开 Internet 了，任何机构、机关、单位、家庭、个人都可以通过 Internet 获取资源并共享信息。新环境下的电子商务应该是基于传统信息技术系统和 Internet 的一种动态商务活动。这种基于 Internet 的电子商务给传统的交易方式带来了一场巨大的革命，所以，支付方式按使用技术的不同大体上可分为传统支付方式和电子支付方式。

新环境下的电子商务利用计算机网络将商务活动涉及的商家、顾客、银行或金融机构，甚至信息卡公司、证券公司和政府都纳入了统一的系统，实现了网上在线交易过程的电子化。信息技术和网络为金融电子化创造了有利条件，电子银行、电子钱包、电子付款以及智能信用卡等已开始应用。本章对传统支付方式和电子支付方式一一进行了介绍。电子支付方式的存在使得电子商务的交易变得快捷，在线订单数激增，那么，接下来就是电子订单的履行环节。新环境下的电子商务势必要求订单履行更快捷、灵活，对客户更具响应性，订单履行效率成为了决定电子商务企业成败的关键。因此，本章对订单履行的任务、流程、遇到的困难等方面进行了介绍。此外，本章末尾还简单介绍了电子商务的物流服务。

Business Terms

①**e-commerce payment system**: It is a system, through which consumers, merchants and financial institutions use secure electronic means to exchange goods or services.

②**insurer**: banks or non-banking institutions that issue e-payment instruments

③**regulator**: usually a government agency whose regulations control the e-payment process

④**authentication**: The act of confirming the truth of an attribute of a single piece of data (a datum) claimed true by an entity. In contrast with identification, which refers to the act of stating or otherwise indicating a claim purportedly attesting to a person or thing's identity, authentication is the process of actually confirming that identity.

⑤**authorization**: The function of specifying access rights to resources related to information security and computer security in general and to access control in particular. "To authorize" is to define an access policy.

⑥**third-party payment**: A kind of trading, in which a certain third-party institution provided with ensured credit standing provide trusteeship services on funds for purpose of trading while sellers and purchasers conduct their settlements on a platform that the third party provides with.

Introductory Case

Alibaba Smashed Singles' Day Sales Record

Alipay. com is a third-party online payment platform. It was launched in China in 2004 by Alibaba Group and its founder Jack Ma. According to an analyst research report, Alipay had the biggest market share in China with 400 million users and control of just under half of China's online payment market in 2016.

Alibaba's 2016 Singles' Day was off to a great start. The company broke RMB 10 billion (US $1.4 billion) in less than seven minutes, and had broached US $5 billion before the first hour was up. As was the case last year, a big majority of the day's sales—84. 3 percent—were coming from mobile devices.

Alibaba smashed its Singles' Day shopping record on Friday by clocking growth of more than 32 percent. It released the official figures for this year which states it sold a record $17. 7 billion in products on Singles' Day 2016. Last year, the 24-hour e-commerce sales event racked up $14. 3 billion GMV in total.

"Back in 2013, $5. 14 billion was our one-day GMV. Now we can achieve it in one hour," said Alibaba Group CEO Daniel Zhang, adding that in the first hour of Singles' Day, orders were coming in 175,000 per second.

Earlier media reports had forecast GMV from Alibaba's 11. 11 Global Shopping Festival, as Singles' Day is officially called, to come at $20 billion in 2016. The figure easily eclipsed $2. 74 billion and $3. 07 billion respectively generated online during the Black Friday and Cyber Monday sales in the U. S. this year. The early figures also included preorders customers made at promotional events earlier in the year to lock in Singles' Day deals. Alibaba said the number of preorders was particularly large this year, "so much so that some Alibaba officials were talking about how the 24-hour sale had become a 24-day affair."

Singles' Day offers didn't only take place online but also offline. Taobao and Tmall sent out many digital coupons on Singles' Day, and those coupons were valid for purchases at participating brands' physical stores as well. For instance, on WeChat, Uniqlo offered select designs at 50 percent off both on Tmall and in-store. Some of the offers are still available after Singles' Day.

It is a successful campaign where brands can capture more of the Singles' Day traffic for themselves instead of only through the e-commerce platform.

The event is more than just shopping; it is a mass participation of people into an event evolving into a season of celebration. A lot of people tune in to live broadcasts for products and hundreds of thousands follow Internet celebrities who use these platforms to sell. Jack Ma feels they are transcending the definition of an e-commerce entity.

"Alibaba is not lacking engineers or customer service representatives. We need economists, sociologists, people with integrated knowledge to deal with challenges," Ma said. Certainly, Alibaba is using technology and data to converge online and offline retail to move beyond simple transactions.

Questions for Discussion

①How did most sales on Singles' Day fulfil in 2015 and 2016?

②How much did Alibaba sell in products on Singles' Day 2016?

③Why is Singles' Day a successful campaign?

9.1 OVERVIEW OF E-COMMERCE PAYMENT SYSTEM

A payment system is any system used to settle financial transactions through the transfer of monetary value, and includes the institutions, instruments, people, rules, procedures, standards, and technologies that make such an exchange possible. E-commerce payment system is an important component of e-commerce systems. It is a system, through which consumers, merchants and financial institutions use secure electronic means to exchange goods or services. E-commerce payment systems have become increasingly popular due to the widespread use of the Internet-based shopping and banking. Any transaction contains one of the most fundamental aspects—the funds transfer. So-called payment refers to the process of transferring funds from the payer to the payee. Payment is of course a critical element in e-commerce. E-commerce payment systems can be any system used to settle financial transactions in e-commerce.

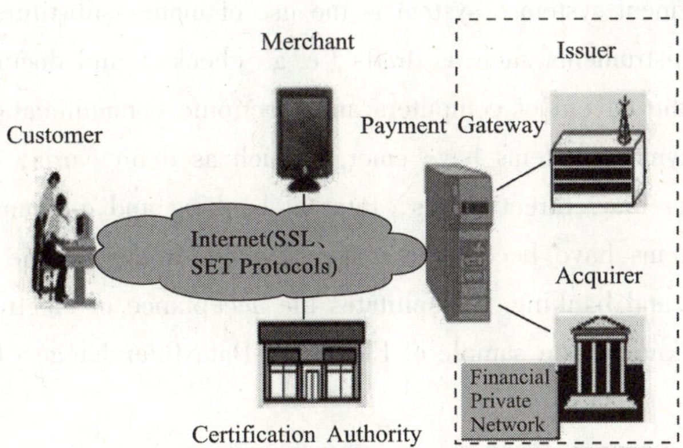

E-commerce Payment System

E-commerce payment system consists of seven parts: the customer, merchant, the customer's bank (also called the issuer), merchant bank (also known as the acquirer), certification authority, payment gateway, financial private network. In addition, It also includes the use of payment instruments and payment protocols to be followed, a combination of parties involved and the means of payment, payment protocols.

Customers use their own payment instruments (such as a credit card, electronic wallet, etc) to initiate payment, which is the starting point.

Merchant in e-commerce payment system offers Internet merchant accounts and merchant credit card processing services.

Customer bank is the bank that provides fund account and network payment tool for customers. In the network payment system that uses bank card as payment tool, the customer bank is also called the issuing bank or issuer.

Merchant banks are banks that provide capital accounts for businesses, because merchant banks operate on the basis of the legitimate accounts provided by the business and are therefore referred to as the acquiring bank or acquirer.

A payment gateway is a merchant service provided by an e-commerce application service provider that authorizes credit card or direct payments processing for e-businesses, online retailers, bricks and clicks, or traditional brick and mortar. The payment gateway may be provided by a bank to its customers, but can be provided by a specialized financial service provider as a separate service, such as a payment service provider. A payment gateway facilitates a payment transaction by the transfer of information between a payment portal (such as a website, mobile phone or interactive voice response service) and the front end processor or acquiring bank.

Financial private network is the internal communication and interbank networks with high security, such as China national advanced payment system, electronic interbank system of the People's Bank of China, bank card authorization system.

Certification body is responsible for issuing digital certificates involved in e-commerce activities to confirm the identity of the parties.

What makes a payment system a system is the use of money-substitutes. Traditional payment systems are negotiable instruments such as drafts (e. g. checks) and documentary credits such as letters of credit. With the advent of computers and electronic communications, a large number of alternative electronic payment systems have emerged such as debit cards, credit cards, electronic funds transfers, direct credits, direct debits, Internet banking and e-commerce payment systems. Electronic payment systems have become increasingly popular due to the widespread use of the Internet-based shopping and banking. It facilitates the acceptance of electronic payment for online transactions. Also, it's known as a sample of Electronic Data Interchange (EDI).

9.2 METHODS OF E-COMMERCE PAYMENT SYSTEM

With the development of society and economy, paying activity also continues to develop. It has gone through five stages; barter exchange, monetary exchange, bank transfer, automatic clearing house and electronic funds transfer (EFT). Now, there are many different ways to pay for products and services in the information age. According to different ways of currency in circulation and payment, methods of e-commerce payment system can be divided into two categories, traditional payments and electronic payments.

9.2.1 Traditional Payment Methods

Each of the following two instruments has its own distinct attributes that have contributed to its popularity as a payment method over many years.

Cash

Cash, legal tender issued by a national authority to represent value, refers to money in the physical form of currency, namely, banknotes and coins. It is the most common form of payment in terms of number of transactions with the features of no transaction fee, being anonymous, low cognitive demands. One of the reasons that has allowed cash to keep the dominate form of payment is the increasing number of automated teller machines (ATMs). Customers have much easier access to money in cash form. But money in cash form is also faced with security risks like easily stolen, limited to smaller transaction and not providing any float. Cash remains the most commonly used payment method, particularly for low-value payments. The cost of cash use is also significantly lower than any other payment method for low-value transactions.

Check

Check is the most common form of payment in terms of amount spent. Funds are transferred directly via a signed draft or check from a consumer's checking account to a merchant or other individual. Not like cash, check is not anonymous because it requires third party intervention (bank's intervention). Checks offer a number of attributes as follows: physical, face-to-face, instant exchange, for example for a property settlement; unlimited additional data to accompany the payment, for instance by attaching the check to an invoice or other information; payment to be made when only limited information is known about the payee; and greater financial control where, for instance, the need for a specific signature (or multiple signatures) provides key account signatories oversight of all outward payments within a business.

9.2.2 Electronic Payment Methods

The term electronic payment can refer narrowly to e-commerce—a payment for buying and selling goods or services offered through the Internet, or broadly to any type of electronic funds transfer. Electronic money (or e-money) is a kind of currency that realizes its function of circulation and payment through electronic information. Electronic payment experiences five stages of development. The first is the stage of bank data processing by stand-alone computers. The second is the stage of bank data processing by bank network computers. The third is the stage of ATM, followed by POS and Internet. With the advent of computers and electronic communications a large number of alternative electronic payment systems have emerged.

E-cash

E-cash is one of the first forms of alternative payment systems and it's a general form that describe any value storage and exchange system created by private entity. It's not really "cash", but the form of value storage and value exchange that have limited convertibility into other forms of value, and requires intermediaries to convert. E-cash is a kind of digital currency, so it is also called digital cash. E-cash was conceived by David Chaum as an anonymous cryptographic electronic money or electronic cash system in 1983. It was realized through his corporation DigiCash and used as micropayment system at one US bank from 1995 to 1998.

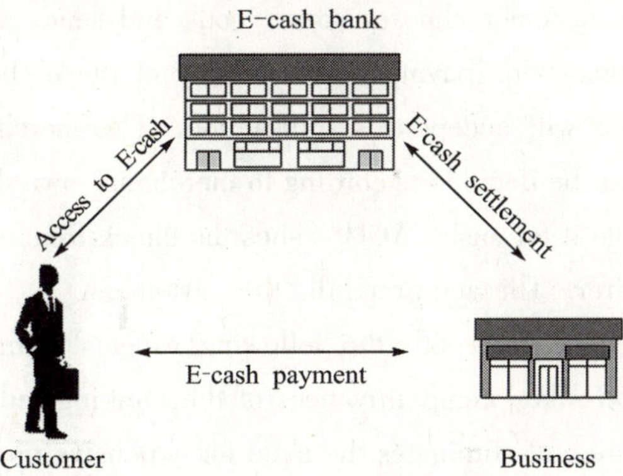

E-cash Payment System

E-cash payment system consists of access to e-cash, e-cash payment and e-cash settlement. The primary function of e-cash is to facilitate transactions on the Internet. Many of these transactions may be small in size and would not be cost efficient through other payment mediums such as credit cards. These types of payments, turning the Internet into a transaction oriented forum, require mediums that are easy, cheap (from a merchant's perspective), private and secure. E-cash is the natural solution, and the companies that are pioneering these services claim that the products will meet the stated criteria. By providing this type of payment mechanism, the incentives to provide worthwhile services and products via the Internet should increase. Another prospective beneficiary from these developments would be Shareware providers, since currently they rarely receive payments. To complete the digital money revolution an offline product is also required for the pocket money/change that most people must carry for small transactions (e. g. buying a newspaper, buying a cup of coffee, etc.). E-cash truly globalizes the economy, since the user can download money into his cyber-wallet in any currency desired. A merchant can accept any currency and convert it to local currency when the cyber cash is uploaded to the bank account. It offers the possibility of maintaining the complete privacy of the client, provided there is an agreement between the bank of issue and the organization from which the goods or services have been acquired. But the main problem of e-cash is that it is necessary that the commercial establishment accept it as payment method. Another problem resides in that at the present time in the development of this model, the client and the salesman have to have accounts in the same bank of issue of the e-cash, which means at the moment the funds emitted by a bank are not valid in other banks. Nevertheless, it is possible that as the use of e-cash extends, there will appear organizations who are dedicated to the interchange of these new currencies between banks.

E-check

The E-check is basically an electronic equivalent of the paper check. Rendering the advantage of paper check, e-check will manage the transfer of funds from one account to another over the Internet.

The process of bank for e-check includes eight steps. The customer visits the merchant's server and gets the inventory. The customer chooses some goods and sends an e-check to the merchant. The merchant verifies the consumers' payment and validity of the e-check via the acquirer. If the check is valid, the merchant will accept this transaction. The merchant sends the check to the acquirer. When to send it can be decided according to merchants' own demands. The acquirer sends the check to ACH to exchange it for cash. ACH cashes the check from customers' acquirer and sends the cash to merchants' acquirer. The acquirer bills the customers.

The advantages of e-check rest with the following aspects. Firstly, it improves the check payments system, enhances the key competitiveness of the banking industry. Secondly, it fits with the present business procedure and eliminates the need for expensive process reengineering. Thirdly, it works like a paper check but in pure electronic form with fewer manual steps. Next, it is designed to meet the needs of businesses and consumers in the 21st century by virtue of the most advanced security techniques. What's more, it can be used by any bank clients who have the check accounts, including those small and medium-sized enterprises that do not possess an electronic payment system. Last, it adds e-commerce function to current bank account.

The disadvantages of e-check mainly involve two aspects. To begin with, e-checks involve the technology of digital signatures. Moreover, the legal validity of digital signatures is ratified by different countries' law regarding digital signatures. In addition, e-checks bring about a series of jurisdiction problems.

E-wallet

An e-wallet serving a function similar to a physical wallet holds credit cards, e-cash, owner identification, and owner contact information. An electronic wallet, also called an e-wallet or a digital wallet, allows people to more conveniently conduct transactions online. Much like a traditional wallet, an e-wallet contains information about its owner. For the consumer, the main advantages of using an electronic wallet is that it can automatically fill out lengthy forms when making online transactions and can also keep personal details more secure. There're two categories of e-wallets applied to different softwares. One is called server-side e-wallet. A server-side e-wallet stores a customer's information on a remote server belonging to a particular merchant or wallet publisher. Another one is client-side e-wallet. A client-side e-wallet stores a consumer's information on his or her own computer.

E-wallets make shopping more efficient and convenient for the customer, the merchant and the bank. Holding e-wallets, consumers enter their information just once and there is no need for them to enter the same information at every web site. A future electronic wallet could maintain records of a consumer's purchases and save the invoice for the consumer. A web robot can be used to suggest where the consumer might find a lower price item that he or she purchases regularly.

However, an attack on an electronic wallet vendor's server or consumer's personal computer will reveal all the sensitive information.

9.3 THE INTERNET AND THE BANKING INDUSTRY

In recent years, the Internet has been embedded in the whole financial system, becoming the living conditions, infrastructure and resource environment of modern finance and influencing the banking industry. Financial services, such as mobile payment and online banking, have developed rapidly because of bringing a new service experience and taking full advantage of the "fragmentation time". And then, with the continuous development of e-commerce and the emergence of the third party payment platform, the third party platform customers continue to increase. E-banking, mobile banking and third party payment are here to be introduced.

E-bank

E-bank is also known as online banking, using Internet technology to provide customers services. Customers can manage the current and fixed deposits, checks, credit card and personal investment conveniently without leaving home. E-bank has been called the "3A Bank", because it has no time and space constraints. It can be used anytime, anywhere, and in anyway to provide customers financial services. Through e-bank, users can enjoy convenient, quick, efficient and reliable service, for example, online transfer, online payment, online purchase fund, online investment management, online pre-paid.

Mobile bank

Mobile bank offers service provided by a bank or other financial institutions via a mobile device such as a mobile phone or tablet, which is a channel for bank to realize its electronic services and allows its customers to conduct financial transactions remotely. It uses software, usually called an app, provided by the financial institution for the purpose. Mobile banking is usually available on a 24-hour basis. Some financial institutions have restrictions on which accounts may be accessed through mobile banking, as well as a limit on the amount that can be transacted.

Transactions through mobile banking may include obtaining account balances and lists of latest transactions, electronic bill payments, and funds transfers between a customer's or another's accounts. Some apps also enable copies of statements to be downloaded and sometimes printed at the customer's premises; and some banks charge a fee for mailing hardcopies of bank statements.

From the bank's point of view, mobile banking reduces the cost of handling transactions by reducing the need for customers to visit a bank branch for non-cash withdrawal and deposit transactions. Mobile banking does not handle transactions involving cash, and a customer needs to visit an ATM or bank branch for cash withdrawals or deposits. Many apps now have a remote deposit option.

Third party payment

Third party payment is an effective way to solve troubles in payment. It can guarantee the goods quality and reliable exchange, and the exchange of a purchase. It will monitor the processes of trade to ensure both buyers and sellers are honest. It offers necessary support for ensuring a successful business in e-commerce. Third party payment platforms are supplied by third party independent institutions, which have already signed contracts with big banks and possessed capability and reputations. These institutions can be classified to service agent organizations with clear payment responsibility. At most circumstances, they only provide supporting services such as e-commerce business or personal e-commerce supporting and application supporting service. So, generally speaking, they are not involved in any specific e-commerce business directly. After selecting the commodities, the customers pay the money through third party payment platform in the transactions. And the third party is responsible for notifying the sellers to deliver the commodities. Once receiving their goods, the buyers tell the third party to transfer the money to the sellers. Third party payment platform brings the following advantages: It reduces the risk of bad credit and the actions such as returning or exchanging merchandise will not be problems any more. It promotes the cooperation between merchants and banks, which are propitious to break the bulwark of bank card; provides increment services and helps the sellers' websites; and provides services such as real-time transaction querying and transaction system analysis.

Third party payment model has become the most popular e-commerce payment model, especially in C2C. Paypal in US and Alipay in China have already achieved great success.

Third party payment system connects to buyers, sellers and financial institutions. Generally, Third party payment system consists of foreground trade components and background management components. The trade components are responsible for dealing with buyers' online transactions, while the latter one is used for dealing transactions with the banks, managing and querying online customers. The system framework is shown below.

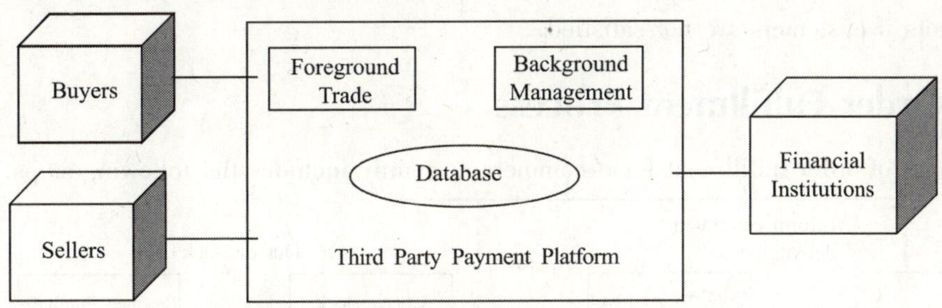

The Third-party Payment System Framework

Buyers and sellers need to register themselves to Third party payment system so that they can obtain their virtual accounts. Connecting these virtual accounts to the real accounts in the bank, the money in the real accounts can be transferred into virtual currency in virtual accounts, which is used for online transactions. Third party payment system achieves this process by building connection between platform and the banks. It also has operations related to virtual money and credit card accounts to provide the capability of transferring between virtual currency and credit card accounts. During the transaction, the money is kept by the third party temporarily who can be seemed as an interceder. If anything goes wrong with the transaction, the third party is responsible for negotiating with both sellers and buyers to decide what to do.

9.4 ORDER FULFILLMENT

Order fulfillment is the complete process from the point of sales inquiry to the delivery of a product to the customer. Sometimes order fulfillment is used to describe the narrower act of distribution or the logistics function, however, in the broader sense it refers to the way firms respond to customer orders. Order fulfillment refers to on time delivery of products to customers' hands after products are ordered by them, but also refers to information offer, such as product installation instructions, necessary training, exchange, and all related customer services.

The key factor of order fulfillment is that goods or services can be submitted to the right place at the right time and at the right price. All the activities needed to provide customers with ordered goods and services, including related customer services. Back-office operations are the activities that support fulfillment of sales, such as accounting and logistics. Front-office operations are the business processes, such as sales and advertising, which are visible to customers.

9.4.1 Order Fulfillment Tasks

Order fulfillment tasks consist of three links: commodity production and organization, transportation and distribution and lastly customer service. Commodity production and organization includes inventory control, supply chain management and electronic and collaborative commerce. Transportation and distribution needs fast delivery products to the customers. Customer service involves remote support for customers to successfully order and use products, to easily exchange or return products if customers are not satisfied.

9.4.2 Order Fulfillment Process

A process of order fulfillment for e-commerce, mainly includes the following steps.

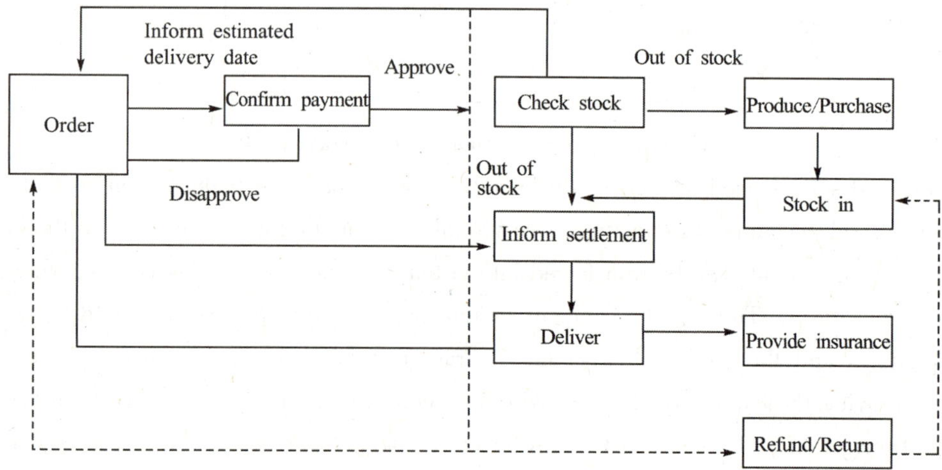

The Process of Order Fulfillment

- **Customer's payment confirmation**

The effectiveness of each payment must be confirmed. In B2B model, it's completed by the companies' financial departments or finance company. In B2C model it generally consists of bank card payments or third party payment platform.

- **Stock check**

Check if the current stock is available, and inform the customer an estimated delivery date according to the current stock, if the customer is not satisfied with the delivery cycle, the order can be cancelled.

- **Delivery arrangement**

If the product is in stock, notify the customer to implement payment, and then arrange delivery.

- **Insurance**

Sometimes the goods need to be insured. Related sectors include the financial sector and insurance companies.

- **Replenishment**

If the product is not in stock, the production enterprises will organize production, while the retail enterprises will make procurement.

- **Return/Refund**

If the customer is not satisfied with the goods, he can exchange or return the goods.

In a broader sense, the possible processes in a logistic-production system are:

- Product Inquiry—Initial inquiry about offerings, visit to the website, catalog request.
- Sales Quote—Budgetary or availability quote.
- Order Configuration—Where ordered items need selection of options or order lines need to be compatible with each other.
- Order Booking—The formal order placement or closing of the deal (issuing by the customer of a Purchase Order).
- Order Acknowledgment/Confirmation—Confirmation that the order is booked and/or received.
- Invoicing/Billing—The presentment of the commercial invoice/bill to the customer.
- Order Sourcing/Planning—Determining the source /location of item(s) to be shipped.
- Order Changes—Changes to orders, if needed.
- Order Processing—Process step where the distribution center or warehouse is responsible to fill order (receive and stock inventory, pick, pack and ship orders).
- Shipment—The shipment and transportation of the goods.
- Track & Trace—Determine the current and past locations of the goods during transit.
- Delivery—The delivery of the goods to the consignee/customer.
- Settlement—The payment of the charges for goods/services/delivery.
- Return—In case the goods are unacceptable/not required.

No matter which process of order fulfillment it follows, traditional order and electronic order have different features, which cannot be ignored. Those two orders' features are listed in the following traditional order and electronic order feature comparison chart.

Traditional Order Fulfillment Feature	Electronic Order Fulfillment Features
▲Orders for all customers in the same way	▲Orders based on each customer
▲Large and palletized orders need less-than-truckload and vehicle transport	▲Smaller orders need unpacking picking, as well as frequent parcel delivery
▲Stable and consistent customer demand for the product, rarely require temporary changes	▲Intermittent and sporadic customer demand for the products, often require temporary changes
▲Individual product campaigns, few returns	▲Bi-directional flow, frequent return
▲Meet customers demand according to the forecasted supply (push)	▲Meet customers demand according to customer's order pulling way
▲Delivery destination is concentrated and standard	▲The starting points and terminal points of delivery scatter due to different orders

Traditional Order and Electronic Order Feature Comparison Chart

9.4.3 Difficulties of Order Fulfillment

- **"Production first" mode vs. "order first" mode**

The first consideration of traditional retail is the production of goods, and then sales to customers in the retail store, while e-commerce focuses on order first, followed by goods production.

And many orders are personalized ones. This makes the supply of products in enterprises a great challenge. It not only requires the enterprise and its supply chain to accurately predict the customer's demand, control inventory, but also requires they have an agile supply chain to respond quickly to changes in customer demand.

- **Products "deliver" vs. products "pickup"**

Customers actually go to retail stores in person to buy and take away their products in traditional retail stores. But e-commerce sales are remote transaction, the enterprise must deliver goods once an order is made. This makes the enterprise face challenges in the delivery of the products to ensure the real-time distribution, but also to reduce the cost of delivery. Because B2C e-commerce always faces small orders, low value transactions and high cost of distribution are not acceptable.

- **"On the spot" service vs. "remote" service**

E-commerce distribution logistics are generally carried out by the third-party logistics company, and e-commerce transactions are remotely realized, which makes the technical support of products differ in the traditional enterprises and in traditional retails. "Remote" service will replace "on the spot" service, the task that the enterprise undertakes is more about training and guidance.

- **Reverse logistics problems**

In traditional retails, when a customer is not satisfied with the purchases, to go to exchange or return is easily realized. While remote trading may probably make it impossible for customs to exchange or return immediately in local places, so "reverse logistics" problems emerge. Reverse logistics are about unsatisfied products purchased by customers will be returned to the enterprises.

9.4.4 Strategic Significance of Order Fulfillment

Order fulfillment is a key process in managing the supply chain. It is the customers' orders that put the supply chain in motion, and filling them efficiently and effectively is the first step in providing customer service. However, the order fulfillment process involves more than just filling orders. It is about designing a network and a process that permits a firm to meet customer requests while minimizing the total delivered cost. This involves more than logistics, and it needs to be implemented cross-functionally and with the coordination of key suppliers and customers.

The order fulfillment strategy also determines the de-coupling point in the supply chain, which describes the point in the system where the "push" (or forecast-driven) and "pull" (or demand-driven see demand chain management) elements of the supply chain meet. The decoupling point always is an inventory buffer that is needed to cater for the discrepancy between the sales forecast and the actual demand (i. e. the forecast error). Typically, the higher the P:D ratio, the more the firm relies on forecasts and inventories. Hal Mather suggests three ways to tackle this "planning dilemma": improve forecasting accuracy or provide for flexibility or build a process to recognize forecasting errors and quickly correct production planning.

It has become increasing necessary to move the de-coupling point in the supply chain to minimize the dependence on forecast and to maximize the reactionary or demand-driven supply chain elements. The order fulfillment strategy has also strong implications on how firms customize their products and deal with product variety. Strategies that can be used to mitigate the impact of product variety include modularity, option bundling, late configuration, and build to order (BTO) strategies—all of which are generally referred as mass customization strategies. The decoupling point can place a much stronger emphasis on supply chain based on the process as well as nature of supply chain configurations.

At the strategic level, the process team designs the operational order fulfillment process. This includes designing the network, establishing policies and procedures, and determining the role of technology in the process. This requires interfacing and communicating with multiple functional areas within the firm, and can be enhanced by working with suppliers and customers to develop a network and a process that meets the customers' requirements in a cost-effective manner. Although many managers consider order fulfillment to fall within the role of the logistics function, it is the integration with other functions in the firm and other firms in the supply chain that becomes key in defining order fulfillment as a supply chain process.

Team should review the marketing strategy, supply chain structure, and customer service goals to determine the order fulfillment capabilities of the firm and the supply chain. By examining the marketing strategy and customer service goals, they are seeking to understand the requirements of the customer and the role that customer service plays in the overall strategy of the firm. To fully understand the customers, the team should interface with the customer relationship management team to understand what is most important to the customer. Often this information is identified through a customer service audit. Together, the two teams will determine which services are necessary to achieve and maintain corporate/supply chain goals.

The order fulfillment process needs to be designed around the customer, but within the limits of the firm's business and marketing of the fulfillment process, the team needs to tradeoff the costs of the solution with the benefits to the customer and the impact on the financial performance of the firm, and its customers and suppliers. The team also needs to understand the firm's order fulfillment budget. That is, determining how much is acceptable to spend on fulfilling the order. A firm might be able to most quickly deliver a product to the customer with an express air shipment, but the costs associated with that policy erodes profits and could be unacceptable. Likewise, financial issues might dictate a minimum order size or something about the selling terms. Throughout the design of the fulfillment process, the team needs to tradeoff the costs of the solution with the benefits to the customer and the impact on the financial performance of the firm, and its customers and suppliers.

The supply chain structure is another important input into the design of the order fulfillment process. Both the sourcing and the distribution sub-networks that are in place impose limits on the cost and the lead-time of the fulfillment process. The team needs to examine the current network to understand its limitations and how cost is added as product moves through the supply chain.

9.5 OTHER SUPPORT SERVICE

The support service in e-commerce operation can be divided into two categories: platform support service and process support service. Platform support service refers to support services related to network business platform, such as business web site construction and maintenance, network security management and online analysis tools. Process support service refers to the support service related to specific business operations process, such as storage, transportation, delivery, payment and information. Whether it is traditional business or e-commerce, the operation of specific business cannot be completed without the support of logistics. Logistics service is very important in the application of e-commerce.

9.5.1 Definition of Logistics

According to the Council of Supply Chain Management Professionals (CSCMP), a professional organization for Logistics and SCM professionals, logistics is defined as: "the process of planning, implementing and controlling the efficient, effective flow and storage of goods, services and related information from point of origin to point of consumption for the purpose of conforming to customer requirements." The goal of logistics is to support procurement, manufacturing and customer accommodation operational requirements.

9.5.2 Logistics Process

Logistics process consists of the following four parts:

Transportation management

It's mainly about the movement of materials, and parts to a warehouse or storage facility within a manufacturing site as well as movement of finished goods to distribution centers and retails sites.

Order management

It involves procurement of SKUs and processing customer orders.

Warehouse management

It needs locating and designing facilities to meet customer service levels.

Inventory management

It requires balancing inventory levels to achieve high customer service levels.

9.5.3 Demands on the Logistics Service

In B2C e-commerce, the easy and fast online ordering make consumers expect of quicker and more reliable delivery. Only through the reliable and high-effective management of the logistics system, vendors could win the market competitive advantages.

The products now are not the focus of vendors' competition; it has been turned to the services, actually the competition of supply chain. The web-based tools to transfer the information between the partners, establish the integrated logistics management system are what vendors must use. They increase the entire supply chain visibility, and coordinate the plan and decision support of all participants in the supply chain.

General speaking, e-commerce creates new e-commerce models and sets high demands on the logistics service, which are listed as follows:

Responsiveness

The request of customers to distribution is often the Just In Time. The delivery in the next day or even the same day has been more popular with customers. It needs better responsiveness of logistics system.

Flexibility

The traditional logistics may fix the optimized facilities and personnel according to the products quantity, peak time and turnover ratio. But e-commerce business is very hard to predict. This needs the quick and effective suitableness of the logistics departments.

Visibility

In order to meet the responsiveness and flexibility requirements of e-commerce to the logistics, the visibility of the whole supply chain must be increased so that the warehousing and transportation information of the goods could be known to guarantee the coordinated operation of the integrated logistics system.

Optimization

To meet the requirement of the customers, enterprises have to set up logistics networks consisting of a lot of small distribution centers in the sales area, which have resulted in the fragmented inventory, higher inventory level, more warehousing facilities and frequent distribution. As a result, the cost is highly increased and the enterprise economic benefit and market competition are affected. Therefore, the supply chain must be optimized to reduce the logistics cost as possible as it can.

So, what kind of practices should be implemented to help logistics companies maintain a well-organized and flexible supply chain that minimizes cost and maximizes profit? Now the logistics companies are facing great challenges in the e-commerce age, and they have to find ways to solve the problems as e-commerce is boosting sharply.

SUMMARY

This chapter mainly discusses issues related to e-commerce payment system, order fulfillment and other support service. E-commerce is the best friend of payment systems. The largest e-commerce markets in the world are USA, China, UK, Japan, Germany and France respectively according to AT Kearney's "The 2015 Global Retail E-commerce Index". The global e-commerce sales volumes reached the level of 840 billion USD in 2014 by more than 20% increase compared to 2013 and this trend is expected to climb up continuously the following years. 2018 will be the year of 1.5 trillion USD sales volumes at global level based on the estimations made. Payment system business has always grown with e-commerce when we check the recent history in business environments. As long as e-commerce systems grow, this situation brings on the market other types of subsystems such as payment systems with cloud solutions in the world (Alibaba. com with Alipay. com, eBay with PayPal, Amazon with Amazon payments, BKM Express solution in Turkey). Today, the new generation was born in technology. E-commerce businesses, payment systems with digital solutions do not refer to them any hesitations or risk that much. Mainly, this'd be very easy and natural for young people as they turn on a switch at home. Therefore, the players in the countries with "young population" or "population growth" will have remarkable market shares in this game in the very near future if they do their strategies and investments accordingly.

Words and Expressions

①**anonymous**: having no known name or identity or known source 匿名的

②**audit**: an inspection of the accounting procedures and records by a trained accountant or CPA 审计

③**boost**: the act of giving a push 推动；改进

④**budget**: a summary of intended expenditures along with proposals for how to meet them 预算

⑤**convertibility**: the quality of being exchangeable (especially the ability to convert a currency into gold or other currencies without restriction) 兑换

⑥**coordinate**: to make (people or things) work together, especially so as to increase effectiveness (使)协调；(使)一致

⑦**currency**: money in any form when in actual use or circulation as a medium of exchange, especially circulating banknotes and coins 货币

⑧**delivery**: the goods that are delivered 递送之物；投递之物；运送之物

⑨**deposit**: a sum of money which is in a bank account or savings account, especially a sum which will be left there for some time 存款

⑩**distribution**: the act of distributing or spreading or apportioning 分发；分派；分送

⑪**guarantee**: to give a security or assurance 保证；担保

⑫**optimization**: the act of rendering optimal 最佳化；最优化

⑬**order fulfillment**: the complete process from point of sales inquiry to delivery of a product to the customer 订单履行

⑭**shipment**: a load of goods sent by ship, train, airplane, or some other vehicle, or the act of sending them (运送的)货物；运送；装运

⑮**stock**: the total amount of goods which are available to sell 库存

⑯**vendor**: someone who promotes or exchanges goods or services for money 供货商；卖方

⑰**warehousing**: the act or process of storing large quantities of goods so that they can be sold or used at a later date 入库；仓库贮存

⑱**withdrawal**: an amount of money that you take from your bank account 取款;提款

Exercises

Ⅰ. **Key Terms**(Explain the following terms.)

①e-commerce payment system

②e-cash

③e-check

④e-wallet

⑤third-party payment

Ⅱ. **Multiple Choice Exercises** (Choose the correct answer to the following questions from A, B, C and D. There is only one correct answer.)

①A payment gateway is a ________ network.

A. retailing　　B. public　　C. private　　D. bank

②________ remains the most commonly used payment method, particularly for low-value payments, but it's easily stolen.

A. Cash　　B. Check　　C. Credit card　　D. Bank card

③What makes a payment system a system is the use of ________.

A. mobile phone　　B. Internet　　C. bank　　D. money-substitutes

④The e-check is basically an electronic equivalent of ________.

A. cash　　B. all payment methods

C. the paper check　　D. electronic wallet

⑤A future electronic wallet could ________ for the consumer.

A. maintain a consumer's purchases and save the goods

B. maintain records of a consumer's purchases and save the invoice

C. maintain records of a consumer's expectation and save the invoice

D. maintain a consumer's purchases level and save the invoice

⑥Mobile bank offers service provided by ________ via a mobile device such as ________.

A. a bank or a mobile company; a mobile phone or telephone

B. a bank or other financial institutions; a computer or a television

C. a bank or other financial institutions; a mobile phone or tablet

D. a bank or a company; a mobile phone or telephone

⑦Which of the following statements is not true about order fulfillment?

A. Order fulfillment is a key process in managing the supply chain.

B. The supply chain structure is another important input into the design of the order fulfillment process.

C. The key factor of order fulfillment is goods or services can be submitted to the right place at the right time and at the right price.

D. Bi-directional flow and frequent return are the features of traditional order fulfillment.

⑧Logistics process consists of ________.

A. transportation management

B. order management and warehouse management

C. inventory management

D. all above

Ⅲ. Review Questions

①What are the methods of payment system for e-commerce?

②What problem is order fulfillment facing?

③What are the demands of customers on logistics service?

Ⅳ. Online Practice

①Please visit different online shopping platforms to list the payment methods they support.

②Please visit one e-tailing platform and make an order to analyze the process of its order fulfillment.

③Try to sell one item in your online WeChat shop. What logistics service are you planning to provide? What payment methods can you accept?

Ⅴ. Case Study

Apply Pay Underperforming in Chinese Market

Feb. 18 marks the first anniversary of Apply Pay's entry into China. Despite being the most popular third-party payment service in the U. S., Apply Pay is currently underperforming its expectations in China. Local payment services utilizing QR codes, such as WeChat and Alipay, are squeezing Apple Pay out of the market, the National Business Daily reported.

According to Analysys, a big data analysis provider, domestic payment service providers took almost 99 percent of the market share in China's third-party mobile service industry in the third quarter of 2016. Of them, Alipay received 50.24 percent of the market share, followed by WeChat's 38.12 percent.

Compared with QR code payments, reliance on hardware has hindered the growth of near-field communication (NFC) payments, which is Apple Pay's chosen mode, a UnionPay insider noted.

Apple Pay only works on iPhone 6 devices and above, which also restricts the number of users.

In addition, the cost to maintain and upgrade the POS that supports NFC payment is high. There are currently about 6 million POS that support NFC payment nationwide. It costs 300 RMB to upgrade a POS, and a new POS costs roughly 600 RMB. It therefore remains a significant challenge to convince shops to upgrade or install new POS in substantial numbers. WeChat and Alipay also offer higher subsidies to shops that use their payment services, which discourages shops from setting up Apple Pay.

As major drivers of Apple Pay in China, UnionPay and several major banking institutions actively promoted the service when it first entered China. But many of these institutions have already shifted their focus to QR code payments.

However, the question remains: Does Apple Pay have a chance to stage a comeback?

"From a technical perspective, NFC payment will have more market space in the future," predicted the UnionPay insider. Li Chao, an analyst with iResearch, remarked that there is good reason for Apple Pay to exist in the Chinese market, as NFC technology offers advantages in security.

Questions for Discussion

①Why did local payment services utilizing QR codes, such as WeChat and Alipay, squeeze Apple Pay out of the market?

②What are the advantages and disadvantages of NFC payment for Apple Pay?

Chapter 10 E-commerce Development and Trends in China

本章导读

中国电子商务的发展起源于1990年EDI标准(U/EDIFACT)首次在我国外贸企业中的应用。随后,我国政府相继实施的"三金工程"为电子商务发展期打下了坚实基础。1995年底,电子商务在中国迅速发展并开始蔓延到社会生活的各个层面。1998年3月,中国第一笔互联网网上交易成功。1999年中国电子商务开始探索并推出大型电子商务项目,进入实际应用阶段。同时,B2B电子商务形式也开始在国内大型企业间逐步应用,网上支付开始试行,电子商务的物流配送也出现可喜的突破。2000年,中国的电子商务发展高度膨胀,随后进入了困难的寒冬时期。2003年开始,跌入低谷的中国电子商务终于反弹,开始进入可持续性发展的稳定时期。2008年以来,我国的电子商务一直保持以较高的速度增长,并受到国家政府的高度重视,开始进入创新发展时期。本章首先将对中国电子商务的发展历程进行简单的回顾,接着介绍我国电子商务发展的现状及特点,分析电子商务发展在促进中国经济转型升级进程中的重要作用。最后,本章将深入探讨中国电子商务发展的趋势。

Business Terms

①**direct employment**: It is the term used for the workers employed directly by those projects, which are designed to promote economic growth and create jobs in specific areas.

②**indirect employment**: It refers to job creation and business growth in the local economy as a result of demand created by some projects.

③**e-government**: E-commerce model in which a government entity buys or provides goods, services, or information from or to businesses or individual citizens.

④**mobile commerce**: It means the delivery of electronic commerce capabilities directly into the consumer's hand, anywhere, via wireless technology.

⑤**social network**: A category of Internet applications that help connect friends, business partners, or individuals with specific interests by providing free services such as photo presentations, e-mail, blogging and so on, through a variety of tools.

⑥**Internet consumer finance**: It refers to consumers buy consumer goods via the Internet loans way of modern financial service, including home loans, student loans, car loans, tourism, etc.

Introductory Case

Online Retailing—New Channel for Western Companies into Chinese Market

On November 11, Todd Fryhover, president of the Washington Apple Commission, joined China's Singles, Day celebration for the first time, hoping to sell 1.2m apples from Washington State in 24 hours. To help him out was the marketing juggernaut of Alibaba, the Chinese e-commerce company, where Washington apples are sold through branded website Tmall.

Singles' Day, which began as a student celebration of singledom in the early 1990s, was reinvented by Alibaba in 2009 as a mass festival of conspicuous consumption, and more and more foreign companies are joining, hoping to use the holiday as a marketing exercise to get their brands out to the Chinese public.

Mr. Fryhover wants everyone in China to have "a repeatable, wonderful experience on Washington apples". China is No. 6 on the list of 60 countries that import apples from Washington's 450 growers, but he thinks it will be No. 1 by next year.

He may be right. By midnight, as a video billboard in Alibaba's Beijing auditorium showed, $14.3bn of merchandise had been bought via Alibaba's platforms in 24 hours.

Western companies are increasingly turning to online commerce, a cheaper and faster way to get to market than setting up store chains or penetrating the opaque retail market in China.

To do this they are learning to love China's Internet conglomerates, informally known as BAT—Baidu, the search company, Alibaba and Tencent, the social media and gaming company. The three have begun to dominate economic life in China with amazing speed, doing everything from retail to finance to transportation, and moving into healthcare and even agriculture.

In just a few years, the BAT conglomerates has been able to monopolise every aspect of daily life that could conceivably be put on the web and sold to the public. "They all want to own the customer, they want to be with them every second of the day, when they watch a video, chat to their friends, buy groceries, or go to a restaurant", says Chris DeAngelis from the Beijing-based Alliance Development Group.

China's Internet giants are becoming what analyst Anne Stevenson-Yang of Capital Research calls "tech Keiretsu", referring to the national champions that dominated the Japanese economy in the 20th century with interests in multiple Industries. "When companies are this big in China, the difference between public and private is not that important," she says. "For all intents and purposes these companies have become the ministry of the Internet."

But fierce competition means foreign sellers have many options for courting Chinese middle class buyers who are looking to buy imported goods abroad due to concerns about home-made counterfeit goods.

Alibaba offers a number of options for sellers, including the free eBay-like platform Taobao, which is basically an online flea market. Most big brands set up on Tmall, which resembles an Amazon market place, a platform where big brands can set up stores and have more control over their sales and supply chains. Tmall's first store from a fortune 500 company was Procter & Gamble (P&G), launched in 2008, which has grown 100 times since then, according to P&G vice-president Jasmine Xu.

This year on Singles' Day Ms Xu says that P&G made its first RMB100m ($16m) in six minutes, compared with eight hours last year. "Tmall is a key platform to drive brand building in addition to sales," she says.

Some merchants have been loath to list on Alibaba, however. It gets vast online traffic, but the pressure to discount and the prevalence of fakes means it is "hard to protect a brand on Tmall," says one consultant.

But there are plenty of alternatives. JD. com, Alibaba's rival, which is increasing its market share, has attracted a number of brands to its online store.

Meanwhile, waiting in the wings is Tencent's social media app WeChat, which has more than 500m users and is growing rapidly. Fearful of flooding the app with advertising and products, Tencent has been holding back on "monetizing" WeChat.

But advertising on WeChat is just one way of getting attention, and many companies have found they can win huge marketing success simply by using WeChat for word-of-mouth marketing.

Fans of English country living, for example, can join a WeChat group devoted to AGA cookers, the iconic English oven brand, watch videos about cooking on an AGA, swap messages about it, and, thanks to the software which embeds the store in the chatroom, even buy one on impulse.

"WeChat is unusually versatile; it's better than Facebook, better than WhatsApp for marketing," says Jim James, head of Eastwest Public Relations in Beijing, which designed the AGA

WeChat group. "China in many ways is more switched on to the Internet than other countries which have had it for longer."

Questions for Discussion

①Why are more and more western companies increasingly turning to online commerce in China?

②What does BAT in China mean?

③Which means would you like to choose when you are purchasing online, through Taobao, Tmall, JD. com or WeChat ? Why?

10.1 OVERVIEW OF THE DEVELOPMENT OF E-COMMERCE IN CHINA

It has been several decades since human beings used electronic communication to carry out trade activities. Back in the 1960s, people began to send business documents by telegraph. In 1970s, people began to make use of the convenient and quick method—fax to replace telegraph. Later, people began to apply email and EDI (Electronic Data Interchange) to the communication within and among enterprises. The development of e-commerce in China started from the initial application of EDI standard (U/EDIFACT) in Chinese foreign trade enterprises. Thereafter, it has experienced the following four stages: the budding stage, developing stage, stabilizing stage and maturity stage.

10.1.1 The Budding Stage(1995-1998)

In 1990, the United Nations has launched EDI standards (UN/EDIFACT), the sole set of standard in the world so far, and promoted it globally, opening a prelude to e-commerce in the world. Similarly, the development of e-commerce in China is also starting from the application of EDI. In 1990, the State Planning Commission, the Ministry of Foreign Trade and China Customs formed a joint group with other departments to make research on the application of UN/EDIFACT standard in China, especially in the international trade and other related fields. Since then, EDI was utilized in foreign trade enterprises.

The early electronic commerce in China is based on national public communication network, represented by the "three gold project" implemented by the Chinese government. It has laid a solid foundation for the development of e-commerce. At the end of 1995, a variety of e-commerce business and network companies, which are based on business websites, began to emerge. In August 1996, Sohu. com was established. In 1997, a large number of website advertisements and publicity emerged, and also many e-commerce terms and concepts began to be spread in China. A lot of large e-commerce projects were launched, such as Chinese Goods Ordering System (CGOS), China Commodity Trading Center (CCEC), Virtual "Canton Fair", and so on, indicating the wide application of e-commerce in China. In December 1998, the establishment of Sina. com has attracted great concern at home and abroad. In the same year, some e-commerce projects began to be launched in Beijing and Shanghai.

At this stage, the main bodies of China's e-commerce are some IT vendors and media, especially some big IT manufacturers led by IBM. They have conducted "enlightenment education" of e-commerce in various ways, stimulating and guiding people's understanding, interest and demand for e-commerce, and promoting the introduction, application and development of e-commerce technology in China.

10.1.2 The Developing Stage (1998-1999)

From 1998, many network service providers, such as ICP and ISP, began to enter the field of e-commerce. New websites and e-commerce projects suddenly increased dramatically, various types of e-commerce information and consulting websites, online shops, online shopping malls, online mail order, online auction sites coming into birth. Many well known websites were established, such as 8848. com, eBay, etc.

Meanwhile, e-commerce began to rapidly expand to more regions, from the original few cities, such as Beijing, Shanghai, Shenzhen, Guangzhou, to other coastal, eastern and central cities.

With the development of B2C and C2C, B2B was also applied gradually. In this year, many e-commerce companies and other industrial and commercial enterprises began to explore the use of B2B. Beijing Electronic Commerce City launched e-commerce between enterprises, and many large domestic enterprises, including Haier Group, began to apply e-commerce within and between enterprises.

E-commerce supporting systems began to take shape at this stage. Online payment was initially tried by China Merchants Bank in 1998 and then entered a diversified practical stage in 1999, the e-commerce payment platform of Beijing Electronic Commerce City being a typical example. The logistic distribution of e-commerce also made a breakthrough in 1999.

At the same time, e-commerce began to be applied in broader areas, e-government, online tax, online education, remote diagnosis being tried in some cities.

10.1.3 The Stabilizing Stage (2000-2007)

In 2000, the number and scale of e-commerce websites in China have entered a period of high expansion, with more than 2,500 websites. The concept of "portal website" was further interpreted as horizontal portal and vertical portal. Several famous portal sites listed overseas one after another, such as sina. com, 163. com, sohu. com, and so on, which has greatly pushed the development of e-commerce in China. However, in the latter half of 2000, NASDAQ stock market continued to fall, bringing a heavy blow to the Internet-based new economy.

B2B got further development in 2000. At the beginning of March, Qingdao Haier and Guangdong Midea announced on the same day stepping into e-commerce; and then Chunlan Group and TCL Group had the similar announcement. Together with some vertical business portals, many network companies provided a platform for transactions between enterprises and its users or suppliers. At the same time, China Electronic Commerce Association (CECA) formally came into being in June 2000.

In 2003, Alibaba Group set up Taobao. com to get into C2C with the investment of 100 million Yuan and the concept of online shopping got more popularity. In the same year, Alibaba launched the "Alipay", with the commitment to providing online payment service on the basis of third party guarantee, formally entering the field of electronic payment. In 2004, the concept "e-businessman" was put forward. In 2005, relying on the huge basis of QQ users, Tencent launched the "Pat Network". In 2006, The First SME E-commerce Application and Development Conference was held in Beijing. In April 2007, PPG received a total of \$50 million of international venture capital. The new direct marketing model of B2C indicated that traditional industries and e-commerce get further integration. In June of this year, the first merger and acquisition case of Industry Web in China was completed, opening the curtain of Industry Webs' integration. In August of the same year, Capital Today invested \$10 million to Jingdong Mall, starting a new era of domestic home appliances.

In this period, Chinese government put forward a series of policies to promote and stimulate the development of e-commerce. In 2001, Provisional Regulations on Internet Banking Management was put forward by the People's Bank of China. The PRC Electronic Signature Law was approved in 2004 and enacted in 2005. In 2005, Guidelines of Electronic Payment (No. 1) was announced, offering comprehensive provisions for norms, safety, technical measures, and accountability of electronic payment. The 11th Five-Year Plan on Electronic Commerce Development was released in 2007, which is the first national development plan on e-commerce. It is the first time to establish strategies and tasks of the e-commerce development at a national policy level.

10.1.4 The Maturity Stage (2008-)

It was the milestone development for e-commerce in 2008. The online shopping transaction exceeded 100 billion for the first time, and B2B market turnover reached 3 trillion Yuan. In 2009, more and more traditional enterprises turned to online shopping. So many giants, such as Founder Group, Legend, Haier in manufacturing, Suning and Gome in home appliance retailing, Cofco in food area, Lining and Septwolves in garment industry, began to make efforts to lead Chinese traditional enterprises to e-commerce marketing era. It will be the general trend of traditional enterprises' shifting to new channels. Therefore, online shopping has enormous development space and potential in the future.

After years of development, e-commerce has entered a booming period since 2010. The sales of major B2C websites almost doubled, and many new B2C platforms and buying sites also sprung up in this year. In 2011, WeChat appeared, and vipshop. com was introduced into the market in the next year. From 2013, cross-border e-commerce and mobile commerce started to emerge.

These years, the nation continues to put forward a series of policies to push the development of e-commerce and the supporting facilities also have got great improvement. E-commerce has entered the stable period of sustainable development.

10.2 CURRENT STATUS OF E-COMMERCE IN CHINA

10.2.1 Rapid Development of E-commerce Market in China

Recent years, e-commerce transactions in China has maintained a rapid growth, the average annual growth rate of which is of 2-3 times. Since exceeding 4 trillion Yuan in 2010, China's e-commerce transaction volume has increased by 2 trillion Yuan per year. It has gradually become an important driving force and engine of national economic growth.

Transaction size of e-commerce

According to the statistics of Chinese E-commerce Research Center, China's e-commerce transaction reached 13. 4 trillion Yuan in 2014. In 2015, the figure raised up to 13. 4 trillion, growing 21. 3% year-on-year. Among them, B2B transactions reached 13. 9 trillion, and online retailing transaction was 3. 828,5 trillion, increasing 39% and 35. 7% respectively. The rapid increasing mainly resulted from the strong support of national polices and the transformation of traditional enterprises into online operations, as well as the soaring number of Internet users.

2011-2016 Chinese E-commerce Transaction Size

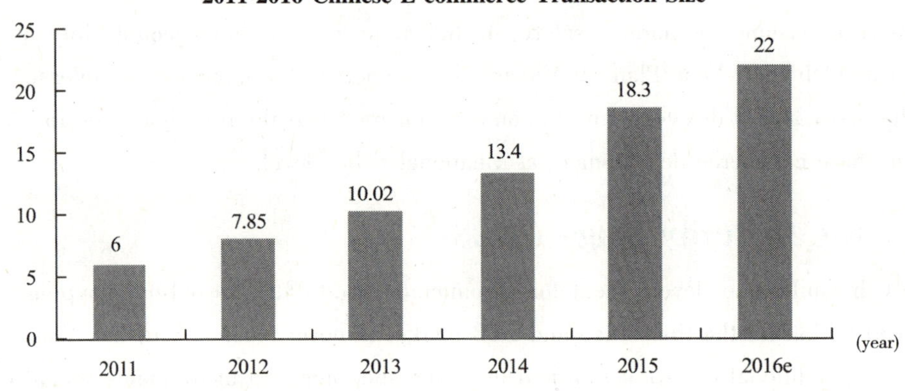

(Transaction amount: trillion Yuan)

Employment size of e-commerce

The rapid development of e-commerce leads to increased demand for talents. Online payment, logistics, personnel management, marketing, finance, online model, industrial park management, all of them are supporting e-commerce industry, creating a lot of new jobs. According to the statistics, till the end of 2015, more than 2. 7 million people were directly employed in the business of e-commerce services, with year-on-year growth of 8%. While, the employment indirectly driven by e-commerce has reached more than 20 million people, an increase of 11%.

B2B transaction

With the support and promotion of the government and the proposal of the Supply-side Reform, B2B business in China is facing new opportunities. Meanwhile, the restructuring of supply chain requires its transformation to demand chain all of these factors have pushed the rapid development of B2B business.

According to the statistics, B2B transactions in 2015 rose to 13.9 trillion, increasing 39% with last year and the revenue of service providers was 22 billion Yuan. As for the B2B market share, Alibaba ranked first, taking up 42% of the market.

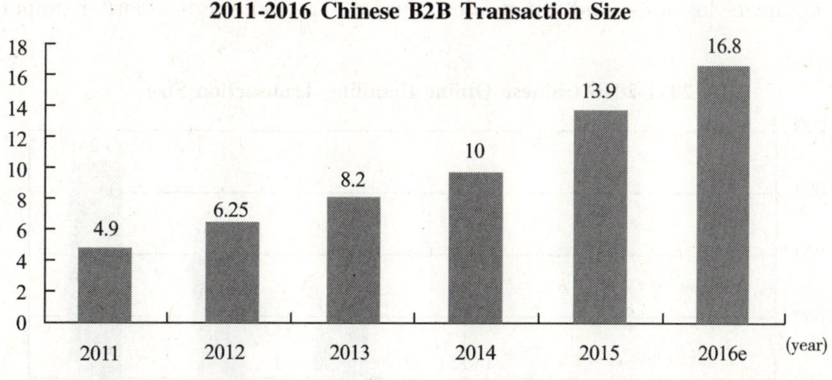

Cross-border e-commerce

In 2015, the government did not only release a lot of policies on the direction of cross-border e-business, it also put forward many specific measures and policy adjustments in various fields. With the gradual deepening of policies and norms, cross-border e-business will get further development.

The statistics of Chinese E-commerce Research Center shows that the cross-border e-business transaction of this year rose up to 5.4 trillion Yuan, with an increase of 28.6% with last year.

Among them cross-border export transactions amounted to 4.49 trillion Yuan, while import amounted to 907.2 billion.

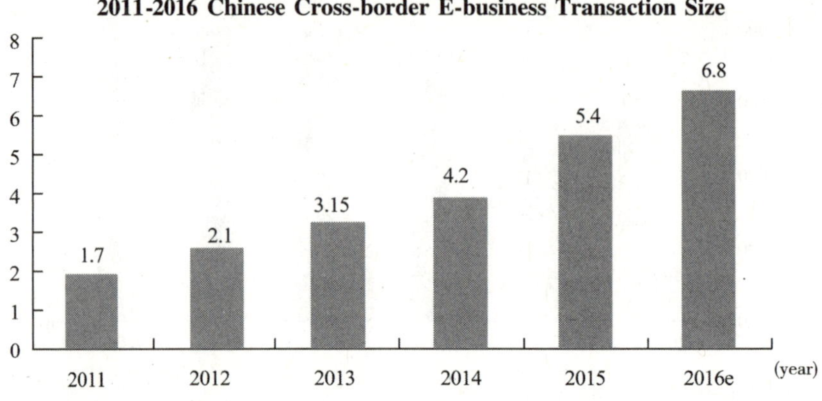

(Transaction amount: trillion Yuan)

Online retailing

According to the statistics, in 2015, the online retailing soared to 3.828,5 trillion Yuan, increasing 35.7% with last year. The following factors has pushed the rapid development of online retailing:

Online retailing market has entered the relative mature stage. It has gone out of the crazy growth phase, returning to a stable range;

The boundaries of different e-business models have gradually blurred, a variety of business models integrated and co-existed;

Almost all the e-business companies are making great efforts to expand the product category, improve and optimize logistics and after-sales service, promote cross-border imports and rural e-commerce.

(Transaction amount: trillion Yuan)

Mobile shopping

Since 2015, many e-business platforms, such as Tmall, Jingdong, vipshop. com, Suning.

com, have made great efforts on mobile terminal, deepening shopping experience and expanding product categories and new business. It is obvious that mobile business will be the major means instead of personal computers.

The statistics of Chinese E-commerce Research Center indicates that the transaction of mobile online shopping reached 2.0184 trillion Yuan in 2015. Compared with the number of 0.9285 trillion in 2014, it had increased by 117.4%. The growth rate is far more than the overall growth rate of online shopping.

2011-2016 Transaction size of Mobile Online Shopping in China

30 000
25 000
20 000
15 000
10 000
5 000
0
116
691
2 731
9 285
20 184
25 420
2011
2012
2013
2014
2015
2016e
(year)

(Transaction amount:0.1 billion Yuan)

Internet consumer finance

With the development of Internet banking, the further upgrading of consumer attitudes, as well as the gradual recognition of the Internet consumer financial services, Internet consumer finance will maintain explosive growth in the next 3 years.

The statistics of 100EC.CN shows that the transaction of Chinese Internet consumer finance soared to 25 billion Yuan in 2015, increasing by 142% with last year.

2011-2016 Chinese Internet Consumer Finance Transaction Size

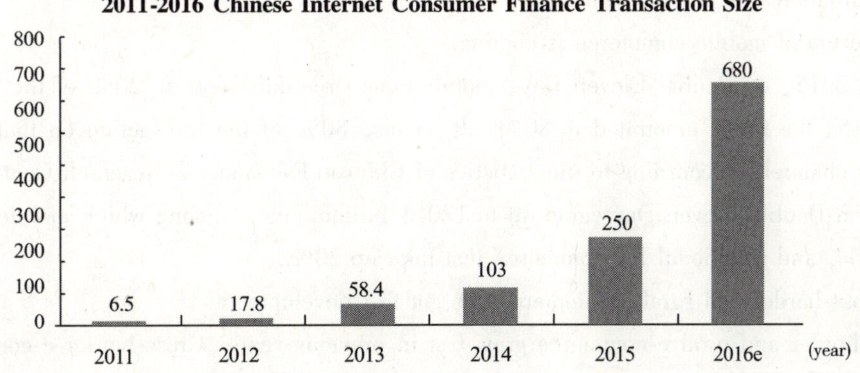

(Transaction amount:0.1 billion Yuan)

10.2.2 Hot Issues of E-commerce Market in China

Concluding the development of e-commerce in previous years, the following issues have attracted public's eyes.

◇ The total transaction of Tmall and Jingdong has exceeded 100 billion Yuan on Double Eleven, the duopoly pattern being formed.

On Double Eleven of 2015, the transaction of Tmall amounted to 91.2 billion Yuan, and Jingdong also surpassed 10 billion. It indicates that the duopoly pattern has been formed, which may not be changed in following 3—5 years.

◇ Big life service platforms have been merged one after another, monopoly and oligopoly taking shape basically.

Many life service platforms have been merged one after another, such as Meituan. com and Dianping. com, Ctrip. com and Qunar. com, Didi and Kuaidadi. com, 58. com and Ganji. com. Baidu invested into Nuomi, and Alibaba supported Koubei. com. Thus, only a few major life service platforms still keep remaining.

◇ E-commerce giants have invested in offline businesses, the integration of online and offline getting into a new era.

Although the bubble of O2O entrepreneurship had retreated, the integration of online and offline became a major event in 2015. Alibaba invested in Suning and Intime Department Store, while Jingdong put investment in Yonghui Supermarket Co. Ltd. The development of e-commerce companies requires their offline channel to get more flows. Offline channel will be the most important entry of flows for these companies.

◇ Traditional brands have accelerated the transformation of e-commerce.

The ranking of transactions on Double Eleven in 2015 indicates that 80% of the top three categories belong to traditional brands, far exceeding Internet marketing brands. While, before 2015, the situation was just the opposite.

◇ The era of mobile commerce is coming.

Before 2015, on Double Eleven Day, mobile commerce only took up 20% of the transaction, while in 2015, the figure amounted to 80%. It means, 80% of the transaction on that day comes from mobile channels. According to the statistics of Chinese E-commerce Research Center, the total transaction on Double Eleven Day came up to 120.1 billion Yuan, among which mobile transaction is up to 80%, and traditional PC commerce just take up 20%.

◇ Cross-border and rural e-commerce has got fast development.

Cross-border and rural e-commerce grew fast in previous years. Cross-border e-commerce rose to 5.4 trillion Yuan, increasing by 28.6% in 2015, and 2.6 trillion Yuan in the first half of 2016, with an increase of 30%. Whereas in the first half of 2016, the online shopping in rural regions has amounted to 31.20 billion Yuan. It is estimated to rise to 64.75 billion Yuan in the whole year.

◇ The whole nation push forward "Internet plus" initiative, Internet penetrating into all areas.

Under the advocacy and promotion of the Prime Minister and the government in the year of 2015, "Internet plus" is not only the government's action plan, but also the focus of enterprise innovation. Internet has penetrated into all walks of society.

◇ Capital has become the strong force of pushing the entrepreneurship and development of e-commerce.

In the year of 2015, many entrepreneurship incubation bases in various areas got rapid development, as represented by Zhongguancun Business Street, Hackerspace, Start-up Cafe, etc. Various kinds of angel funds and private equity (PE) has become the powerful force of industry transformation and upgrading of M&A.

10.3 CHARACTERISTICS OF E-COMMERCE DEVELOPMENT IN CHINA

At present, the development of e-commerce is stepping into a new era of intensive innovation and rapid expansion, gradually becoming the significant engine of stimulating the demand for consumption, promoting the upgrading of traditional industry and developing modern service industry. In all, it has following characteristics:

◇ China's e-commerce continues maintaining rapid growth with huge potential. Recent years, the transaction of e-commerce has maintained the rapid growth rate. Online retailing is developing especially rapid, which can be indicated in previous analysis. There is no doubt that e-commerce is becoming an important driving force to promote the rapid and sustainable growth of the national economy.

◇ The application of e-commerce has been expanded. Recent years, the service industry and enterprises have accelerated their pace of informatization, thus the demand for e-commerce applications has become increasingly strong. A lot of traditional industries have made good achievements in the application of e-commerce. Rural informatization has made gratifying achievements. With the innovation of e-commerce application mode, a number of Taobao stores have emerged. Some villages have applied e-commerce with their own characteristics around their resources and market advantages. Traditional retailers are moving into e-commerce. Other industries, including post, tourism and insurance have put their efforts into e-commerce on the basis of their existing informatization construction.

◇ The service industry of e-commerce has developed rapidly, a fully functional system taking the primary shape. The development patterns of service industry are evolving. B2B and B2C have being accelerated their integration, and transformed from information platform to transaction platform. The retail e-commerce platform has developed vigorously, which includes three forms: the integrated platform with comprehensive coverage of products, the vertical platform with the focus on market segmentation and the gradual transformation of large enterprises' own websites to third party platform. As for supporting services, many great changes have arisen. Various aspects of supporting function are increasingly independent, showing a high degree of division of labor. The new generation of information technology has got rapid application in e-commerce services. Apart from Internet of Things, Big Data is gradually making data mining play its function on precision marketing. In addition, the function of e-commerce platform is becoming more and more comprehensive. To support e-commerce service, some new services are created around the online transaction, such as net bargainer, online modeling, operating services and outsourcing of online stores, etc.

◇ Cross-border transaction has developed rapidly. Under the worldwide sluggish economic situation, China's small and medium-sized foreign trade enterprises are still developing fast, keeping an average annual growth rate of 30%. Authorities concerned are stepping up efforts to improve supporting policies and measures on platform, logistics, payment and settlement of cross-border online transaction. Various new models appeared, such as one-stop promotion, platform operation, the combination of online shopping business and exhibition, and so on. More "made in China" products have been sold into foreign markets through online platforms, which has effectively promoted the development of cross-border e-commerce.

In addition, the environment for the development of e-commerce is constantly improving. The awareness of e-commerce application in the whole society continues to increase, and the application skills have been improved effectively. The mechanism of jointly promoting the development of e-commerce among relevant departments has been preliminarily established. A series of polices, rules and standards on electronic certification and online shopping have been introduced, carrying out active exploration in building a good environment for e-commerce development.

10.4 TRENDS OF E-COMMERCE DEVELOPMENT IN CHINA

As a new industry, e-commerce has gradually stepped into mature and stable development stage. According to the analysis of of Chinese E-commerce Research Center, the development of e-commerce may have the following trends:

◇ Cross-border e-commerce will keep the rapid development in following years.

With the enhancement of international purchasing power, the increasing of Internet penetration rate, the improvement of logistics and online payment, cross-border e-commerce will continue to maintain rapid growth in future. Cross-border exporters are expanding from Guangdong, Jiangsu, Zhejiang provinces to the midwest China. The exporting products are extending from low gross margin standard products of 3C to some new categories, such as clothing, outdoor supplies, health beauty, Home & Garden, auto parts, and so on, which will provide a new space for the export of e-commerce in China. Besides, with the constant joining of new markets, such as Brazil and Russia, the popularization and development of Internet technology, the continuous improvement of infrastructure and the continuous releasing of policies, the development space of online export will be further expanded.

Countries with minor languages will become a new regional growth point of cross-border e-commerce. The traditional export markets center on four countries: the United States, Britain, Australia and Germany. However, since two years ago, the export to some countries with minor languages, such as France, Italy, Spain and Southeast Asia, has got rapid growth. These countries have become a new growth area of cross-border e-commerce in future.

Traditional foreign trade enterprises will become the mainstream of cross-border e-commerce. Recent years, more and more traditional foreign trade enterprises have started cross-border e-commerce, and B2B has become their major marketing channel. These enterprises will deal with foreign consumers directly to establish and upgrade their brands, as well as enhances the core competitiveness.

◇ E-commerce market in rural area has got rapid growth, the rate of which is faster than that of cities. and this trend will continue.

The entering of rural market has achieved initial success, which has, to some extent, changed the consumption habits of rural users, improved logistics construction, and enhanced the demand for e-commerce in rural areas.

The statistics of Chinese E-commerce Research Center shows that the size of online shopping market in rural areas rose to 181.70 trillion Yuan in 2014, and 353.00 trillion in 2015, with an increase of 94.3% with last year. In the first half of 2016, the figure has already amounted to 321 trillion Yuan, and it is estimated to rose up to 647.50 trillion at the end of this year.

The rapid growth of rural residents' consumption demand and the constant investment of government and e-commerce enterprises have greatly promoted the development of e-commerce in rural areas. However, poor infrastructures of rural e-commerce, lack of talents, and immature business model have constrained its development. To solve these problems, the government and enterprises should cooperate together to actively support and vigorously promote the relevant projects.

◇ O2O model of retail industry has great potential in future.

In past few years, the number of "Internet plus" startups increased significantly, and mobile apps are booming. From the point of consumers, the most popular O2O models are applied to catering takeout, tourism, online comments and taxi-hailing; while as for the app which is not in use but will be considered in the future, the application may focus on supermarket and convenience purchasing, as well as fresh food purchasing.

In the digital era, although consumers' purchasing model has changed a lot, convenience, comfort and price can still exert great influence on their purchasing-decision. They do not want to give up the experience of consumption, but also wish to enjoy the convenience of online shopping.

◇ Mobile commerce will explore new models of consumption and marketing.

With the popularization of smart phones, mobile shopping market in China has maintained rapid development. According to the statistics of Chinese E-commerce Research Center, the transaction of mobile online shopping reached 201.84 trillion Yuan in 2015 and 160.70 trillion in the first half of 2016. The mobile buyers are mainly people at the age of 26—35 (accounting for

53%), or people with bachelor degree or above (accounting for 80%).

Mobile shopping has diverse models, and the application related to different scenes has become a new growth point of promoting traffic. In the year of 2015, those websites related to the application in different contexts, such as Meituan. com, Dianping. com, Ctrip. com, have already promoted the increase of network traffic. It is obvious that mobile shopping is closely connected with shopping contexts.

Another exploring model of mobile e-commerce is the socialization of online marketing, which means some social elements, such as following, sharing, communication, discussion and interaction, are applied to the process of mobile transaction. The proportion of "enter through clicking friend's sharing" has increased from 12% in 2014 to 23% in 2015. Whereas, the utilization of other mobile entrance has decreased significantly or just remained barely even.

SUMMARY

This chapter mainly discusses issues related to the development of e-commerce in China, including the history, the current status, the characteristics and trends. E-commerce in China started from the initial application of EDI standard in Chinese foreign trade enterprises and then experienced four stages: the budding stage, developing stage, stabilizing stage and maturity stage. Recent years, e-commerce transactions in China has maintained a rapid growth, which can be shown in the growth of the total transaction size, employment figure in e-commerce field, B2B transaction, cross-border e-commerce, online retailing, mobile shopping and online consumer finance. E-commerce has gradually become an important driving force of national economic growth. As the environment for the development of e-commerce is constantly improving, in future, service industry, cross-border and rural e-commerce will keep the rapid development. Mobile e-commerce will explore new models of consumption and marketing.

Words and Expressions

①**acquisition**: something such as a building, another company, or a piece of land that is bought by a company, or the act of buying it 收购

②**app**: software designed to run inside a web browser or on smartphones and other mobile devices 应用程序

③**bargainer**: negotiator of the terms of a transaction 讨价还价者

④**big data**: a term for data sets that are so large or complex that traditional data processing application software is inadequate to deal with them 大数据

⑤**CAGR**: compound annual growth rate 复合年增长率

⑥**entrepreneurship**: skill in starting new businesses, especially when this involves seeing new opportunities 创业精神

⑦**Internet plus**: the application of the Internet and other information technology in conventional industries 互联网 +

⑧**merger**: the combination of two or more commercial companies (企业等的)合并

⑨**network traffic**: also data traffic, the amount of data moving across a network at a given point of time 网络流量

⑩**online shopping**: a form of electronic commerce which allows consumers to directly buy goods or services from a seller over the Internet using a web browser 网上购物

⑪**provider**: a group or company that provides a specified service 供应商

⑫**settlement**: the process of exchanging the consideration for financial instruments once a transaction has been executed 结算

⑬**SMS**: short message service 短信服务

Exercises

Ⅰ. **Key Terms** (Explain the following terms.)

①EDI

②e-government

③mobile commerce

④social network

Ⅱ. **Multiple Choice Exercises** (Choose the correct answer to the following questions from A, B, C and D. There is only one correct answer.)

①The development of e-commerce in China started from the initial application of EDI standard ________.

A. online retailing　　B. internal management of enterprises

C. in Chinese foreign trade enterprises　　D. Both A and B

②Which bank of the following is the first one who introduced the online payment business in China ________.

A. Bank of China　　B. China Construction Bank

C. China Merchants Bank　　D. Industrial and Commercial Bank of China

③The rapid increasing of the e-commerce transaction in China is mainly resulted from ________.

A. the strong support of national polices

B. the transformation of traditional enterprises into online operations

C. the soaring number of Internet users

D. All of them

④The rapid development of cross-border e-commerce in China is mainly because ________.

A. authorities concerned are stepping up efforts to improve supporting policies and measures

B. the awareness of e-commerce application in the whole society continues to increase

C. the application skills of e-commerce have been improved effectively

D. all of them

⑤Which of the following is not the trend of e-commerce development in China?

A. Cross-border e-commerce will keep the rapid development in the following years.

B. E-commerce market in rural area will continue to get rapid growth.

C. O2O model of retail industry has great potential in future.

D. Mobile commerce will be replaced by other new forms.

⑥What is the feature of e-commerce development in China these years?

A. The application of e-commerce has been expanded.

B. The service industry of e-commerce has developed rapidly.

C. Cross-border transaction has developed rapidly.

D. All of them.

⑦Chinese traditional export markets does not include ________.

A. the United States　　B. Japan

C. Australia and Germany　　D. Britain

⑧Which of the following can exert great influence on consumers' purchasing decision?

A. Convenience.　　B. Comfort.

C. Price.　　D. All of them.

Ⅲ. Review Questions

①How many stages has the development of e-commerce experienced in China?

②What are the characteristics of the development of e-commerce in China?

③What are the trends of the development of e-commerce in China?

Ⅳ. Online Practice

①Online retailing has been developing fast in China in recent years, represented by the sharp sales increase of Tmall, Jingdong and Vipshop. com. Please visit these three sites, analyze their services and features, and summarize the trends of online retailing.

②Please visit one life service platform, such as Meituan. com, Dianping. com, Ctrip. com. And then analyze their features and models.

③E-commerce market in rural area has got rapid growth in China. Please visit some relevant sites, and then analyze the characteristics and trends of rural e-commerce.

Ⅴ. Case Study

10 Key Factors of Success for E-commerce in China

With 243 million of e-shoppers and an annual increase of 30 million new users, China e-commerce is taking more and more share in the global e-commerce market.

What are the key factors for e-commerce business in China?

1. Localization in China

Website hosted outside of mainland China takes a very long time to charge.

A good e-commerce website in China requires host in China. And an ICP certificate is also very important in order to have less chance to be censured by the government. All the successful e-commerce website in China are host in China with ICP.

One of the best Chinese search engines is Baidu. Nevertheless some negative feedbacks exist about Chinese hosts regarding instability problems or suspected to provide IPs to the governments or to sell IP to competitors.

2. Logistic

One challenge is to be able to deliver products to the entire country. Delivery is not an easy work to do, and all the companies in the field are fighting over prices and profits are low. With an average 3—4 Yuan's margin in this sector (according to the Association of Logistics China), it remains a challenge for many companies.

3. The Price

Internet in China today almost equals to a place where consumers can find the lowest prices. Chinese consumers will compare a large number of websites before making a choice price oriented.

Solutions: bring prices beating all competitors on a unique product in the whole country (exclusive offer).

4. Gaining Confidence of Cyber-Consumers

Chinese consumers remain very cautious due to the number of scandals in the country. Consumers take trust rating as the KPI on Taobao is the best example of it.

It is important for a website to work on its image, to gain the trust of users. Cross-media campaigns are often useful to gain notoriety. For example VANCL used Hanhan as brand ambassador and have launched classic advertising campaigns.

5. Your Website Should Respect Chinese Standards

Chinese buyers do not use PayPal but Alipay or Tenpay. Concerning delivery for small amounts in China, many websites make it possible to pay at the reception.

The design of the website also have some convention to follow. For instance a Chinese website will use a smaller typography, more informations on one page, with a larger variations in color codes. It is preferable not to copy and paste a western version of your website which will probably not appeal to people who already accustomed to the Chinese pattern of design.

6. A Streamlined Purchase Process

Three steps represents an average for most of Chinese e-commerce websites. A website that takes more than 5 steps before buying is considered too complex by Chinese netizens. Display time of websites in China is much longer than what we know in the West, so the less pages are, the better for Chinese netizen. With the rapid development of China's e-commerce, streamlining the purchasing process remains an objective.

7. How to Increase Your Conversion Rate?

Professional photos can improve the conversion rate in B to C business (and even in B to B).

Videos are necessary to show the features of your products. Chinese are very pragmatics.

Descriptive texts are needed to foster consumers' awareness. For example, in the field of wine, the best performing sites are those that explain the history of the wine with tasting guides.

Please check the following example: a Tmall shop designed for Afu Mythical.

8. Promotion

Chinese people in real life have a habit of buying by negotiating price. For many Chinese the price without bargain is an unfavorable deal. This phenomenon is even more popular online.

For example, the Singles' Day organized by Taobao proposed discounts that have attracted millions of orders per day.

9. Visibility

The most difficult task for a website is to attract visitors. How to increase your traffic? This target can be achieved via a good SEO or SEM campaign.

SEM: search engine marketing campaigns, i.e. pay per click, are effective in some areas and less in others. For Baidu, these campaigns have the advantage to make you appear in the 11 first natural results. But the price of the click can be very high for certain sectors. For instance you may have to pay 25 Yuan for keywords such as buy "wine" or "cosmetic".

SEO: the best way to gain visitors economically, and therefore to foster your sales. SEO in China is mainly on Baidu (80%) and a little on Google. com. hk.

Social Networks: community management is another tool to attract traffic for your website. It's a good way to build a customer loyalty. Once a site is running and generate sales, a good integration of social networks will be very interesting.

10. Instant Messaging

Very few Chinese use email. Indeed they prefer instant messaging to communicate directly with the salesman. Generally, Chinese websites include QQ messaging or click to WeChat' systems.

In China SMS or phone calls are frequently used to confirm an order, when in western countries the email remains the most widely used communication tool.

Chinese people often have various email addresses they do not consult. Mass emailing in China is rather inefficient. On the contrary promotional campaigns sent on mobile shows an extraordinary efficiency nowadays.

Conclusion: E-commerce in 2012 generated more than 1,000 billion Yuan of transactions (45% for B2C and 55% for B2B) (source: iResearch) and will remain a huge market for western brands.

Questions for Discussion

①What are the key factors of success for e-commerce business in China?

②What are the main processes to increase the traffic of a website?

Chapter 11 Electronic Commerce Laws

本章导读

电子商务法是指调整平等主体之间通过电子行为设立、变更和消灭财产关系和人身关系的法律规范的总称；是政府调整、企业和个人以数据电文为交易手段，通过信息网络所产生的，因交易形式所引起的各种商事交易关系，以及与这种商事交易关系密切相关的社会关系、政府管理关系的法律规范的总称。本章介绍了电子商务法的概念与分类，电子商务法的调整对象和范围及其在法律体系中的地位、性质和作用；也阐释了电子商务法的基本原则、性质与特点。最后本章讨论了我国当前电子市场潜在的风险，通过提出建议，以加深对电子商务立法的理解。

Business Terms

①**oligopoly market**: The oligopoly market is a mixed market between monopolistic competition and monopoly. It is a market form in which a market or industry is dominated by a small number of sellers (oligopolists). Oligopolies can result from various forms of collusion which reduce competition and lead to higher prices for consumers. Oligopoly has its own market structure.

②**EC-logistics**: It refers to using electronic means, in particular the Internet technology, to complete the whole process of logistics coordination, control and management. So as to achieve all the intermediate process services from the network front-end to the client.

③**civil aviation law**: It is a law which is in order to safeguard the national sovereignty of territorial airspace, the rights of civil aviation, civil aviation safety and orderly operation. It can protect the legitimate rights and interests of all parties involved in civil aviation activities, and promote the development of the civil aviation industry law.

④**maritime law**: It refers to the floorboard of legal norms for the specific social relations, such as the loss of or damage to or loss of or damage to the ship or other property or casualty caused by an accident which is caused by an accident in the sea or other navigable waters.

⑤**electronic commerce disputes**: In the process of merchandise sales, suppliers, carriers and demander have different views on the transport effects, the duties and obligations set out in the contract.

⑥**the right of consumers' personal information privacy**: The right of privacy is a kind of personality right which is enjoyed by the natural person, and has a personal information, private activity and private field which is independent of the public interests.

⑦**anti-monopoly law**: It is a part in order to prevent and stop the monopoly behavior, protecting fair competition in the market, enhancing economic efficiency, safeguarding the interests of consumers and social public interests, promoting the healthy development of the socialist market economy and the development of law.

Introductory Case

In May 30th, at the 2017 Beijing international service trade fair, the 2017 China e-commerce conference, *New Business: Electricity Supplier Integrity and Business Model Innovation*, was opened. The forum was sponsored by the China Business Culture Research Association, Peking University, Guanghua School of Management and Beijing daily newspaper group.

The forum called on the community to fully understand the significance of strengthening the integrity in the field of e-commerce, to promote clear supply side structural reform, expand the effective supply, accelerate the transformation of economic development mode, enhance the driving force of economic development, solve the problem of lack of trust in e-commerce transaction parties. Electronic business has an important role in promoting public entrepreneurship and innovation.

The forum invited the main person in charge of the industry authorities, associations and judicial organs. This forum carried on a thorough discussion on how to innovate the market supervision mode, to build enterprise credit system under the environment of e-commerce; how to rectify and regulate the market order, to create e-commerce development environment of honesty and trustworthiness; how to promote the integrity of electronic commerce; how to formulate relevant laws and regulations and standards and so on. Meanwhile, the organizers also invited a number of well-known domestic electricity supplier business leaders, to discuss how to build an electricity supplier integrity system for the healthy development of online shopping environment.

Statistics from the Ministry of Commerce show that in 2016, China's online retail transactions amounted to 5 trillion and 160 billion Yuan, an increase of 26.2%. Among them, the amount of online retail transactions of physical goods was 4 trillion and 190 billion Yuan, an increase of 25.6%, and the total retail sales of consumer goods in the same period increased by 15.2%. Online retail market continues to maintain high growth. At the same time, the integrity problems such as counterfeiting, malicious fraud, false propaganda and violation of privacy have become increasingly prominent in e-commerce. In accordance with the Party Central Committee and the State Council's decision to deploy, and to vigorously promote the integrity of e-commerce system construction, we should give full play to the role of the government in organizing, leading and promoting, and also to the role of the market mechanism, encouraging and supporting the active participation of social forces, such as credit service institutions, and jointly to promote the formation of working force.

Questions for Discussion

①What is the current urgent problem of e-commerce in our country?

②Can you make some suggestions for the standardization of e-commerce in China?

11.1 OVERVIEW OF EC LAWS

Electronic commerce law refers to generic terms of the law which adjusts the social relations in the electronic commerce activities. It is a new legal field. In recent years, many countries and international organizations in the world have made a lot of regulation of e-commerce legal norms. That forms many legal documents of electronic commerce. According to an uncompleted statistic, dozens of countries and regions have enacted and promulgated the substantive e-commerce law so far. Since 1980 to now, many scholars of the world have already begun the investigation of electronic commerce law. It has accumulated a large number of practical cases. Above all, the globalization of electronic commerce law's legislation fully reflects the critical fuction to regulate the electronic commerce activities between the countries.

11.1.1 The Regulating Object of Electronic Commerce Law

Any legal operation department and legal field's regulating object will always be social relation. With the development of electronics and communication technology, the forms of commercial transaction have also become more and more diverse. Securities trading, paper circulation, the operation of the company, banking, insurance, investment and other industries can't do without electronic means. If there is no special electronic commerce law to adjust it, it may seriously hinder the development of commercial relations. In other words, the relation of electronic transaction has become a social relation which must be regulated by the law. It is one of the major reasons of electronic commerce law's emerging.

11.1.2 The Status of Electronic Commerce Law

The position of e-commerce law refers to its position in the whole legal system. It should be a new legal department in a new situation. The content of e-commerce law covers every aspect of social life. It is not something that any existing legal department can accommodate. The criterion for judging the existence of a legal department is to see if he has a particular object of adjustment. The three segments of electronic commerce, the social relationships arising from information flow, logistics and capital flows, are the special adjustment objects of electronic commerce law. The common of its adjustment objects is that they all move through the network. So electronic commerce law is an all-new and independent legal operation department.

11.1.3 The Subject of Electronic Commerce Law

The development of e-commerce is the result of the collaboration of various subjects, such as the government, enterprises and consumers. It can't be lack of participation and support of either party.

In a framework for global electronic commerce, the US government said that business is the main part of e-commerce. But this framework's publishment has already indicated that the government is responsible for the development of e-commerce.

For the other two types of subjects in e-commerce activities, obviously, the enterprise is the main body of the market and the main force of e-commerce. It is both an initiator and a consequence taker. And consumers are the ultimate service goal of e-commerce. It is also the source of innovation in business models.

11.2 THE CHARACTERISTICS OF ELECTRONIC COMMERCE LAW

The electronic commerce law has the following characteristics:

11.2.1 Internationalism

IT information technology' development promotes the process of economic globalization and market integration. Electronic commerce has been a cosmopolitan economic activity. Therefore, its legal framework should not be restricted to the rang of one country. In the cyber space, traditional management method isn't suited. And it is uncertain that whosever law is fit for electronic commerce. Hence we need to formulate a commonly used law to solve joint legal issue and make a clear distinction of legal liability. Finally electronic commerce law need to fit the demand of all over the world. So internationalism is one of the characteristics of electronic commerce law.

11.2.2 Technicality

Electronic commerce is produced by modern high-tech. Its activity needs Internet to achieve. Electronic commerce law serves as a supervisor of this activity. It is also indispensable for it to have this characteristic. electronic commerce law makes reasonable stipulation for the technical question of electronic commerce. And that will make electronic commerce go on the track of sound progress.

11.2.3 Openness

Electronic commerce law is a developing law. So we have an open attitude to any technological means and information media and all the ideas and skills which are beneficial to the development of electronic commerce. It is always reflected in the openness of electronic commerce's basic definition and legal structure.

11.2.4 Security

Computer networks' technicality and openness make huge vulnerablility its characteristic. Electronic commerce law is responsible for solving the security issue of electronic commerce. It effectively prevents various kinds of cyber crime by the means of ordering the activity of electronic commerce. So security is one of the characteristics of electronic commerce law.

11.2.5 Collaboration

Electronic commerce's collaboration is from the complexity and dependence of its technological means. Such as Access Serve provided by Web Service, Digital Certificate offered by Certification Authority and Delivery Activity supplied by Third-Party Logistics. And that makes complexity a characteristic of electronic commerce's business transaction. It asks for full-scale legal regulation and the adhibition of ample subject knowledge.

11.2.6 Procedural

In the electronic commerce law, there are a large number of procedural stipulations. Those are used to solve the pro forma issue of business and don't involve the contents of transaction.

11.3 THE BASIC PRINCIPLES OF ELECTRONIC COMMERCE

The basic principles of the electronic commerce law mean three aspects. First it refers to the generality of non laws. Second, it is a general provision as provided for by law. Third, it have legally binding, although it is not stated in the legal text. For example, electronic commerce law's pricinple of trade freely is served as the standard of other articles.

11.3.1 Trading Self-restraint

It is the basic property of the trading law that the litigants are allowed to determine the rules of transactions by the agreement. So, in the processing of electronic commerce law's legislation, we should be guided by the principle of autonomy. Reserve sufficient space for the parties to express their wishes in full and provide substantial protection. Electronic commerce subjects have the right to decide whether they will do business or not, with who and how. This fully embodies the autonomy of e-commerce. Any transaction that is contrary to the will of the parties is invalid.

11.3.2 Equality of Eevidence

Electronic signatures and electronic documents shall have the same legal status as written signatures and written documents. The electronic documents of electronic commerce include electronic commerce contracts and electronic bill flowing in electronic commerce. Electronic documents are quite different from traditional paper documents. The essence of an electronic document is a set of electronic information. It has broken through the definition of documents by traditional laws. In the electronic commerce, traditional paper documents, such as trade contract, insurance policy, bill of lading, invoice, will be replaced by electronic files stored in the computer. These electronic documents are the electronic evidence in the evidence law. Legal provisions on electronic evidence are gradually being added to the laws of many countries. Electronic evidence has acquired the same legal status as the traditional written evidence.

11.3.3 Neutrality

Above all, the basic goal of the electronic commerce law is to establish a fair trading rule in e-commerce activities. This is the inevitable embodiment of the commercial security principle from the commercial law in the electronic commerce law. In order to realize the balance of the interests of all parties involved in the transaction and achieve a fair goal, we must accomplish the following:

Technical neutrality

The electronic commerce law must allow the use of current technology to solve problems like electronic signatures. New technologies must also be adopted.

Media neutrality

It is the concrete expression of the principle of neutrality in various communication media. It focuses on the carrier of information, such as wireless communications, cable communications, television, radio, mobile phones, the Internet and so on. Electronic commerce law treats these media with a neutral principle. Various media are allowed to fuse with each other and promote each other. That can make full use of all kinds of resources.

Implementation neutrality

It refers to the implementation of the e-commerce law and other relevant laws cannot do one thing and neglect the other. In our country, the legal treatment of e-commerce activities and transnational e-commerce activities should be treated equally. In particular, we cannot attach more importance to the legal effect of the traditional written environment than electronic commerce. Law shall be uniform and impartial. Determine the implementation of the law with specific environmental characteristics.

Equal protection

Electronic commerce law should do the same protection to both businesses and consumers. Because the e-commerce market is international, under the condition of modern communication technology, fragmented and closed e-commerce market cannot survive.

11.3.4 Protect the Legitimate Rights and Interests of Consumers

With the development of electronic commerce market, all countries have enacted laws concerning the protection of consumers' rights and interests. Efforts are made to achieve balanced protection between the two sides of the transaction. But these laws that protect consumer rights are rules for traditional forms of trade. In the electronic commerce environment, its strength does not match its ambitions. Therefore, electronic commerce law must be established for the protection of consumers' interests for electronic commerce. International rules must also be coordinated, in order to let the consumer make a trade operation and protect their rights and interests.

11.3.5 Safety Principle

To ensure the security of e-commerce is not only its primary task, but also one of its basic principles. Electronic commerce, with its efficient and quick features, stands out in various forms of business transactions. Efficient and fast electronic commerce must be based on security, not only the security of technology but also the law's guard. The e-commerce law consistently runs through safety principles and concepts, such as the recognition of the effectiveness of the message data, the elimination of legal uncertainty in the manner in which electronic commerce operates, and the operational standards established according to e-commerce activities.

11.4 EC THIRD PARTY LOGISTIC LAWS

11.4.1 EC Third-party Logistic Laws' status and Characteristics

Our country is lack of the basic law of the third party logistics.

In the course of the third party logistics operation, different problems need different laws to regulate, and there is no law applicable to all cases. Therefore, a full range of legal system is needed. For example, "general principles of the civil law" and "contract law" apply to adjust the relationship between the third party logistics contract. "Company law" applies to the enterprise's establishment, change, termination and so on. These laws can play a basic role in the guidance and protection of the development of the third party logistics.

The legislation of the core transport links of logistics is scattered.

The core of logistics transport links of the basic law is "civil aviation law", "maritime law" and "railway law". But it lacks the legal provisions of road transport and inland waterway transport. In this case most of the logistics activities either adapting to the "contract law" in general, or to a number of administrative rules and regulations issued by China's traffic management department.

Third party electronic logistics is a fusion of onerous contract and bilateral contract.

The bilateral contract means that the parties to the contract have the obligation to each other. Onerous contract refers to the rights that the parties bear the equal value of the contract. Third party logistics enterprise is responsible for the acceptance of goods, the extraction of goods and timely reporting to the customer the progress of the relevant logistics services, to ensure that goods are delivered to the designated location in a timely manner, to protect the buyers and sellers of the information, and to collect the corresponding remuneration.

Third party electronic logistics often involves many kinds of contract relations.

Electronic commerce in the third party logistics enterprises transformed from the traditional private transformation, the operation of the standard is not standardized, loose internal management. When many third party logistics enterprises are busy, they will pass the cooperation which need to be signed between the two sides of other cooperative enterprises, which produces more than two kinds of cooperation contracts. This leads to a long chain of cooperation, uncontrollable risk and the decline in the quality of service and loss of the long-term development of the third party logistics enterprises.

11.4.2 Legal Problems in the Third Party Logistics Enterprises

It's difficult to determine the jurisdiction of electronic commerce disputes.

Firstly, it is difficult to establish the jurisdiction of the dispute between the third party logistics enterprises and sellers. Secondly it is also difficult to establish the jurisdiction of the dispute with the buyer. The main reason is that our country's law on the litigation jurisdiction caused by the contract dispute has a clear regulation: The court exercises jurisdiction over the place where the defendant is located or where the contract is performed. This shows that the real transactions in the dispute are easy to establish jurisdiction. But the third party logistics runs through the middle link, and the electronic commerce regulatory system cannot keep up with the speed of the development of the commercial economy. There is no way to regulate the occurrence of disputes, unable to define the responsibility of the dispute, as well as to determine the specific jurisdiction of the court.

China's law does not specify the nature of the third party logistics contract.

Third party logistics business is a link in the whole industry chain link, involving many aspects of the rich variety of business. On the basis of traditional business transportation, information management, principal-agent, consulting services and other services are derived. At the same time, China's "contract law" does not make clear provisions on the third party logistics contract. If by any chance, electronic commerce third party logistics dispute happens, the contract content will be very confusing.

The burden of dispute is hard to collect.

Contract between third logistics enterprises and both sides of supply and demand is stored in the computer in the form of electronic document. But there is a possibility of tampering with electronic data. In the event of a dispute, the seller is difficult to find evidence to prove that the goods are damaged in transit, and litigation failure will be the end because the evidence is difficult to collect.

11.4.3 Legal Countermeasures to Regulate the Third Party Logistics

- Constructing the system of the third party logistics laws and regulations, strengthening the legal system of the government regulation.
- Transforming the government functions in the field of third party logistics management, delegating administrative examination and approval authority.
- Constructing the legal system of the third party logistics and promoting the policy orientation of the market reform.

11.5 EC THRID-PARTY PAYMENT LAWS

Third party payment platform is a new thing in the development of online shopping transaction. It is not only related to the success or failure of each transaction, but also related to the safety of a large number of funds and social stability. The legal relationship between both sides of business and the third party payment platform can be explained by the agency relationship. At the macro level, we need to control the operation and financial risks of the third party payment platform.

11.5.1 The Legal Relationship of the Third Party Payment Platform

Firstly, from the legal relationship between the seller and the third party payment platform, it should belong to the contractual relationship. Through the participation of the third party payment platform, the seller increases its transaction credit, which makes it possible for the network transaction between the seller and the consumer. In addition, the accumulation of credit evaluation by the seller and the buyer in the long-term trading process, the third party payment platform provides a valid proof of the seller's credit.

Generally, the legal relationship between the seller and the third party payment platform is relatively clear. But in reality, the seller may be individual network operators, and the third party payment platform is usually a strong service provider, or even a dominant operator. Therefore, there is a significant difference between the actual strength of the two. Thus, the third party payment platform may use its advantage position to delay the payment of goods, etc. This is the one aspect that needs the law to relieve.

Secondly, the legal relationship between the buyer and the third party payment platform should belong to the legal relationship between the third party and the trustee. Third party payment platform replaces the seller and collects payment, waiting for the buyer to confirm the payment of the order to the seller after the transfer of the goods.

In this process, the issue of capital ownership is essential. One view believes that in order to protect the interests of the buyer, it should be modeled on the securities companies trading patterns. Set up a separate trading account in the third party trading platform for each buyer to determine the account of the funds for the buyer. Another view is that the third party payment platform should be similar to the commercial bank. When the funds go into the platform, its ownership has been transferred. At present, the first view is generally supported, for it is conducive to consumer protection. But in accordance with the basic rules of currency ownership, ownership and possession of money cannot be separated. When the currency is transferred, the ownership of the money should be transferred too. Moreover, to determine the funds in the name of the buyer, if the buyer does not pay the purchase price, it will be difficult to complete the case of the transaction. Even if the securities companies are still in the presence of the company's misappropriation of customer funds and other circumstances, in electronic transactions to protect consumers is not enough to be a reason for the support of buyer control the fund.

In the end, it is a kind of legal technology to regard the relationship between the two parties and the third party payment platform as agent. But it still has difference between purely agents. Third party payment platform in the transaction process should be fair to the seller and the buyer, not be partial to favor the seller, thereby enhancing the buyer's confidence in the completion of the transaction.

11.5.2 Legal Regulation of the Third Party Payment Platform

- The key question is not to deny the legal status of the third party payment platform, but to strengthen its supervision to prevent financial risks.
- As the third party payment platform is related to the development of network transactions, involving financial security and other issues, to make clear legal provisions are necessary. Access

qualification should include the following major issues: the need to have necessary financial support; the need for personnel and equipment conditions; the need to have a reasonable organization and management system.

- Third party payment platform is not allowed to divert funds from the buyer to obtain the transaction. We can consider the establishment of other appropriate security system. In the use of limited funds for other matters, it should establish a more stringent control mechanism, to ensure that the large amount of payment has a real trading base. At the same time we need to monitor the transfer of funds of the payment platform's major shareholders and other related accounts, in order to detect abnormal trading situation in a timely manner. In the aspect of establishment of other security system, we may consider the profit from the network transaction payment to deduct a certain percentage of funds to set up the security fund, in order to respond to the crisis of individual payment platform. Only a certain relief mechanism has been established in advance, in order to ensure the healthy and orderly operation of the third party payment platform.
- In the division of supervision, there are views that it should be regulated by the China Banking Regulatory Commission(CBRC) and the Ministry of supervision. But the two sector cooperation is bound to produce coordination costs, thus affecting the efficiency. In accordance with China's current institutional settings, CBRC will be more responsible for efficient. Of course, in the case of design related matters, the CBRC may lead with other departments to develop regulatory documents to be specified.

11.6 EC MARKET RISK AND MARKET SUPERVISION LAWS

11.6.1 Potential Risks in the Online Retail Market

With the improvement of people's living standards and the popularity of the Internet, online shopping patterns have been gradually recognized by people. But the long distance payment shopping has some inevitable risks. The potential risks of the online retail market mainly include five categories: the risk of e-tailing provider; online retail transaction object risk; the risk of after-sale protection; payment security risk; the risk of personal privacy information.

The risk of e-tailing provider

- Risk of confusing transaction object.
- Risk in infringement of real name.
- Online store missing risk.

Online retail transaction object risk

- Online shoppers is difficult to guarantee the right to know about the net goods.
- Confusing the smuggled goods to earn the difference.
- Attract consumers with low price and use accessories to make huge profits.

The risk of after-sale protection

- To return goods is difficult.
- Lack of after-sales service.

Payment security risk

- Online banking risk.
- Third party payment risk.

The risk of personal privacy information

In the general rules of civil law of our country, there is no provision for the right of privacy. But it cannot be denied, at this stage the majority of Internet users' privacy is in crisis. In online shopping, some businesses, use the consumer's information to establish a database in order to expand sales. What is more, in order to make profits, some sell the consumer information to others. In addition, the consumer's password of credit card account is often tampered with or stolen. If all these problems cannot be solved in a timely and effective way, it will certainly restrict the development of online shopping in the future.

11.6.2 Analysis of the Economic Cause of Supervision in the Online Retail Market

Market failure: the market failure constitutes the premise of regulation economics. If there is no market failure, there is no need for government regulation. Market failure is relative to the "market success" in economics. If there are monopoly of large enterprises and excessive market at the same time, the allocation of social resources lose efficiency. The principle of justice of social consumption is also destroyed. Market failure is mainly manifested in the public goods, externality, market forces and information asymmetry, etc.

- Public goods: Public goods are things that members of society can share. Strictly speaking, public goods are non competitive and non exclusive.
- Externality: Externality refers to the behavior of individuals and firms that has a direct impact on others, but they do not pay or receive compensation. Market economic activity is based on reciprocity, so the interests of the people in the market are essentially related to the interests of money.
- Monopoly: Oligopoly and complete monopoly may make the allocation of resources lack of efficiency. Correction of this situation depends on the power of the government. The government intervention is mainly on the market structure and enterprise organizational structure, to improve the economic efficiency of enterprises. Anti-monopoly is essential to maintain the normal operation of market economy. It is no exaggeration that the anti-monopoly law is the market economy under the conditions of the "economic constitution".
- Information asymmetry: Because economic activity is different, some people can use information superiority to cheat, which will harm the right transaction. When people are worried about the serious impact of fraud transactions, the market will lose the normal role of market

allocation of resources, the function of failure.

Regulation failure: Corresponding to the market failure, the government regulation may also appear regulation failure. The main reasons leading to the failure of regulation are the duration of the regulation, the interests of their own, limited rationality, limited information and so on. Sometimes, there is a "regulatory capture"—the regulator is regulated by the "buy" phenomenon. If the market failure and regulation failure coexist, it should be terrible. But in reality, the situation is often not the case, because the government regulation is subjective.

11.6.3 The Policy and Suggestion of Online Retail Market Regulation

Consumption is an important part of social reproduction, and also an important part of improving people's living standard. The steady and healthy development of trade and circulation areas is about the overall situation of a country's economic and social stability. It is imperative to strengthen supervision from the following aspects:

Formulate online retail industry standards

In today's world, the standardization level has become the core competitiveness of the basic elements of the region. An enterprise, even a country, must be in an invincible position in the fierce international competition. It is necessary to understand the important significance of the standard to the national economy and social development. The essence of the standard is unity, the unity of things and concepts of the provisions of the standard; the task is to regulate the standard, which is the object of the adjustment of a variety of economic objects. Therefore, the development of online retail industry standards is to guide, promote and regulate the healthy development of the retail industry, a basic work.

Guard against the monopoly of online retail industry

Monopoly is the enemy of the healthy operation of the market economy. All countries in the world will maintain anti-monopoly as important work for the healthy operation of the economy. The reason for the government to take anti-monopoly measures is to protect the market competition, because competition is beneficial to economic growth and the maintenance of consumer interests. But the competition process often causes the change of the market structure. It is easy to cause the individual monopoly group to dominate the market, until the new competitor breaks the market structure. The main function of the anti-monopoly law is to reduce the adverse effects of price control, limited production, hostile takeover or vertical integration, and protect the normal operation of the market.

Strengthen the management of the industry and improve the ability to avoid risks

There are two definitions of risk: one is that the risk is not definite; the other is that the risk is the uncertainty of the loss. Risk management is how to reduce the risk to the lowest management process in an environment where there is a certain risk. It includes a measure of risk, assessment, and contingency strategies. The ideal risk management is a series of priorities of the process, a variety of contradictions. To guide the healthy development of online shops and orderly development, we must implement the system from the source.

SUMMARY

Through the study of this chapter, we understand that the e-commerce law is a general term for the regulation of social relations arising from business activities. This is a new comprehensive legal field. It includes a lot of content: such as data messages, electronic contracts, electronic signatures, electronic certification, e-commerce, logistics and e-commerce security. With the rapid development of e-commerce in China, it is not difficult to find that there are always disputes about transactions. At the same time, China's e-commerce market has many hidden dangers. Therefore, China still needs to perfect relevant laws to provide a more fair and secure market environment for the development of e-commerce.

Words and Expression

①**auction price**: the highest price in which goods are auctioned 拍卖价格

②**capital flows**: the transfer of capital, including loans, aid and investment, etc. 资本流动

③**company law**: The company law is a general term for the establishment, activities, dissolution and other foreign relations of various companies. 公司法

④**general principles**: the general guidelines or general outline 总纲

⑤**general provision**: a preamble to laws, regulations, and articles; a general summary of textual materials; a short narrative 总则

⑥**information flow**: It refers to a set of information moving in the same direction in space and time. 信息流,数据流

⑦**legal evidence**: Its basic connotation is that the proof power of all evidence and the choice and application of evidence are prescribed by law in advance. 法定单证

⑧**main force**: a person or organization that describes one or more prices in a market or stock 主力

⑨**market failure**: Market failure refers to the fact that the market cannot allocate goods and services efficiently. 市场失灵

⑩**media**: a means of a tool used by buyers and sellers or between them 媒介

⑪**monopolistic competition**: It is the market phenomenon that a lot of manufacturers produce and sell similar but not identical products. 垄断性竞争

⑫**national economy**: The national economy refers to the interrelated population formed by the social production departments, circulation departments and other economic sectors within a modern country. 国民经济; 民族经济

⑬**retail market**: a place where buyers and sellers carry out retail transactions 零售市场

⑭**securities trading**: the act of transferring securities to other investors in accordance with the rules of trading 证券交易

⑮**shopping mall**: It refers to the huge scale, shopping, leisure, entertainment, catering to one, including department stores, hypermarkets, as well as many professional retail stores, including super business center. 大型购物中心

⑯**supply and demand**: The relation between market supply and demand refers to the relation and restriction between commodity supply and demand under the condition of commodity economy. 供求

⑰**third party logistics**: It is relative to the shipper of the first party and the consignee of the second party. Through its cooperation with the first or second parties to provide its specialized logistics services, it does not own goods and does not participate in the sale of goods. 第三方物流

⑱**transaction credit**: It refers to the form of credit that is mutually supplied between the business enterprise and the commodity transaction. It is based on mutual trust between businesses. 交易信用

⑲**wireless communications**: the way to communicate by radio waves 无线通信

Exercises

Ⅰ. **Key Terms** (Explain the following terms.)

①principle of autonomy

②market failure

③public goods

④regulation failure

⑤consumers' right to know

Ⅱ. **Multiple Choice Exercises** (Choose the correct answer to the following questions from A, B, C and D. There is only one correct answer.)

①Which of the following innovations has not been mentioned in Section 11.2?

A. Formulaic. B. Technical.

C. Security. D. Neutrality.

②Which of the following is not the ingredient of Principle of Neutral?

A. Technical neutrality. B. Media neutrality.

C. Implement neutrality. D. Autonomy neutrality.

③Which one is not the potential risk in the online retail market?

A. The risk of receipt. B. The risk of e-tailing provider.

C. The risk of after-sale protection. D. The risk of personal privacy information.

④Which suggestion of online retail market regulation is not right?

A. Establish online retail industry standards.

B. Strengthen industry management and improve the ability to avoid risks.

C. Be aware of the monopoly of Internet retailing.

D. Let it develop by itself.

⑤Which one is right according to Section 11.4?

A. There is excellent electronic logistics laws and regulations in our country.

B. Different problems need different laws to regulate in the course of the third party logistics operation.

C. Third party electronic logistics is a kind of onerous contract or bilateral contract.

D. China's law has already specified the nature of the third party logistics contract.

⑥Which of the following is not a legal problem in the third party logistics?

A. It's difficult to determine the jurisdiction of electronic commerce disputes.

B. There is no inspection mechanism.

C. China's law does not specify the nature of the third party logistics contract.

D. The burden of dispute is hard to collect.

⑦The key point of the legal regulation of the third party platform is ________.

A. let it develop

B. Put severe pressure on it

C. deny its legal status

D. strengthen supervision and guard against financial risks

⑧Which of the following is true?

A. Public goods are things that are not to be shared.

B. Monopoly: Oligopoly and complete monopoly may make the allocation of resources lack of efficiency.

C. Market failure is mainly manifested in the aspects of public goods, externalities, market forces and information symmetry.

D. Government regulation can not be out of regulation failure.

Ⅲ. Review Questions

①What is the principle of electronic commerce law?

②How to deal with the influence of oligopoly market?

③How to protect the consumer's personal privacy information better?

Ⅳ. Online Excerise

①Register as the user with a false name on the site of Taobao.

②Do the 7 days unconditional return on the site of Taobao.

Ⅴ. Case Study

Case playback: Last December 11th, the driver of the car, Mr. Luo, drove a small car from east to west at the Dongying junction of Chaoyang District airport. He collided with an electric bicycle coming from the north to the south. Cycling is a teenager under 18 years old, with a more than 40 year man behind. In the accident, the electric bicycle fell to the ground and the man was injured, a grade ten disability.

Because the intersection monitoring couldn't be retrieved, the traffic control department couldn't determine who was responsible for the accident. Therefore, the traffic control department had to recommend the two sides to the court proceedings. Thus, the injured man, Mr. Gou, and Mr. Luo, the vehicle rental company and the insurance company all went to the court. Mr. Gou asked for medical expenses, nursing fees, disability compensation, the living expenses and so on, totaling 220 thousand Yuan.

On October 15th, 2015, this dispute went to the substantive trial in Chaoyang Court. The agent of Beijing Tongda infinite Technology Co. Ltd., who was applied for the additional co-defendant, also participated in the trial. According to Tongda Company's opinion, they only provided information and Internet services to promote bilateral transactions, and therefore should not bear any responsibility for the accident.

Questions for Discussion

①Study the case and think about why it is difficult to deal with e-commerce disputes.

②What issues should we pay attention to in the legislation of e-commerce in China?

Chapter 12 Online Marketing Research and Advertisement

本章导读

网络市场调研是利用互联网系统地进行营销信息的收集、整理、分析和研究的过程，以及利用各种搜索引擎寻找竞争信息、客户信息、供求信息的行为。市场调研对于营销管理来说，其重要性犹如侦查之对于军事指挥。作为市场营销活动的重要环节，市场调研给消费者提供了一个表达自己意见的机会，使他们能够把自己对产品或服务的意见、想法及时反馈给企业或供应商。通过市场调研，能够让生产该产品或提供服务的企业了解消费者对产品或服务质量的评价、期望和想法。本章将主要介绍电子商务领域的市场调研，包括市场调研的重要性、调研的过程、网络调研的方法等。网络广告就是在网络上作的广告，是通过网络广告投放平台，利用网站上的广告横幅、文本链接、多媒体的方法，在互联网上刊登或发布广告，再通过网络传递到互联网用户的一种高科技广告运作方式。与传统的传播媒体广告及近年来备受垂青的户外广告相比，网络广告具有得天独厚的优势，是实施现代营销媒体战略的重要部分。本章将探讨电商领域中的网络广告，包括网络广告的方法以及在线广告的策略。网络市场调研和网络广告对于营销管理有着极其重要的作用，提供作为决策基础的信息，可以弥补信息不足的缺陷，了解外部信息；可以了解市场环境变化，了解新的市场环境，推广新的产品信息等。

Business Terms

①**ad-as-a-commodity**: It means people are paid for the time that is spent viewing an ad.

②**affiliate marketing**: It is a marketing arrangement by which an organization refers consumers to the selling company's web site.

③**focus groups**: a group of people together in a room (usually physically, although technology is making virtual or online focus groups more feasible)

④**marketing research**: It is defined as the systematic design, collection, analysis and interpretation of data and findings relevant to a specific marketing situation facing the company to support decision-making.

⑤**primary research**: It involves the collection of original primary data by researchers. It can be accomplished through various methods, including questionnaires and telephone interviews in market research, or experiments and direct observations in the physical sciences.

⑥**search engine optimization (SEO)**: It is the process of affecting the visibility of a website or a web page in a web search engine's unpaid results—often referred to as "natural", "organic", or "earned" results.

⑦**secondary research**: It is simply the act of seeking out existing research and data. Secondary data could be US Census data, Twitter comments, journals, and much more. The best thing about secondary research is that it is often free and it usually can be done quickly.

⑧**web advertising**: It is also called online advertising or Internet advertising or web advertising. It is a form of marketing and advertising which uses the Internet to deliver promotional marketing messages to consumers.

Introductory Case

Market Research Was Born in the Field

Procter & Gamble was the venue for the origin of systematic market research. Along with brand management, field research is the life-blood of consumer product companies and both began at Procter & Gamble.

It may seem like an obvious idea now, but field research was revolutionary in its time. For decades following the Great Depression, companies had a patriarchal orientation to product development, advertising and sales.

Products were developed in company laboratories that were considered to be scientific and objective. Companies developed products to meet generic needs and marketing underscored that if customers would just buy and use the advertised products, all would be well.

The missing element in this research and development approach was the research. On the watch of Neil McElroy, Procter & Gamble connected the dots. If Procter & Gamble wanted to know what customers wanted, in order to be able to sell it to them, the company would need to hear directly from the consumers. Procter & Gamble was predominantly a consumer products manufacturer and, as such, the majority of the company's customers were homemakers.

Hundreds of women were recruited to conduct their ordinary domestic activities with Procter & Gamble products, and to report the results of their experiences with the products.

The information gained through these field research studies was used to improve Procter & Gambles' existing products and to inform the development of their new products. The scientific mind behind this systematic approach to consumer research was a D. Paul Smelser. A Johns Hopkins University graduate with a Ph. D. in economics, he was Doc Smelser to the other executives at Procter & Gamble.

First hired by Procter & Gamble to work in a new business unit set up for commodities market analysis, Doc Smelser pushed the corporate culture at Procter & Gamble in a number of ways. Where executives at Procter & Gamble wore a conservative uniform of suits, Smelser showed up in sporty garb. With his feisty nature, he pulled no punches and he periodically posed sales and marketing questions to senior executives without preamble.

The cerebral Smelser was intrigued when executives couldn't answer questions about how Procter & Gamble products were being used or not used. He harbored a notion that a company should know a great deal about product use in order to conduct effective marketing.

By 1925, Smelser had sufficiently unsettled leadership at Procter & Gamble to bring about the establishment of a formal Market Research Department headed by none other than Smelser. Until his retirement in 1959, Smelser developed the market research department into a sophisticated and scientific business unit.

The Procter & Gamble field researchers, who conducted innovative door-to-door interviews with consumers, were carefully selected for their positions. Like the people hired to work in Disneyland, or the Harvey girls of the famous Fred Harvey restaurants in the late 1800s, the Procter & Gamble field researchers were selected on the basis of the impact they would have on the consumers they contacted in the field.

Smelser hired predominantly young female college graduates who were modestly attractive and projected a wholesomeness that Smelser considered appropriate for the Procter & Gamble products. This hand-picked research corps was intended to be skillful at obtaining frank and honest responses from the consumers in the field who agreed to participate in the market research efforts.

The army of Procter & Gamble field researchers knocked on doors and peppered willing homemakers with questions about each and every domestic chore for which the company either had a product or was considering a product launch. To create an informal conversational tone that was non-threatening (while being rigorously effective), the field researchers did not carry any clipboards, writing implements, lists or forms of any kind. The field researchers had to have perfect recall of tons of detailed information that they gleaned from their conversations with the homemakers. Once they were back in their cars, these amazing researchers recorded all that they remembered and had learned.

Smelser's field research outcomes were deep and broad, resulting in astonishingly comprehensive sets of overlapping data. Doc Smelser worked at Procter & Gamble for 34 years, and during that time, 3,000 women and a smattering of men conducted field research.

The researchers learned about Procter & Gable's products and about competitors' products. The company developed a competitive edge from the strength of this research, which propelled Smelser into the advertising realm. With the same intense focus Smelser had shown in his efforts to develop field research, he got to know advertising media backward and forward. Smelser could quote precise audience numbers to astonished radio station managers who didn't know such facts.

Questions for Discussion

①Why did Procter & Gamble Company do market research?

②How did Procter & Gamble Company do market research?

③What's the result of Procter & Gamble Company's market research?

12.1 THE IMPORTANCE OF MARKETING RESEARCH

Marketing research is defined as the systematic design, collection, analysis and interpretation of data and findings relevant to a specific marketing situation facing the company to support decision-making. Marketing research is necessary because of the uncertainty that surrounds most business decision-making and it can provide a large quantity of reliable information and so reduce risk.

It provides important information to identify and analyze the market need, market size and competition. Thus, marketing research is also a very important component of business strategy.

Why do marketers do marketing research?

Marketers have many questions they would like answers to:

—What doubts do consumers have about our products?

—Does it pay to introduce new packaging?

—Why is our sale declining?

—Which regions/countries should we expand in?

—How effective was our recent advertising campaign?

The functions of marketing research:

- Identify potential traditional and electronic markets;
- Meet customer requirements;
- Create customer satisfaction through finding out customers' wants and needs.

12.2 THE MARKETING RESEARCH PROCESS

The market research process is a systematic methodology for informing business decisions. The figure below breaks the process down into six steps:

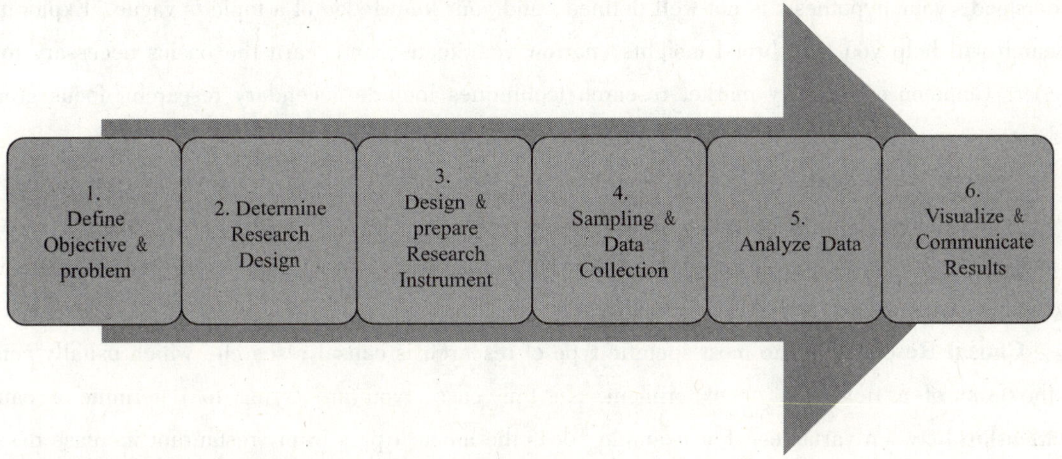

Step 1. Define the objective & your "problem"

Perhaps the most important step in the market research process is defining the goals of the project. There is typically a key business problem (or opportunity) that needs to be acted upon, but there is a lack of information to make that decision comfortably; the job of a market researcher is to inform that decision with solid data. Examples of "business problems" might be "How should we price this new widget?" or "Which features should we prioritize?"

By understanding the business problem clearly, you'll be able to keep your research focused and effective. At this point in the process, well before any research has been conducted, you can to imagine what a "perfect" final research report would look like to help answer the business question (s). You might even go as far as to mock up a fake report, with hypothetical data, and ask your audience: "If I produce a report that looks something like this, will you have the information you need to make an informed choice?" If the answer is yes, now you just need to get the real data. If the answer is no, keep working with your client/audience until the objective is clear, and be happy about the disappointment you've prevented and the time you've saved.

Step 2. Determine your "research design"

Now that you know your research objects, it is time to plan out the type of research that will best obtain the necessary data. Think of the "research design" as your detailed plan of attack. In this step you will first determine your market research method (will it be a survey, focus group, etc.?). You will also think through specifics about how you will identify and choose your sample (who are we going after? Where will we find them? How will we incentivize them?). This is also the time to plan where you will conduct your research (telephone, in-person, mail, Internet, etc.). Once again, remember to keep the end goal in mind—what will your final report look like? Based on that, you'll be able to identify the types of data analysis you'll be conducting (simple summaries, advanced regression analysis, etc.), which dictates the structure of questions you'll be asking.

Your choice of research instrument will be based on the nature of the data you are trying to collect. There are three classifications to consider:

Exploratory Research—This form of research is used when the topic is not well defined or understood, your hypothesis is not well defined, and your knowledge of a topic is vague. Exploratory research will help you gain broad insights, narrow your focus, and learn the basics necessary to go deeper. Common exploratory market research techniques include secondary research, focus groups and interviews. Exploratory research is a qualitative form of research.

Descriptive Research—If your research objective calls for more detailed data on a specific topic, you'll be conducting quantitative descriptive research. The goal of this form of market research is to measure specific topics of interest, usually in a quantitative way. Surveys are the most common research instrument for descriptive research.

Causal Research—The most specific type of research is causal research, which usually comes in the form of a field test or experiment. In this case, you are trying to determine a causal relationship between variables. For example, does the music I play in my restaurant increase dessert sales (i. e. Is there a causal relationship between music and sales?).

Step 3. Design & prepare your "research instrument"

In this step of the market research process, it's time to design your research tool. If a survey is the most appropriate tool (as determined in step 2), you'll begin by writing your questions and designing your questionnaire. If a focus group is your instrument of choice, you'll start preparing questions and materials for the moderator. You get the idea. This is the part of the process where you start executing your plan.

By the way, step 3.5 should be to test your survey instrument with a small group prior to broad deployment. Take your sample data and get it into a spreadsheet; are there any issues with the data structure? This will allow you to catch potential problems early, and there are always problems.

Step 4. Collect your data

This is the meat and potatoes of your project; the time when you are administering your survey, running your focus groups, conducting your interviews, implementing your field test, etc. The answers, choices, and observations are all being collected and recorded, usually in spreadsheet form. Each nugget of information is precious and will be part of the masterful conclusions you will soon draw.

Step 5. Analyze your data

Step 4 (data collection) has drawn to a close and you have heaps of raw data sitting in your lap. If it's on scraps of paper, you'll probably need to get it in spreadsheet form for further analysis. If it's already in spreadsheet form, it's time to make sure you've got it structured properly. Once that's all done, the fun begins. Run summaries with the tools provided in your software package (typically Excel, SPSS, Minitab, etc.), build tables and graphs, segment your results by groups that make sense (i. e. age, gender, etc.), and look for the major trends in your data. Start to formulate the story you will tell.

Step 6. Visualize your data and communicate results

A great way to present the data is to start with the research objectives and business problem that were identified in step. Restate those business questions, and then present your recommendations based on the data, to address those issues.

When it comes time to presenting your results, remember to present insights, answers and recommendations, not just charts and tables. If you put a chart in the report, ask yourself "what does this mean and what are the implications?" Adding this additional critical thinking to your final report will make your research more actionable and meaningful and will set you apart from other researchers.

While it is important to "answer the original question", remember that market research is one input to a business decision (usually a strong input), but not the only factor. So, that's the market research process. The figure below walks through an example of this process in action, starting with a business problem of "how should we price this new widget?"

12.3 MARKETING RESEARCH APPROACHES IN EC

There are several ways to categorize the various market research methods. The vast majority of techniques fit into one of six categories: ①secondary research; ②surveys; ③focus groups; ④interviews; ⑤observation; or ⑥experiments/field trials.

The most basic classification of market research is primary and secondary research. Secondary research happens to be the first of six market research methods. The other five are all different flavors of primary research.

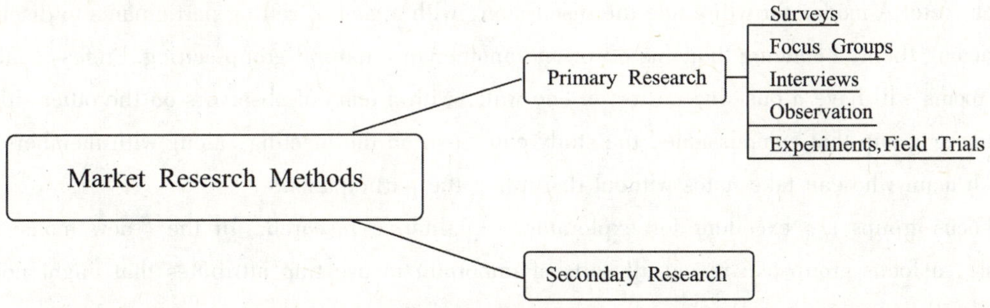

Secondary market research

Secondary research is simply the act of seeking out existing research and data. Secondary data could be US Census data, Twitter comments, journals, and much more. The best thing about secondary research is that it is often free and it usually can be done quickly. The job as a secondary researcher is to find existing data that can be applied to your specific project. It is possible that you might not be able to find secondary data that is suitable for your research needs. If that's the case, you'll need to conduct your own primary research and that's why we'll find the other five market research methods.

Primary market research

Primary research involves the collection of original primary data by researchers. It can be accomplished through various methods, including questionnaires and telephone interviews in market research, or experiments and direct observations in the physical sciences.

◇ **Primary market research method #1—surveys**

Surveys are perhaps the most widely known and utilized method when it comes to market research. Surveys come in a wide variety of shapes and sizes, from that little "feedback card" on the table at your favorite restaurant to those never-ending web surveys that make you want to punch your computer.

Surveys can be used effectively for satisfaction research (customers or employee), measuring attitudes, pricing research, fact gathering (e. g. the census), and much more. You'll find surveys administered in all sorts of ways, including snail mail form, web forms, face-to-face (that guy at the mall with the clipboard), over the phone (the guy who calls during dinner), on the sidebar of a blog, and even on mobile devices via text message or otherwise. Surveys can be self-administered (the respondent reads and answers questions alone) or a person who records your answers can administer them.

◇ **Primary market research method #2—focus groups**

Focus groups involve getting a group of people together in a room (usually physically, although technology is making virtual, or online focus groups more feasible). These people fit a target demographic (e. g. "mothers under 40 with an income over $50k", "college males who play 8 or more hours of video games a week", etc.) depending on the product or service in question. Participants are almost always compensated in some way, whether it be a money, coupons, free products, etc. A moderator will guide the discussion, with a goal of getting participants to discuss the topic among them, bouncing thoughts off of one another in a natural group setting. Professional focus group rooms will have a one-way mirror on one wall, with a team of observers on the other side. The company or group that commissioned the study can sit-in on the meeting, along with members of the research team who can take notes without disrupting the participants.

Focus groups are excellent for exploratory, qualitative research. In the "new mouse trap" example, a focus group can reveal all sorts of important mouse trap attributes that might not have been considered otherwise. Focus groups are great tools to use prior to a survey, because it will inform your survey questions to be more specific and targeted. Focus groups can also be beneficial after a survey, as a way to dive very deep into a topic that came up in the survey. For example, an employee satisfaction survey may reveal "cafeteria food" to be a big issue. A follow up focus group with a handful of employees will allow the employer to understand that issue much better (What is the problem with the food? Is it the taste, price, healthiness, temperature, something else?).

◇ **Primary market research method #3—interviews**

Like focus groups, individual interviews are a qualitative market research method. To simplify things, think of individual interviews as focus groups with only one participant and one moderator (interviewer). There is a wide spectrum of interviewing formats, depending on the goal of the interview. Interviews can be free flowing conversations that are loosely constrained to a general topic of interest, or they might be highly structured, with very specific questions and/or activities (e. g. projective techniques such as word association, fill in the blank, etc.) for the subject.

Like focus groups, interviews are useful for exploratory research. Use this market research method when you are interested in digging into a specific issue very deeply, searching for customer problems, understanding psychological motivations and underlying perceptions, etc.

◇ **Primary market research method #4—experiments and field trials**

Experiments and field trials involve scientific testing, where specific variables and hypotheses can be tested. These tests can be conducted in controlled environments or out in the field (natural settings). This form of market research is always quantitative in nature. Experiments and field trials can be a hairy topic with lots of jargon, but here's a simple example that demonstrates an effective online experiment: In his first presidential campaign, Obama used "A/B testing" to optimize his campaign donation page. Some website visitors would see one image and others (at random) would see a different image. The webpage team was able to measure, which image was resulting in more donations, and they could quickly decide to use the more favorable image for all users. By employing this simple market research experiment on which website images performed better, Obama was able to maximize contributions in a major way. Another example might be a cereal company making two different packaging styles and delivering each one to limited test market stores where their individual sales can be measured.

◇ **Primary market research method #5—observation**

Observational research can come in a different shapes and sizes. In general, there are two categories: strict observation with no interaction with the subject at all, or observation with some level of intervention/interaction between the researcher and subject. The greatest benefit of this technique is that researchers can measure actual behavior, as opposed to user-reported behavior. That's a big deal, because people will often report one thing on a survey, but behave in another way when the rubber hits the road. Observational research is a direct reflection of "real life", so these insights are often very reliable and useful.

There are many examples of observational research. Here are a few:

Usability testing—Watching a subject use a prototype device is one form of observational research. Again, this can be done with or without intervention.

Eye tracking—Let's say you have come up with a website. You might ask people to navigate your website, and you will use eye tracking technology to create a "heat map" of where their eyes go on the website. This information can be used to re-design and optimize the page elements.

Contextual inquiry—This is a hybrid form of research that involves interviewing subjects as the researcher watches them work or play in their natural environment.

In-home observation—Watching a family member go through the morning routine in their home might turn up useful insights into pain-points that need solving.

In-store observation—Simply watching shoppers in action is another form of observational research. What do shoppers notice? How do they go through a store?

Mystery shoppers—This involves hiring a regular person to go into a store and pretend to be an everyday shopper. They will then report on aspects of their experience, such as store cleanliness, politeness of staff, etc. In the case, the mystery shopper is the researcher and the store is the subject being observed.

Methodology	Qualitative or Quantitative?	Typical Cost	Typical Time	Comments
Secondary Research	can be either	typically free or low cost	short	usually a great place to start, but often not detailed or specific enough
Surveys	quantitative	varies widely, key costs include participant incentives, survey design and survey administration	medium	excellent for measuring attitudes across a large population and for answering specific questions
Focus Groups	qualitative	medium, key costs include focus group moderation and participant incentives	medium	good for exploratory research
Interviews	qualitative	similar to focus groups, but can be much cheaper depending on the audience and interviews	short-medium	also good for exploratory research, along with deep dives into specific topics
Experiments and Field Trails	quantitative	often the most expensive method	usually long	used for scientifically testing specific hypotheses
Observation	usually qualitative	medium, relative to the other options	medium	good for measuring actual behavior, as opposed to self-reported behavior

12.4 WEB ADVERTISING

Web advertising, also called online advertising or Internet advertising or web advertising, is a form of marketing and advertising which uses the Internet to deliver promotional marketing messages to consumers. Consumers view online advertising as an unwanted distraction with few benefits and have increasingly turned to ad blocking for a variety of reasons.

Like other advertising media, online advertising frequently involves both a publisher, who integrates advertisements into its online content, and an advertiser, who provides the advertisements to be displayed on the publisher's content. Other potential participants include advertising agencies who help generate and place the ad copy, an ad server that technologically delivers the ad and tracks statistics, and advertising affiliates who do independent promotional work for the advertiser.

12.5 ONLINE ADVERTISING METHODS

Online advertising methods include email marketing, search engine marketing (SEM), social media marketing, many types of display advertising (including web banner advertising), and mobile advertising.

Last year Internet ad revenue hit $31bn. Q4 saw the best quarterly result ever at $9bn with a 20% increase on spend from the same period in 2010. Figures from the Internet Advertising Bureau, which is the trade association for online advertising showed:

- 46.5% of the spend was on search advertising on websites such as Google;
- About 8.1% was on online classified advertising;
- 34.8% was on display advertising which includes banners and digital video commercials.

Five of the best online advertising methods today

◇ Websites and blogs

Most online advertising is geared to direct people to your website, a central hub if you will. A large percentage of Internet users use the Internet as their preferred choice to find information about goods and services. Your website or blog is a permanent shop window that is available 24 hours a day 7 days a week. Tip: Just having a website or blog does not mean you will get traffic, leads, sales. You need to be 100% clear on the purpose of your blog before starting.

◇ Social media websites

Social media websites such as Facebook and YouTube are constantly seeking to increase their advertising revenues. Both provide full details of their advertising possibilities on their websites.

Facebook allows you to select your audience by location, age and interests and to test out simple image and text based ads. It suggests that companies advertising on Facebook can:

- Advertise their own web pages.
- Create demand for their products by creating relevant adverts.
- Publicize an event such as a product launch or anniversary.

Payment is either made by "pay per click" or by "impression" (visitors see the ad whether they click it or not). You can set a daily budget that can be adjusted up or down at any time.

YouTube offers a host of resources such as "how to" guides and advertisers playbooks that will show you exactly how to set up and run your first successful marketing campaign with it.

Twitter also recently announced that it allows users to place self serve ads. Any Advertising on social media networks should only be undertaken as part of a coordinated social media strategy.

◇ Banners and display advertising

Display banners, or banner ads, were the first major method used for online advertising. By 2009, they had dropped to less than 23% of online advertising spend, as pay per click or keyword advertising became the predominant force.

Display banners still have merit and are good for special offers or for reinforcing a brand. Banner ads are small adverts that normally come in various rectangle forms. They appear on websites and serve as a link directly to the advertiser's website: When you click on a banner your browser instantly redirects you to that site.

The popularity of banner ads is partly due to fact that they are simple to produce and publish. They are also highly measurable. Depending on the ad and the producer or service, advertisers can calculate the cost per sale—this is the amount of advertising money that is spent to make one sale.

◇ Pay per click (PPC) or keyword advertising

Search engines and many websites (including social networks sites such as Facebook and YouTube) carry small adverts with embedded URL's. When someone clicks on these adverts, the company that put them there is charged. This is considered by many to be the best online advertising method by far and has been growing at a remarkable rate. Unlike traditional advertising, pay per click is user activated. Users like it, because it costs them nothing and they only use it if there is something that attracts them.

The advantage of pay per click for advertisers is that they only pay for the actual click through to their site. With other methods of advertising, both offline and online, you have no particular idea of how much it will cost you to attract each visitor. A user that clicks through into your site is likely to be interested in what you have to say, because these users are actively looking for information or researching what you have to say, your product service or offering.

The largest pay per click advertiser by a long way is Google and they have a large library of information available to walk small business owners through the process of starting a successful PPC campaign.

◇ Search engine optimization (SEO)

With the huge increase of companies operating online and selling on the Internet there has been a dramatic increase in the competition between companies to get visitors to their websites. When carrying out research most people will only look at the first page of search results and quite often only the first two or three.

Search engine optimization (SEO) is the process of affecting the visibility of a website or a web page in a web search engine's unpaid results—often referred to as "natural", "organic", or "earned" results. In general, the earlier (or higher ranked on the search results page) and more frequently a site appears in the search results list, the more visitors it will receive from the search engine's users, and these visitors can be converted into customers.

12.6 ONLINE ADVERTISING STRATEGIES

An advertising strategy is generally tailored to a target audience perceived to be most likely out of the population to purchase the product. Advertising strategies include elements such as geographic location, perceived demographics of the audience, price points, special offers, and what advertising media, such as billboards, websites, or television, will be used to present the product. There are four online advertising strategies as follows:

Affiliate marketing

Affiliate marketing is a marketing arrangement by which an organization refers consumers to the selling company's web site.

Ads-as-a-commodity

Ad-as-a-commodity means people are paid for the time that is spent viewing an ad, for example, Mypoints. com, Clickrewards. com, etc.

Viral marketing

Viral marketing is word-of-mouth marketing by which customers promote a product or service by telling others about it.

Customized ads

Customized ads are filtering irrelevant information by providing consumers with customized ads can reduce this information overload.

SUMMARY

This chapter mainly discusses issues related to online marketing research and advertisements. First of all, marketing research is defined as the systematic design, collection, analysis and interpretation of data and findings relevant to a specific marketing situation facing the company to support decision-making. Marketing research is necessary because of the uncertainty that surrounds most business decision-making and it can provide a large quantity of reliable information and so reduce risk. Marketing research involves six steps. Moreover, there are several ways to categorize the various market research methods, including secondary research, surveys, focus groups, interviews, observation and experiments/field trials. Secondly, web advertising, also called online advertising or Internet advertising or web advertising, is a form of marketing and advertising which uses the Internet to deliver promotional marketing messages to consumers. There are five best online advertising methods today, including websites and blogs, social media websites, banners and display advertising, pay per click and keyword advertising, and search engine optimization. Also, four online advertising strategies are discussed, including affiliate marketing, ads-as-a-commodity, viral marketing and customizing ads. Online marketing research and advertisements are critical to marketing and management. What's more, marketers need to update their knowledge everyday to meet the dramatic changes in electronic commerce field.

Words and Expressions

①**affiliate**: an organization which is officially connected with another, larger organization or is a member of it 成员组织;附属机构

②**banner**: a long strip of cloth with something written on it, usually attached to two poles and carried during a protest or rally 横幅,标语

③**commercial**: an advertisement that is broadcast on television or radio 商业广告

④**demographics**: the statistics relating to the people who live there 人口统计学特征

⑤**exploratory**: serving in or intended for exploration or discovery 探索性的

⑥**incentive**: a positive motivational influence 刺激,激励

⑦**maximize**: to make as big or large as possible 使最大化

⑧**questionnaire**: a written list of questions which are answered by a lot of people in order to provide information for a report or a survey 调查问卷

⑨**quarterly**: a quarterly event happens four times a year, at intervals of three months 按季度的

⑩**qualitative**: relating to the nature or standard of something, rather than to its quantity 定性的

⑪**quantitative**: relating to different sizes or amounts of things 定量的

⑫**respondent**: a person who replies to something such as a survey or set of questions 回答者

⑬**routine**: the usual series of things that you do at a particular time 惯例,常规

⑭**segment**: to divide the market into separate parts, usually in order to improve marketing opportunities 细分

⑮**spreadsheet**: a computer program that is used for displaying and dealing with numbers 电子制表程序

⑯**survey**: to find out information about people's opinions or behavior, usually by asking them a series of questions 调查

⑰**track**: to investigate someone or something, because you are interested in finding out more about them 跟踪,追踪

⑱**usability**: the quality of being able to provide good service 可用性

⑲**viral marketing**: a marketing technique that uses pre-existing social networking services and other technologies to produce increases in brand awareness or to achieve other marketing objectives 病毒式营销

Exercises

Ⅰ. **Key Terms** (Explain the following terms.)

①marketing research

②exploratory research

③descriptive research

④secondary market research

⑤affiliate marketing

Ⅱ. **Multiple Choice Exercises** (Choose the correct answer to the following questions from A, B, C and D. There is only one correct answer.)

①Which one is not the function of marketing research?

A. Identify potential traditional and e-markets.

B. Meet customer requirements.

C. Create customer satisfaction through finding out customers' wants and needs.

D. Design a revenue model for the company.

②The goal of ________ is to measure specific topics of interest in a quantitative way.

A. market research　　B. exploratory research

C. descriptive research　　D. casual research

③Primary market research method includes the following except ________.

A. surveys　　B. focus groups

C. interviews　　D. online materials

④Which of the following is not the online advertising method?

A. Websites and blogs.　　B. Social media websites.

C. Banners and display advertising.　　D. Television advertising.

⑤________ is the process of affecting the visibility of a website or a web page in a web search engine's unpaid results—often referred to as "natural", "organic", or "earned" results.

A. Banners and display advertising

B. Search engine optimization

C. Websites and blogs

D. Social media websites

⑥Which of the following is ad-as-a-commodity?

A. Walmart. com.　　B. Amazon. com.

C. Tmall. com.　　D. Mypoints. com.

⑦________ is a marketing arrangement by which an organization refers consumers to the selling company's web site.

A. Affiliate marketing　　B. Viral marketing

C. Customizing ads　　D. Ads-as-a-commodity

⑧________ is filtering irrelevant information by providing consumers with customized ads which can reduce this information overload.

A. Banners and display advertising
B. Search engine optimization
C. Websites and blogs
D. Ads-as-a-commodity

Ⅲ. Review Questions

①Why do companies do market research?

②What is the difference between primary market research method and secondary market research method?

③What are the online advertising methods?

Ⅳ. Online Practice

①Online research is popular recently. Please use one or two market research methods to conduct an online market research about the satisfaction of personal computers online.

②Build an online store on the website of Taobao. Then try to do search engine optimization for your products online.

③Try to design a market research plan for P&G Company with your team members. Then conduct the market research online, analyze the data, and complete a research document.

Ⅴ. Case Study

Market Research Case Study—Starbucks' Entry into China

Starbucks has developed an internationalization strategy to enable the company to open stores and franchises in countries across the globe. Market research is the core market entry strategy Starbucks is employing. This case study will consider how market research has strengthened Starbucks' entry into the Chinese markets.

Starbucks' entry into emerging and developed markets is informed by market research. Starbucks conducted market research to enable deeper understanding of the Chinese markets, and the way that capitalism functions in the People's Republic of China (PRC). China contains a number of distinct regionally-based markets, a factor that makes market research crucial to launching new stores and franchises in China. A deep understanding of intellectual property right laws is critical to successful market entry in emerging markets.

Starbucks articulated an entry strategy that would address the dominant Chinese markets and that was designed to be as inoffensive with respect to the Chinese culture as possible. Instead of taking the conventional approach with advertising and promotions—which could have been seen by potential Chinese consumers as attacking their culture of drinking tea—they positioned stores in high-traffic and high visibility locations. Moreover, Starbucks deliberately began to bridge the gap between the tea drinking culture and the coffee drinking culture by introducing beverages in the Chinese stores that included local tea-based ingredients.

Market research supported the development of Starbucks' competitive internationalization strategy. The overarching competitive strategy was to create an aspirational brand. Prospective Starbucks customers in China could look forward to what Starbucks refers to as the Third Place experience. The Starbucks experience conveys status that is highly appealing to those aspiring to western standards or to climbing the ladder in their own culture.

Market research indicates that brand consistency is important to Starbucks' customers. When Starbucks opens a new store in an emerging market like China, the best baristas are sent for the launch and to conduct training of the baristas who will carry on when once the launch has completed.

It is essential to understand the intellectual property rights laws and licensing issues when planning market entry in an emerging market. Starbucks has used intellectual protection laws to prevent its business model and brand from being illegally copied in China. Four years after opening its first café in China—in 1999—Starbucks had registered all its major trademarks in China.

The organization and structure of Starbucks' global operations was informed by market research. The organizational strategies employed by Starbucks were derived from Starbucks' experiences in other emerging markets supported an early recognition that China is not one homogeneous market. The organizational strategies employed by Starbucks addressed many Chinese markets. The culture dominant in northern China differs radically from the culture in the eastern parts of China, as reflected in the differences in consumer spending power inland, which is considerably lower than the spending power in coastal cities. The complexity of the Chinese markets led to regional partnerships to aid in Starbucks' plans for expansion in China; the partnerships provided consumer insight into Chinese tastes and preferences that helped Starbucks localize to the diverse markets.

Northern China—joint venture with Beijing Mei Da coffee company

Eastern China—partnered with Taiwan-based Uni-President

Southern China—worked with Maxim's Caterers in Hong Kong

Starbucks' competitive advantage is built on product, service, and brand attributes, many of which have been shown through market research to be important to Starbucks' customers. Starbucks' global brand is valuable and maintaining brand integrity is a fundamental focus in Starbucks' internationalization efforts. The baristas in China acted as brand ambassadors to help embed the Starbucks culture in the new market and ensure that high standards for customer service and product quality are maintained at each new and established local store.

Starbucks' ability to address changing markets is honed by effective and ongoing market research. Establishing and maintaining a global Starbucks brand does not mean having a global platform or uniform global products. Starbucks' marketing strategy in China was based on customization in response to diverse Chinese consumer target segmentation. Starbucks created extensive consumer taste profile analyses that are sufficiently agile to enable them to change with the market and to create an attractive East meets West product mix. Moreover, the localization effort is sufficiently flexible to permit each store to have the flexibility to choose from a wide beverage portfolio.

Questions for Discussion

①What does Starbucks get by doing market research?

②How do you think of Starbucks' marketing strategy in China?

Chapter 13 Online Travel Agent

本章导读

随着电子信息技术的发展与应用,网络成为旅游业重要的营销渠道。旅行社通过网站可以发布旅游线路信息、游程安排的细节,并开展在线预订与组团;酒店可以通过网站直销或者分销来提高入住率;景区景点可以通过网站利用虚拟现实技术充分展示资源魅力,销售电子门票;旅游中介企业可以通过网站,在旅游供给与旅游需求之间搭建中介桥梁,提供翔实、即时的代理产品信息,并实现在线销售。这些具有旅游产品销售功能的旅游网站,为旅游者提供了便捷、高效、经济的服务,促进了在线旅游市场的扩大与旅游电子商务的发展,形成了旅游OTA,即 Online Travel Agent。随着人们可自由支配收入的提高,闲暇时间的增多和交通运输的现代化,在线旅游消费市场快速增长,风险投资和其他产业不断涉足旅游 OTA,旅游 OTA 形成了一个庞大的产业群,市场竞争也越演越烈。

Business Terms

①**OTA**: It refers to the travel consumer booking travel products or services from travel service providers through the network and paying through the network too.

②**integrated portal's tourist channels**: Websites offering a wealth of tourist information. However, the tourism information and services provided by it are relatively lack of professionalism, authority and comprehensiveness. Therefore, the competitiveness of tourism is relatively weak.

③**tourism service trade**: Tourism service trade is a kind of international service trade. It refers to the activities of tourist employees in one country or region using controllable tourism resources to provide tourist services and receive remuneration to other tourist services in other countries or regions. Service trade in tourism includes both inbound and outbound trips by foreign tourists.

④**experience**: It means using your own life to feel the truth, feel the life, and leave a deep impression.

⑤**the chain of tourism industry**: The supply chain formed by tourism, accommodation, catering, entertainment, sightseeing, shopping and other tourist elements.

⑥**overseas tourism**: It means that people go out of the country, go to other countries and regions with different cultures, and enjoy different forms of foreign tourism.

⑦**information quality**: It refers to the ability of information to meet the needs of different customers.

⑧**product innovation**: Tourism products are the combination of tourist attractions and services offered by tourists through the exploitation and utilization of tourism resources. That is, the total number of services needed to provide a tourist with a tourist destination.

Introductory Case

Ctrip-Leader of China Online Travel Service

In October 1999, Ctrip Website officially opened, becoming China's first travel service company built on the platform of e-commerce. The project was supported by the Xuhui District science and Technology Commission of Shanghai as a high-tech project in the same year. As the leading online travel service company in China, Ctrip. com is a successful integration of high-tech industries and traditional travel industry, providing a set of hotel reservation, ticket booking, holiday booking, travel management, preferential business and tourism information, the full range of travel services to more than 90 million members worldwide. It is internationally known as the Internet and traditional tourism seamless integration of the model.

With the advent of the world network information age, the integration of tourism and e-commerce has become an inevitable trend. The application of the electricity supplier in the tourism industry has become an important measure to build regional e-commerce demonstration cities and a new growth point of economic development. At present, China's tourism service trade industry has established the basic way to change the tourism industry to the modern service industry with the information technology. According to the China Electronic Commerce Research Center monitoring data, in 2014 online travel market transactions amounted to 277 billion 290 million Yuan, an increase of 27.1% over 2013. Therefore, it is of great significance to explore the impact of e-commerce on tourism service trade.

Although the current coverage of Ctrip has been higher, but if you can not provide consumers with more value-added services, if you can not further improve the performance price ratio, rising space will be limited. The essence of Ctrip is an intermediary, but with the Internet as a tool. As an intermediary, the biggest risk lies in the direct transaction between the two sides of the intermediary and bypassing the intermediary. Airlines and hotels are also opening their own online booking business. In order to avoid the loss of the intermediary part of the profits, Ctrip needs to provide more value-added services. It is reported that, including Air China, Shenzhen Airlines, seven or eight airlines are also in contact with Taobao, ready to open direct stores on the platform this year. In addition, in less than a year, the country has more than 55 cities; more than 100 ticket agents opened the Taobao store. Today, Taobao has become the second largest Internet ticket booking platform after Ctrip.

Even though Ctrip is now the leading travel agency in China, it faces the pressure and challenge from all walks of life.

Questions for Discussion

①What advantage does Ctrip have?

②What are the challenges that Ctrip faces?

③How to deal with the challenges?

13.1 OVERVIEW OF ONLINE TRAVEL AGENT

OTA, whose full name is Online Travel Agent, is a professional term in the tourism e-commerce industry. It refers to the travel consumer booking a travel product or service from a travel service provider, and checking out by online payment or down payment. That means all travel agents can carry out product marketing or product sales through the Internet. The emergence of OTA put the traditional travel agency sales model on the network platform. This makes the transmission of the line information more extensive and more convenient for the guests to consult and order.

13.2 THE CATEGORY OF ONLINE TRAVEL AGENT

OTA has the characteristics of multiformity of investment subject and the trait of diversification of capital. To research its competitive situation and competitive characteristic better, we divide OTA into two major categories based on whether it is relying on the tourism entity industry. One type is online travel direct selling network which is built by the tourism supply enterprise, such as hotels, airline companies and tourist attractions. Another is online travel intermediary network. But this kind of network is controlled by risk investment or other industries and they have no direct background in the tourism industry. Now online travel intermediary network is the main force of OTA. It is mainly divided into the following categories: integrated portal's tourist channels, comprehensive tourism website, tourism vertical website, travel recommendation website and travel reviews website.

13.2.1 Integrated Portal's Tourist Channel

Portal websites are websites that provide comprehensive Internet information resources. In China, typical portal websites include Sina, Netease and Sohu. They all involve the content of tourism in different degree. Taking Sina as an example, the interactive service community provides tourist information, such as accommodation, catering, leisure, air tickets, train tickets and so on. Compared with the professional tourism websites, the tourism information and services provided by the portal website are relatively lack of professionalism, authority and comprehensiveness, and the competitiveness of the tourism industry is relatively weak. But the information of the portal website is large and complete, which decides that the tourism information and service is the essential content of its website construction. Portal websites rely on their rich information resources to attract a large number of Internet users, and their travel channels also have higher traffic volume and click through rate. The development of portal website and tourism channel supplement each other.

13.2.2 Comprehensive Tourism Website

In the early stage of the construction of a comprehensive tourism website, it basically takes VC as the capital injection form. They exist in the form of purely tourism supply and demand intermediaries, and in the early stages of their development there is no entity tourism enterprise to support them. The comprehensive tourism website brings together various kinds of tourism supply factors, such as tourist traffic, tourist hotels, tourist catering, tourist shopping, tourist resources, tourist routes and so on, and provides online booking business. Most of the comprehensive tourism website take proxy commissions as the source of profit and occupy most of the share of online travel booking business.

13.2.3 Tourism Vertical Website

A vertical web site is a web site that focuses on specific areas or specific requirements and provides full depth information and services related to this domain or requirement. Tourism vertical website business develops vertically. Its service of segment market is more specific. Market segments can be based on product types, such as travel, vacation, hotel accommodations, geographical resources and consumer preferences. Vertical web site is represented by Tuniu. com. In addition to the vertical meaning of the business segments, the vertical web site also has a technical vertical meaning. Qunar. com and Kuxun. cn are the representatives of the technical tourism vertical search engine website. They do not have a complete library of tourist product information. They capture relevant product information in terms of tourist search terms and sort them by price to facilitate travelers' choice.

13.2.4 Travel Recommendation Website

The travel recommendation website is represented by Travelzoo. It collects tourist information and provides the quality tourism product information to tourists after confirming the correctness and validity of the product information. Travelzoo does not sell tourism products directly. It is a neutral attitude, according to the tourism consumption index system to screen product information.

13.2.5 Travel Reviews Website

Travel reviews website is represented by Daodao. com. It is the Chinese travel review website developed by Expedia Trip of Advisor. While recommending tourist products, it also sets up a tourist evaluation column, which allows tourists to leave messages on the Internet. It brings together many consumer experience information to help later tourists to screen. Daodao. com also offers travel guides and self-help guides to help travelers develop travel plans and provide booking links.

13.3 THE DEVELOPMENT STRATEGY OF OTA

Online travel booking market development is very fast, and in order to compete for market share, tourism OTA competition will be heating up. Review the past competition situation, the development of tourism OTA should pay attention to the following basic strategies.

13.3.1 Provide Comprehensive and Extensive Information

Comprehensive and rich tourism information can attract more tourists, and effectively enhance the stickiness of tourist websites and the loyalty of tourists. The powerful database of tourist websites is the basis of providing information consultation service and tourist reservation service. According to the needs of the target tourists, the travel websites should classify the information and links according to the product column of the website, and set up the station search engine at the same time, so as to facilitate the inquiry and choice of the tourists. Tourism websites should pay great attention to the visual effects of information display, and display detailed information about scenic spots, accommodation, transportation and consumption comments in terms of text, pictures, audio and video materials. In addition, the travel website also establishes the information consultation, the friendship link, in order to facilitate the visitor to roam outside this station.

13.3.2 Achieve Low Cost Intermediary Profits

Since the use of the Internet is distributed to the use of terminals, the information transfer is free of charge, and the number of information exchanged and the number of exchanges are unlimited, and there is no geographical restrictions on the dissemination of information. Tourism websites can make full use of the characteristics of network information dissemination, and combine various tourist resources together. Utilizing the low cost advantage of the hypostatic store management, the intermediary service between the tourism supply and the travel demand is carried out, and more profits are given to the customers. This makes the owners and consumers of tourism resources benefit, thus establishing the existence value of the intermediary and making profits.

13.3.3 Meet the Individual Needs of Customers

In order to avoid homogeneous competition, tourism websites must pay full attention to the personalized needs of tourists, and the more they can meet the individual needs of tourists, the easier it is to reach a deal. Tourist websites should provide a wide range of tourist product materials, and be processed into individual tourism products for potential tourists to design personalized tourist routes according to their personal travel needs.

13.3.4 Select Targeted Markets

Using the unlimited network marketing advantages of time and space, the tourism website can extend the market access further, and the correct target market positioning will bring good economic benefits. The target market can be divided into geographical, age, product preferences, price preferences and other indicators. For example, customers can be divided into ordinary customers and business customers, while business travelers can be divided into individual customers and company team customers, and the company team customers can be divided according to the size of the company. Since 1990s, the individual has become the mainstream of tourists. There are two kinds of individual: One is to start the registration group, and one after the arrival of the group. Compared with the traditional stores, travel agencies detailed travel information provided by the Internet has advantages. In terms of departure or destination, individuals can quickly come into the group, economies of scale.

13.3.5 Build a Brand

Tourism OTA business model is easy to copy, so homogeneous competition is very fierce. The development of tourism e-commerce must attach great importance to the brand construction, improve brand reputation and customer loyalty, promote repurchase repeat, effectively consolidate the existing market, and further expand the market through word of mouth.

For brand building and brand maintenance, the most critical factor is to provide good service. In the homogeneous competition of tourism integrated websites, there is no secret of winning. Only by providing excellent booking service can the existing competitive advantages be further consolidated. Quality reservation service to be accurate, effective and in place, we must emphasize the standardization of service processes, fine and systematic. For a long time, the tourism industry service quality in China has being criticized, so the travel booking service and reception service combination should be made of high quality brand. Thus tourism website can also have strong position in the high-end market. The business model of large-scale tourism integrated website is simple, easy to be copied and produce homogeneous competition, but the brand advantage of high-quality service is difficult to overstep.

13.4 THE ONLINE TICKET BUSINESS OF OTA

13.4.1 The Influence on Trade in Tourism Service

Change propaganda way and make online marketing more effective

Compared to traditional travel agencies, OTA has built an information bridge between itself and consumers through Internet technology. Consumers can query whatever information they want at any time and place. Survey shows that foreign tourists understand the tourist routes mainly in the following ways: website advertising (29.8%), friend recommend ation (27.6%), magazine and newspaper advertising (17.6%), search engines (13.1%) and television (11.8%). Internet allows consumers to get information and enjoy more discounts. It reduces middlemen and cost.

Enlarge the market scale and increase the turnover

E-commerce makes the tourism target market not limited to the region, but open to the global market. It uses the Internet to realize free communication and information sharing across time and space.

Speed up the circulation of information and enhance the competitiveness of tourism service trade

In the information age, the basis of competition is to reduce the cost of information. The rapid development of Internet technology provides an opportunity for the upgrading and transformation of tourism industry. First, it can expand the target market and connect directly with the international market. Then, it connects consumers and travel agencies directly, reducing intermediate costs. Finally, tourism e-commerce can achieve two-way communication between enterprises and consumers. The travel agency can understand consumer demand timely and accurately grasp the market trend through the Internet. Consumers can obtain information and feedback in a timely manner through the network. Two-way information exchange will improve the satisfaction of tourism products and enhance the competitiveness of tourism service trade.

Optimize the structure of tourism industry and promote the sustainable development of tourism industry

The rapid development of the third industry provides a wider space for the development of tourism. First, it constantly meets the needs of society and the coordinated use of resources. On the other hand, it adjusts the relationship between the tourism industry and other industries and deepens cooperation among these industries. This makes tourism service trade more reasonable and advanced, so as to maximize social utility. In the future, increasing the added value of individual products, improving the utilization rate of tourism resources and realizing the effective combination of resource utilization, development and protection will promote the sustainable development of tourism.

13.4.2 Experience Economy

The so-called "experience" refers to the use of people's own life to feel the facts, perception of life, leaving an impression. With the improvement of living standards, people's consumption concept is changing, and more and more people are no longer satisfied with traditional tourism. "Experience of rural life in the farmer's home", " Crossing the western desert like a professional explorer", " As a soldier", this "experiential tourism" is quietly prevalent.

The key of modern tourism experience, the era of experience economy lies in the "three quality": perceivability, understandability and participation. The ultimate goal of experience tourism is "three senses": freshness, intimacy and satisfaction. The core driving force of consumer buying experience tourism is "three demands": seeking compensation, seeking liberation and stimulating. Development of experiential tourism through the "three quality" make tourists get "three senses", to meet the "three demands", and follow the following five principles:

Thematic principle

Theme is the basis and soul of experiencing tourism. The more distinct the theme, the more able to arouse and stimulate the senses of visitors.

Difference principle

The principle of difference means that we should strive for unique personality, to maintain the freshness of the experience. Constantly bring visitors different experience and feelings, to meet their personalized needs.

Participation principle

Participation can eliminate the gap between the tourist consumer and the experience, and enhance the intimacy of the experience.

Authenticity principle

Authenticity means that the development of experience tourist attractions should maintain its naturalness as much as possible.

Challenging principle

Challenging tourism activities can make tourists reach the state of oblivious of oneself. In the challenge of self and breakthrough limit, visitors can win victory and achieve a sense of achievement.

13.4.3 The Chain of Tourism Industry

Tourism industry chain is divided into broad sense and narrow sense. The broad sense tourism industry chain includes all sectors and enterprises related to tourism economic activities. These departments and enterprises form a relation of division of labor and cooperation in the process of taking different value creation functions. The narrow sense of tourism industry chain is generally considered to only provide tourism products and tourism services related enterprises.

The composition of online tourism industry chain mainly depends on the tourism products and services. It takes the advantages of online travel industry as the core, and other related industries as a supplement.

In general, the industrial chain upstream of the online travel industry include: tourism products suppliers, agents, network marketing media and end users of a total of four parts. Of course, the online travel industry chain in the operation also involves logistics, financial payment, insurance, communications and other auxiliary link.

13.4.4 Construction of Evaluation System

According to the service characteristics of e-commerce tourism website, we can talk about the factors that affect its service quality, summarized as the following 7 points: reliability, responsiveness, ease of use, security, empathy, trust and quality of information.

Evaluation Index System

Main Dimension	Minor Dimension
Reliability	Fulfillment of commitments Commitment to timeliness System stability
Responsiveness	Complaint handling speed Transaction request processing speed Types of contact
Ease of use	Clear navigation Web loading speed System operability
Security	Security mechanism Transaction security Privacy of individual
Empathy	Emphasis on customer needs Personalized service Care about customers

Main Dimension	Minor Dimension
Trust	Transaction fairness Company reputation Product quality
Quality of information	Information comprehensiveness Information authenticity Information update

13.5 THE CROSS-BORDER ONLINE TRAVEL

Four Aspects of Cross-border Online Travel:

Family outings are hot

Research shows that parent-child travel has become the mainstream travel mode of post-80s. 71.6% of the post-80s parents expressed hope to travel with their children and share the joy of traveling with their children. Among them, Five family destinations with higher happiness are: Japan (45.8%), the United States (36%), Australia (34.4%), Taiwan (32.5%), Thailand (32%). Family tourism will be more and more important in domestic and international tourism holidays. According to the survey, there are three focuses for family outings: service facilities, security and non-stop flights. Users generally need good resort hotels for children, facilities for children, and safety, which is an important standard for hotels. Among them, children's playground, parent-child activities and outdoor experience are the minimum requirements for children's facilities. Therefore, it is necessary to fully understand the specific needs of consumers when organizing family travel and family tourism.

More mobile terminal booking travel products behavior

One of the highlights of the online travel industry in 2014 is the popularity of mobile terminal bookings. Survey shows that 46.5% of users in the past year with mobile terminals (mobile or/and tablet PC) booked travel products. 76% users said they would consider or continue using the mobile terminal in the next year. Among them, 85% can accept more than 600 Yuan products, with mobile booking. The proportion of users who do not intend to use mobile terminals only 11.6%. This shows that mobile payment in terms of security and ease of use has been widely recognized by users, and its future is huge.

At present there is no domestic mobile terminal sales accounted for total online travel than authoritative data, but the Emarketer figures show that in the first half of 2014 of the United States online travel, the mobile terminal travel booking has growth of 20%, while the PC side is only 2%. In addition, data from Emarketer in April 2014 show that 25% of users have booked travel at least once in the past 12 months, using tablets and smartphones, and next year the rate is expected to rise to 30%.

However, there are still some obstacles of booking travel products via smart phones, including instability and other issues. Once problems such as speed instability have been resolved, mobile booking accounts for a disruptive change.

The rise of theme tourism

Survey found that Chinese tourists for overseas deep travel and tourism are in a significant increase. More than 50% of respondents want to improve the intrinsic quality of travel and leisure, and would like to spend more on hotels, restaurants and entertainment on the trip instead of shopping. And nearly 70% of respondents want to schedule their own rhythm and control the pace of travel. Only 19.4% of users would like to visit more scenic spots. For the beach, gourmet tourism, self driving, cruise, historical sites, local cultural experience and other topics of tourism, the user will be more than 30%. These are higher than last year's survey results, which is about 10%.

People are beginning to be fed up with the free travel of machines and drinks offered by the online travel platform. Especially for a white-collar worker who has high language ability, high frequency and well-informed travel needs characteristic, cost-effective products. Because they are busy, they can't deal with everything by themselves like many budget travelers. As a result, customized travel products, new lines, new locations, and personalized tours to popular scenic spots will be welcomed. Some exclusive overseas tours, such as Tokyo dining, a one-day tour in Sydney, and value inn darwin in popular locations, have all been welcomed. Users also show a significant interest in some of the characteristics of tourism last year: eco-tourism, medical tourism, such as plastic surgery and physical examination, health vacation, education, training, tourism, overseas study tours, outdoor sports. It shows that the interest of overseas tourists in China has shown a trend of diversification and theme. These special tourism projects are still a small minority. But since social media has narrowed the distance between users and online travel services, the long tail market has been able to break the regional ladder more and gather enough users. Undoubtedly, for those start-up companies, vertical online travel platform is a big positive, which can be carried out with Ctrip and other OTA differentiated competition.

The flourishing age of online outbound travel

According to iResearch online travel data in 2016, 89.7% of users in the past six months had travel behavior and outbound travel accounted for 21.6%. Of these, 18.7% of people travel abroad for the primary purpose of consumer shopping. With the improvement of people's income level and leisure time and with the United States and Japan taking the lead in relaxing the visa threshold for Chinese residents since 2015, it is becoming more and more convenient for people to apply for visas from different countries. Outbound travel will also have greater room for improvement.

13.6 THE CONTRACT OF TICKET BUSINESS BETWEEN TRADITONAL TOURISM AND OTA

Due to the development of information technology and Internet, the rapid rise of online travel agencies has brought unprecedented pressure to traditional travel agencies. Under the background of booming tourism industry in our country, the competition between the two sides is becoming more and more fierce.

13.6.1 Problem Analysis of OTA and Traditional Travel Agencies

Traditional travel agency's problems

Quality is unstable and it is difficult to quantify. The travel service industry lacks a relatively uniform service standard, and the product quality of travel agencies is always different from man to man.

Lack of control of terminal resources. The business chain is too long. Tourism involves five basic elements: food, shelter, travel, shopping and entertainment. Therefore, a good tourism service is bound to have quality of each link and the link between each other. Any link problem can lead to lower product quality. This also determines the difficulty of the travel agency's control over the provision of terminal services. Lack of control is one of the problems faced by travel agencies.

Today, the degree of homogenization of products increases and vicious competition is intensified. Travel products of traditional travel agencies are easily copied, and the coincidence rate of products is high. Homogenization of products will lead to vicious competition or unfair competition in the industry. And this brings about the reduction of the profits of traditional travel agencies and the degradation of the industry, which is not conducive to the long-term operation of the industry.

OTA's problems

Lack of safety. An open network platform will cause some customers to have some worries about their security, such as personal information theft and tampering, system resource leak and so on. All these problems will hinder the development of tourism e-commerce to a certain extent.

Price competition is too fierce. Most e-commerce platforms are still at a junior or intermediate level. So the obvious duplication of construction, the lack of personalized content, and similar products and business models exacerbate the price competition. In addition, the competition between the big OTA has become increasingly fierce, and the price war continues.

The cost of e-commerce platform construction and operation is higher. The establishment of network platform, operation and maintenance, talent recruitment, supplier cooperation, product involvement and promotion, continuous investment and many other complex problems need a lot of financial support.

13.6.2 The Competitive Relationship Between Traditional Travel Agencies and OTA

The rise of OTA has a great impact on the traditional tour agencies. Travel agencies rarely receive orders from groups, mostly some individuals. Now, the arrival of the "comfortable age" makes the self-help tour and self-driving tour continue to heat up. National Tourism Administration pointed out that in the 2014 spring festival tourism, free travel accounted for 60%. Most of the tickets, hotels and air tickets are settled through the Internet platform. The change from team travel to the individual makes travel agency operation pressure is tremendous. But OTA is in the condition of temperature rise period.

The dependence of tourism products on traditional travel agencies has declined. In the era of traditional travel agencies, most of the tourists' tickets, hotels and transportation services are completed through travel agencies. The emergence of OTA makes the dependence of the supply of tourism products on traditional travel agencies significantly lower. The bargaining power of traditional travel agencies has fallen, resulting in higher purchasing costs. OTA not only has transparent product information, but also has a convenient operating platform. Its competitiveness is strong.

13.6.3 The Cooperative Relationship Between Traditional Travel Agency and OTA

Under the fierce competition between OTA and traditional travel agencies, the future of tourism will be the integration of travel agencies and network platforms. That is to say, online tourism enterprises and traditional tourism enterprises will not be purely competitive relations. The following are the corresponding analysis of the pros and cons of OTA in traditional travel agencies:

Brand influence

Through long-term operation and long-term expansion, traditional travel agencies have established a clear brand identity, good reputation, stable supplier cooperation relationship and tourist resources. And this is what the emerging OTA lacks, and it can be said that the vast majority of OTA is still in the brand building and customer building period.

Targeted service

Traditional travel agencies can provide tourists with guaranteed services. This service is mainly reflected in the face-to-face communication between travel agencies and tourists, as well as the service of tourist guides and after-sale services in the course of tourism. And these targeted services are the inadequacies of OTA. The network marketing platform is lack of direct communication with tourists, and can not really integrate into the tourism activities to provide timely help for tourists.

Convenience of information

Traditional travel agencies provide tickets, accommodation, transportation costs and other related content. Through the integration of the purchased products, the travel agency will sell the products and make a profit. Tourists lack the means to fully understand the information. Under the Internet era, the development of OTA enables visitors to quickly search through the web page or through the form of mobile clients, and to understand the basic information of tourism products, and compare products online. This kind of operation is more convenient and more competitive.

Through the previous analysis, it is not difficult to find that the advantages of traditional travel agencies are the disadvantages of OTA, and the advantages of OTA are the disadvantages of traditional travel agencies. This is an important basis for cooperation between the two sides. In August 1, 2014, China International Travel Service Corp and leisurely travel officially reached a cooperation agreement. The integration of online and offline makes use of the advantages of online leisurely network, and leisurely network will introduce a large number of international tourism products. To achieve complementary advantages of resources, the cooperation model of "traditional hostel + online travel agency" is worth popularizing.

SUMMARY

This chapter mainly discusses the related issues of online travel agency. OTA refers to the provision of travel products and services to consumers via the Internet. OTA can be divided into tourism direct selling network and tourism intermediary network according to whether or not the entity is attached to the tourism industry. Nowadays, the rapid development of Internet technology provides an opportunity for the transformation of China's tourism industry. It directly connects the travel agencies with the consumers, reduces the intermediate links and greatly reduces the cost. Efficient two-way communication is also conducive to enhancing the competitiveness of China's tourism service trade. In addition, with the continuous improvement of people's living standards, people's concept of tourism is also changing. People are gradually not satisfied with the traditional sightseeing tours, and experiential travel is gradually gaining favor. This also shows the continuous innovation of tourism products. Besides the vigorous development, OTA still has many challenges. So the development strategy of OTA is also discussed. What's more, OTA has its advantages and disadvantages over traditional travel agencies, but perhaps the combination of these two is a new tourism business model to conform to the market. At the end of this chapter, we also discuss the four major trends of today's overseas travel to enrich the knowledge of the students.

Words and Expressions

①**capital injection**: The majority shareholder of a listed company sells its assets to a listed company. 资本注入

②**competitive situation**: It is the influence of each respect in competition. 竞争态势

③**construction and operation**: e-commerce platform maintenance, reconstruction, expansion, and network product development and profitability 运营建设

④**development strategy**: Development strategy is the theoretical system about how to develop an enterprise. 发展战略

⑤**down payment**: A sum of money or an alternative that is paid as security in advance of the contract or before it is performed. 预付定金

⑥**driving force**: Generally it refers to factors that force others to act. 驱动力

⑦**evaluation system**: Service evaluation system is a kind of evaluation system to improve service quality of service personnel. 评价系统

⑧**existing market**: It usually refers to the market that the enterprise has in the economic activity.

现有市场

⑨**flourishing age**: a period of rapid development or climax 盛世

⑩**homogeneous competition**: market competition behavior on the basis of product homogeneity 同质竞争

⑪**interactive service**: A communication network that uses digital transmission and digital switching to provide end-to-end digital connectivity and supports both voice and non-voice services. 交互型业务

⑫**intrinsic quality**: It refers to the quality of the product produced by the producer, and is the intrinsic attribute of the product. 内在质量

⑬**market access**: It refers to the extent to which a country allows foreign goods, services and capital to participate in the domestic market. 市场准入

⑭**market share**: It refers to the proportion of sales (or sales) of an enterprise in the market for similar products. 市场占有率

⑮**mobile terminal**: a computer device that can be used while moving 移动终端

⑯**risk investments**: It refers to all investments with high risk and income. 风险投资

⑰**segment market**: It refers to the marketing of a product divided into several consumer groups of market classification, through market research, according to consumer needs and desires, buying behavior and buying habits and other aspects of the difference. 细分市场

⑱**two-way communications**: In two-way communication, the sender and receiver of information are in constant exchange. 双向沟通

Exercises

Ⅰ. **Key Terms** (Explain the following terms.)

①OTA

②experiential tourism

③the chain of tourism industry

④brand effect

⑤vertical website

Ⅱ. **Multiple Choice Exercises** (Choose the correct answer to the following questions from A, B, C and D. There is only one correct answer.)

①Which one provides the online booking service to the customers?

A. OTP. B. OTA. C. Travel agency. D. Travel reviews websites.

②________ exists in the form of purely tourism supply and demand intermediaries, and in the early stages of their development there is no entity tourism enterprise to support them.

A. Integrated portal's tourist channels B. Comprehensive tourism website

C. Tourism vertical websites D. Travel recommendation websites

③Accroding to 13.4.3, which one is not right?

A. There is no link between the sectors and enterprises related to tourism economic activities in different value creation processes.

B. Tourism industry chain is divided into broad sense and narrow sense.

C. The narrow sense of tourism industry chain is generally considered to provide tourism products and tourism services related enterprises.

D. The narrow definition of tourism industry chain, from the perspective of tourism supply, includes before, during, and after sale stages of tourism products and services.

④Which one of the following isn't contained in reliability?

A. Fulfillment of commitments. B. Commitment to timeliness.

C. System stability. D. Privacy.

⑤Which of the following isn't contained in the development strategy of OTA?

A. Provide comprehensive and extensive information.

B. Achieve low cost intermediary profits.

C. Meet the individual needs of customers.

D. Analyze market.

⑥Which of the following is not the principle of experiential tourism?

A. Thematic principle. B. Fair principle.

C. Participation principle. D. Challenging principle.

⑦OTA's problems contain lack of security, fierce price competition and ________.

A. unstable mass

B. lack of control of resources

C. high cost of e-commerce platform operation

D. long business chain

⑧Which one is not right according to 13.6.3?

A. Online tourism enterprises and traditional tourism enterprises will not be purely competitive relations.

B. Traditional travel agencies have a good brand effect.

C. OTA lacks targeted services.

D. The convenience of traditional travel agencies is comparable to that of OTA.

Ⅲ. Review Questions

①Why do more and more people choose online travel agencies?

②What is the classification of OTA?

③What are the four major trends of outbound travel agencies?

Ⅳ. Online Practice

①Visit several traditional travel agencies and analyze the pros and cons of their service.

②Use Ctrip to search for local travel products or services and try to book some service.

③Summarize and analyze the respective advantages and disadvantages of OTA and traditional travel agencies through the above two practices.

Ⅴ. Case Study

Qunar Denies CCTV Report of Fake Flight-delay Insurance

NASDAQ-listed Qunar. com Inc, a Chinese online travel service provider, refuted on Sunday a report by China Central Television (CCTV) on the same day that alleged that flight-delay insurance products bought by customers on the company's site have "disappeared".

The company said that the online system of China Pacific Insurance (Group) Co (CPIC), the provider of the insurance products, had suffered a malfunction, causing insurance buyers to be unable to trace their bills on CPIC's website via the codes auto-generated on Qunar, according to a post on its Sina Weibo account on Sunday.

The system is still being repaired by press time, a customer service staff with CPIC told the Global Times Sunday.

Qunar's explanation has not convinced some analysts, who believe that it may just be an excuse.

As an online travel agent (OTA), Qunar is responsible for ensuring that all products and services offered on its website must function well, said Zhao Zhanling, a legal counsel with the Internet Society of China.

The company should have been informed of CPIC's system failure right away, Zhao told the Global Times Sunday.

Qunar's statement came immediately after CCTV reported Sunday morning that the company sold "fake" flight-delay insurance products, citing Web users' complaints.

A Web user named Wang Zheng was quoted by CCTV on Sunday as saying that he had bought a 20 yuan ($3.26) flight-delay insurance coverage with a Shenzhen—Hangzhou flight ticket in October, but could not find his insurance bill on CPIC's official website.

Consumers who bought such products on Qunar but failed to find their insurance bills on CPIC can still receive normal insurance service, said Qunar.

Zhao noted that if consumers filed a lawsuit over this matter, Qunar would have to take on some joint liability.

This is not the first time that online travel services have been the subject of fake insurance allegations.

Qunar's major rival Ctrip. com International, also listed on NASDAQ, was sued by a couple in 2009 for selling counterfeit insurance offered by a third-party insurance agent and was required to pay 2,200 yuan in compensation.

"China's OTA is always a mixed market with the lack of strict regulation, making it possible for some profit-pursuing OTAs and third-party insurance agents to offer fake insurance on behalf of established insurance companies," said Wei Changren, general manager with Beijing-based Jinlü Consulting.

Wei believes that as a US-listed company, it is unlikely that Qunar would have committed the acts in the CCTV report.

"But it is hard to say in the future (if regulations are not strengthened). In order to offset the loss caused amid increasing marketing costs and declining agent commission fees, companies like Qunar may take advantage of weak domestic rules," Wei told the Global Times Sunday.

Qunar recorded a 421.6 million yuan net loss in the second quarter of 2014, compared to a loss of 41.2 million yuan in the same period of 2013, attributing the increased loss to investment in product development and marketing efforts, read a financial report issued in August.

Questions for Discussion

①What are the current problems with online travel agents in China suggested in the case?

②As consumers, how can we deal with or prevent such problems?